I0819105

STEVE JOBS IN EXILE

STEVE JOBS IN EXILE

The Untold Story of NeXT and the Remaking of an American Visionary

GEOFFREY CAIN

PORTFOLIO | PENGUIN

Portfolio / Penguin
An imprint of Penguin Random House LLC
1745 Broadway, New York, NY 10019
penguinrandomhouse.com

Most Portfolio books are available at a discount when purchased in quantity for sales promotions or corporate use. Special editions, which include personalized covers, excerpts, and corporate imprints, can be created when purchased in large quantities. For more information, please call (212) 572-2232 or email specialmarkets@penguinrandomhouse.com. Your local bookstore can also assist with discounted bulk purchases using the Penguin Random House corporate Business-to-Business program. For assistance in locating a participating retailer, email B2B@penguinrandomhouse.com.

Photo captions for photographs by Doug Menuez adapted from *Fearless Genius: The Digital Revolution in Silicon Valley 1985–2000* by Doug Menuez, published by Atria Books, an imprint of Simon & Schuster, LLC, 2014.

Book design by Alissa Rose Theodor

LIBRARY OF CONGRESS CONTROL NUMBER: 2025045169
ISBN 9780593716694 (hardcover)
ISBN 9780593716700 (ebook)

Printed in the United States of America
1st Printing

The authorized representative in the EU for product safety and compliance is Penguin Random House Ireland, Morrison Chambers, 32 Nassau Street, Dublin D02 YH68, Ireland, https://eu-contact.penguin.ie.

For Gözde, my wife and partner in braving this wilderness together.

For Daphne, our daughter, who arrived as the final pages took shape.

I didn't see it then, but it turned out that getting fired from Apple was the best thing that could have ever happened to me. The heaviness of being successful was replaced by the lightness of being a beginner again, less sure about everything. It freed me to enter one of the most creative periods of my life.

STEVE JOBS, STANFORD UNIVERSITY
COMMENCEMENT ADDRESS, JUNE 12, 2005

Midway upon the journey of our life
I found myself within a forest dark,
For the straightforward pathway had been lost.

DANTE'S *THE DIVINE COMEDY*

CONTENTS

PART TWO

PART THREE

FOREWORD

Sometimes, losing a bet can pay off. After too many drinks at a bar in Buffalo while playing pool, I scratched on the eight ball and doubled down—only to lose again. Broke and out of options, my penance was to drive the victor's potbellied stove to Silicon Valley. It was the summer of 1976 and I had just graduated from college. I never looked back.

Several months later, I started my first job in the Valley selling business recording products for Sony. That very same week, Apple moved out of Steve's parents' garage and rented its first office space next door to Sony's.

Standing outside our respective offices, Steve and I struck up a conversation. It was April 7, 1977. He had longish greasy hair in those days and a beard. I remember him wearing Birkenstocks, blue jeans with holes—and needing a shower.

He was curious about Sony's products and the brand, so I handed him a product brochure. Flipping through it, he asked why our products cost more than those of competitors.

I replied, "Because they're Sony's."

He grinned, nodded, and walked off with a bounding gait.

As he left, I could see him rubbing the brochure between his fingers, gauging the quality of the paper. That simple act clued me in on a trait of his I would come to appreciate over the years: his focus. When you were talking to him, he had a great way of removing everything around and just looking at you. When faced with a business problem, he knew how to cut out distractions and reduce it to its very essence. And when it came to matters of design, like logos and paper quality, he was always a critic.

Later, when we worked together at Apple and NeXT, I would travel with him around the world. Wherever we went, Steve's focus followed. When we were walking down the street in another city, he might see a car and point out something about its design to me: the shadow cast by the curve of a fender, the shape of a headlamp, and even the choice of paint color best suited to a particular model. He was perpetually searching for insight and seeking excellence.

His focus made him different from anyone else I've worked with. It was a superpower. But like a lot of strengths, it could be a double-edged sword. He sometimes let his focus get in his own way. At NeXT, it led him to obsess maniacally on many of the wrong things, relentlessly pursuing perfection at the expense of his company's viability.

It could also make him bruising to work for. He didn't know how to exempt anyone from his exacting—and often changing—standards, whether they were waiters, top corporate lieutenants, or university presidents. He struggled to show others grace.

Over the next few years following that first interaction, Steve and I ran into each other from time to time as Apple grew. When we spoke, our conversations were invariably about Sony products. His curiosity about the brand and our technology never wavered.

In December 1980, on the day Sony announced the 3.5-inch floppy disk drive, Steve recruited me to join Apple. Having been inside nearly every company in the Valley by that time as a Sony salesman, I was interested in being a part of Apple's culture as much as its blossoming success, as demonstrated by its IPO. While I wasn't familiar with the dynamics of the emerging personal computer industry, I felt confident I could get up to speed quickly. I mentioned to Steve my interest in graphics, at which point he alluded to Apple working on "a better way" to interact with computers. I also knew a fair amount about microprocessors and the semiconductor industry.

So, I took a pay cut and joined the company. What ensued was a decade-long professional relationship and a friendship that changed the course of my life.

At Apple, I started as the market development manager for the Personal Office Systems Division, which was building the Lisa computer, and wound up establishing Apple's Education Marketing Division. In between those two roles, Steve recruited me again and I spent several years in his nascent Macintosh Division, where I designed and established the Apple University Consortium and the branding of the Wheels for the Mind initiative. The consortium placed nearly fifty thousand Macs in the hands of students by one month in late summer of 1984 and made Apple a major player in the higher education market. Education was very important to the company as well, growing to become two thirds of Apple's business by 1985. This effort also pioneered the practice of personal computer manufacturers selling directly to their customers.

In early 1985, Steve was pushed out of Apple. He called me later that year. "I'm going to start a new company focused on higher education," he said. "I want you to come with me."

That same day, I met Steve at his home in Woodside for a walk, which was his favorite way to have deep conversations. He described to me the vision for what would become NeXT: He wanted to build on our work together at Apple and develop a powerful computer for higher education institutions. The relationships and market expertise that I had developed at Apple would be essential for the venture.

The decision to join Steve's new company didn't necessarily make sense on paper. I had a great job running education marketing at Apple.

Building a start-up would be a real risk—success wasn't guaranteed, and Steve did not yet have his legendary reputation.

But if I didn't join and the company succeeded, I would have missed the chance of a lifetime. And if they failed without me, I would always wonder if I could have made a difference. In the end, I knew I had to do it.

Within days, my five cofounders and I left our jobs at Apple and joined Steve to work out of his barely furnished house. Though we were united by our conviction that starting the company was the right thing to do, we had no real plan. We had only each other, our respective skills, our accumulated experiences, and some seed funding from Steve's personal bank account.

It was an exhilarating time.

For all the books and movies that have been made about Steve, and about Apple, most fail to document the real story of this period of his life—and of NeXT. Too often, these years are breezed over or airbrushed.

As we often discussed at NeXT, growing a company is like polishing rocks in a tumbler. Over time, the mix and grit change into a shiny, well-functioning team. Along the way, though, things can be rough. You're crashing into each other, experiencing ups and downs. By overlooking this discomfort, these narratives ignore the role that the NeXT years played in both Steve's leadership development and the eventual outcome: In the late 1990s, NeXT's core technology became essential to Apple's survival.

Perhaps part of the impulse to skip this story is because NeXT was—spoiler alert—never a huge market success. NeXT had all the ingredients to succeed. We were at the right place at the right time, we had a world-class team, and we were building technology that was years ahead of the rest of the industry. If history had gone differently—and if Steve had been more willing to take advice—I believe NeXT and its operating system, NeXTSTEP, could have become *the* industry standard, taking the place that Microsoft Windows eventually occupied.

Instead, we faced persistent challenges. Our computers were expensive, slow to come to market, and barely worked once they did. Meanwhile, Steve sabotaged important business and distribution relationships. NeXT existed on the perpetual verge of bankruptcy and on the wheel of Steve's ever-shifting standards. Many of the original team, including me, left as a result of our frustrations with him. But despite these problems, NeXT succeeded in laying the unseen foundation for everything that came after for Apple and for the technology industry at large.

This book is about how those contributions took shape. It's also about how Steve evolved. I saw his growth firsthand, and I experienced growth of my own as a result of our collaboration. It was an active push and pull between us. At Apple, I had learned that our working relationship would only succeed if I treated him as an equal and was clear, direct, and assertive with him. Steve knew that too.

When we started NeXT, Steve was eager to focus his energy on developing his public presence. I told him that wouldn't work. Until we had a product to sell, Steve *was* the product—and we would have to be judicious about how we deployed him. I believed that the most strategic use of Steve's persona was to present him with an air of mystery, which meant not talking all the time. That was a foreign idea for Steve.

As we discussed this point on a walk one day in the Stanford Research Park hills, where we had rented our first office space, I could sense that he was struggling to express something. This was unusual for Steve. After I pushed him to share what was bothering him, he finally said to me, "Sometimes, I think you want to do my job."

"No, I don't," I replied immediately. And it was the truth. "Only you can be you," I said.

I understood this fact well. When I was in college, my independent study and thesis work focused on charismatic leadership theory. The recent ratification of the Twenty-sixth Amendment, which extended the franchise to eighteen-year-olds, had piqued my interest. It led me to study the organizing principles and leadership of Bob Dylan as well as the giants of the civil rights and women's rights movements. I wanted to understand the method behind their magic. How did they grow their audience, while staying current with changing times? One thing I discovered was that transformative leaders always return to an origin story or a core concept, again and again.

For Steve, his core was the Macintosh.

Released in 1984, the Mac revolutionized the computer industry with its graphical user interface. Before that, users had to interact with computers not by mouse, but via command-line interface, typing instructions that the computer would then execute. As its famous tagline said, the Mac made personal computing accessible "for the rest of us."

Improbable as it seemed at the time, NeXT enabled Steve to return to the Mac and emerge as a charismatic leader.

By the mid-1990s, the Mac was in serious trouble—the product line was a mess of unappealing options, its operating system was badly out of date, and Apple itself was nearly bankrupt. When he returned to Apple in 1997, Steve and his capable team integrated NeXT technology into the Mac and propelled it back into a leading position.

NeXT allowed the Mac to live. And it allowed Steve to etch himself into the annals of history.

Having left NeXT in 1990, I watched from the outside as Steve managed Apple's remarkable transformation. Meanwhile my own experience at NeXT—and my relationship with Steve—remained fundamental to my life's work even as I took a job working for Microsoft to help Steve's rival, Bill Gates, normalize business relationships with Apple and the rest of the computer industry as it settled its lingering antitrust case.

I spent nearly seventeen years at Microsoft. Following that, in 2018, I took over the leadership of the Computer History Museum, which I was proud to run until 2025. In that time, I dedicated myself to developing our collective understanding of the history of computing and its implications for the human condition.

I believe NeXT is a major part of that story. It's why I decided to share the source materials for this book, which I collected during my time at NeXT. I am thrilled that they have come to life in the capable hands of Geoffrey Cain.

It was a privilege to be a part of NeXT, and I hope you are able to derive value from reading about our trials and tribulations, just as my fellow NeXT alumni and I did living them.

Before I turn it over to Geoff, I want to highlight an underappreciated part of every technology story. And that is: family. Not corporate family, but the wives, husbands, children, partners, parents, and chosen family members who support founders and builders as they do great work.

I know that I would not be writing this foreword without my own family. And I am certain Steve would not have become the person he did without his.

When we first founded NeXT, Steve didn't have much family to speak of. At times, it led to contention between Steve and me. It was important to me to spend time with my wife and young sons. But Steve made it difficult. He often demanded the leadership team appear in person for weekend meetings, whether on holidays or family birthdays. I did my best to draw boundaries.

After I left the company, Steve began to understand why. During the later NeXT years, he got married, had his second, third, and fourth children, and learned what it meant to be a father. In this same window, both of his adoptive parents died.

When his father passed away, in 1993, the loss affected Steve deeply, and he invited me to the burial. There were less than ten people present. Soon after that, we had breakfast together. As was typical, Steve arrived a little late. But this time, with an unusual opening remark.

"You were right," he declared with that same old grin.

"About what?" I said, incredulously, recalling the many years of argument and struggle as we built NeXT.

"Family," he said.

We talked for a long time that morning, with little mention of products, but great enthusiasm for the life lessons that only family can deliver. It is my belief that Steve's success and the eventual success of Apple emanate from this balance and the commitment to and trust in others that he learned from his family.

It's a lesson we should all heed.

DAN'L LEWIN
FORMER CEO, COMPUTER HISTORY MUSEUM
COFOUNDER, NeXT COMPUTER

PART ONE

1

SIBERIA

"I'm asking Steve to step down," Apple CEO John Sculley told the company's board of directors, "and you can back me on it . . . or you're going to have to find yourselves a new CEO."

It was April 11, 1985, and long-simmering tensions between John Sculley and Steve Jobs had finally erupted. It marked a stunning reversal. Just two years earlier, Steve had handpicked and personally recruited John from PepsiCo. Apple had grown into a billion-dollar company, and Steve, along with the board, felt that John would be the right person to provide the company with "adult supervision" as its CEO. After John joined, Steve remained chairman of the board and head of the Macintosh unit, where he led the development of the company's flagship personal computer.

John's working relationship with Steve began as trusting and close. The two shared private talks and meals. They seemed preternaturally aligned on most parts of Apple's corporate strategy.

But the relationship soured as the company's fortunes declined. Apple computers weren't selling. John struggled to put forward a clear vision to boost sales. And Steve—convinced of his own brilliance—was impossible to manage. He had recently told an executive, "I am the board."

But the duly elected members of Apple's board begged to differ—they dressed down both John and Steve over the situation. Now John wanted Steve out entirely. He asked that Steve be removed from his operational role and stripped of all decision-making authority.

Steve was livid. He reminded the board members that Apple was his baby—the company he had built from nothing out of his parents' garage. He remained indispensable, he told them, as nothing less than Apple's beating heart and its intellectual force. But only one person could lead Apple, and John wanted it to be him. "I had given Steve greater power than he ever had and I had created a monster," John recounted later.

Just over a year before, on January 24, 1984, Steve had launched his brainchild into the world: the Macintosh. Steve called it the "computer for the rest of us" and claimed that its simplicity and ease of use would revolutionize the personal computer industry. For the first one hundred days, it posted strong shipments and looked poised to succeed.

But regular customers were put off by the Mac's serious limitations. Though simple to use, the Mac had no hard drive, extremely limited functionality, and was priced at a jaw-dropping $2,495 (almost $8,000 in 2026 dollars). By 1985, Apple had run through early adopters, and the remaining shoppers turned to the lower-priced alternative, the Apple II. Mac inventory piled up, budgets spun out of control, and the company struggled to come up with a dazzling new product. An industry-wide slump made the problem worse.

For the first time in its short history, Apple was in real trouble. By early 1985, IBM—the computing giant that dominated corporate

America—and its imitators had captured nearly half the personal computer market, up from about a third just months earlier. These "clone" computers ran the same software as IBM's machines but cost far less. Apple's market share remained stuck in place, exposing the failure of the company's Macintosh gamble.

Things got so bad that Steve and John entered secret talks to sell the company to General Electric. According to journalist Frank Rose, the conglomerate hired Texas-based businessman H. Ross Perot to meet with Apple's leadership and investigate the company as an acquisition target. In the end, GE decided against buying. But Ross was impressed with Steve, a connection that would later prove important when Steve needed investors.

Ross's fascination with Steve followed a pattern. Many in Apple's orbit lavished attention on Steve while overlooking John's contributions to the company, fueling an emerging rivalry between the two that was exacerbated by Apple's shaky market position.

To fix the problem, Steve told employees that he believed Apple should play in the big leagues. So far, the company had focused on the consumer market. If Apple made a more powerful computer for corporate customers, Steve believed it could take on IBM. So he began to develop the Macintosh Office, an upgraded version of the Mac specially designed for office settings.

John was not on board. He thought Steve's plans were unrealistic. The Mac was designed to be a simple device for drawing and typing at home. Its architecture was not built for pressure-cooker corporate environments with complex demands. Even engineers in Steve's own department argued that the project lay beyond their capabilities. Steve forged ahead anyway.

Steve also liked that releasing the Macintosh Office would give Apple a chance to recreate its *1984* commercial from the year before, which had introduced the original Mac and become an instant classic. Apple tasked Chiat/Day, the same firm behind the *1984* spot, to develop a follow-on.

Chiat/Day's concept: convince business leaders that they were on a slow march off a cliff if they didn't buy the Macintosh Office. On Super Bowl Sunday, January 20, 1985, Steve and John went to Stanford Stadium to watch the premiere of their new commercial together.

The ad, titled "Lemmings," aired during a break in the fourth quarter. The dystopian spot opens on a line of blindfolded, suit-clad office workers marching toward the edge of a cliff as they whistle an eerie, minor-key version of "Heigh-Ho" from *Snow White and the Seven Dwarfs*. One by one, the lemmings step off the edge and fall to their deaths. The last lemming in the line stops just before the edge, removes his blindfold, and gazes over the abyss.

"You can look into it," announces a somber voice, "or you can go on with business as usual." Text flashes: The Macintosh Office.

As the lemmings fell, the eighty-four thousand fans in Stanford Stadium went uncomfortably silent. Apple's top duo began to experience a sinking feeling themselves. John felt certain the reaction portended hard times for the product.

Sure enough, Apple released the Macintosh Office three days later to muted press coverage and weak sales. Worse, John's fears about Apple's capacity to deliver the product were realized. The technical heart of the product—Apple's much-hyped file server—was severely delayed and not yet ready to ship.

The bad sales numbers drove further division behind the scenes as Apple employees began splintering into factions. At one point, a contingent supporting John stormed the Human Resources Department to complain about Steve overstepping his area of control. Meanwhile Steve undermined John at every turn, badmouthing him to colleagues and challenging his every decision. Steve's acolytes accused John of lacking vision and misunderstanding technology products. They felt that he was turning Apple into yet another boring, bureaucratic corporation.

With so much open dissension, no one knew who was really running the company.

In response, John—the Wharton-trained, former PepsiCo president—

made a plan to reshape Apple's corporate hierarchy. From its earliest days as a start-up, the company had relied on flat management. This had facilitated scrappiness and the creative exchange of ideas when Apple was young. But as it grew, John watched the lack of structure fuel chaos and infighting. He believed that a mature Apple needed centralized leadership to succeed. So he moved to combine the product divisions under one C-suite that would report up to him.

The plan sounded simple enough. But John faced one big obstacle: bringing Steve to heel. Under his proposed reshuffle, Steve would become one of three coequal product executives. On the back side of his office door, John hung a graphic outlining his mission: a simple pyramid with himself perched at the top.

Steve wasn't having it, particularly as his respect for John dwindled. John's attempt to impose order was failing and tensions kept ratcheting. On February 7, when an anonymous caller made a bomb threat targeting John's and Steve's personal homes, a rumor circulated inside Apple that it had been orchestrated by Steve to seek revenge. "Guards with rifles were sleeping on our sofa," John admitted to a pair of journalists. The threat turned out to be a hoax, but the suspicions among staff illustrated how deep the rift had become.

Two weeks later, Steve threw himself a thirtieth birthday bash at the St. Francis Hotel in San Francisco's Union Square. For someone who was known to say, "Never trust anyone over thirty," the milestone prompted reflection. As Steve wrote on the table cards: "You've helped me acquire my habits (good and bad). Thank you for joining me tonight to celebrate thirty more years of living with them."

Steve arrived an hour into the event, clad in a black tuxedo, in accordance with the party's black-tie dress code. John set aside his differences and rose to give Steve a toast, calling him "technology's foremost visionary."

Then a jazz singer took the stage, sporting a red tuxedo.

"I'm Ella Fitzgerald," she said, "and for some reason a young man here wants me to sing happy birthday to him for his thirtieth birthday."

Few at the party would forget hearing Ella sing to Steve. But for the legendary chanteuse, it was just another gig. After singing a jazzy rendition of "Happy Birthday," she left the building. To Ella, "he was just a rich guy named Steve," wrote David Bunnell, the founder of *Macworld*, the magazine devoted to Apple and the Macintosh, who covered the party. Then members of the San Francisco Symphony orchestra took over the music. Steve departed soon after.

To attendees, the event felt distant and sad. "Steve doesn't have any real friends," Mike Murray, who marketed the Mac, had told David before the party.

The next month, March 1985, John and Steve barely spoke to each other. Steve told anyone who would listen that John was clueless. Apple managers complained that Steve's perfectionist tantrums were making it impossible to meet product deadlines. They urged John to enforce discipline over the chaos, to step up as CEO.

Something had to be done. So Jay Elliot, Apple's human resources chief, brought John to Steve's office to hash things out. Outside the windows, rain poured. Inside, things quickly went south.

"Sculley just started hollering at [Steve]," Jay recalled. John blamed Steve for the Mac Division's poor sales and lambasted him for undermining his authority.

Steve started shouting back, saying that John was the real source of Apple's problems. The Mac Division was one thing, Steve said, but John simply couldn't lead the company. Then came Steve's stinger: He said he regretted ever hiring him as CEO.

And then, Steve burst into tears.

"I knew at that moment that Sculley had him," Jay said, "because Sculley would go to the board and say, 'This guy is out of control.'"

A few weeks later, the night before the fateful April 11 board meeting, John did exactly that. He proposed to the board that Steve be transferred from his post as leader of the Mac team to a newly invented, completely powerless unit tasked with dreaming up far-off ideas.

For three hours, from 6:00 p.m. to 9:00 p.m., Steve and John went back and forth, arguing for their professional lives. After taking a break for the night, the pair picked up at 9:00 a.m. the next day and fought before the board for another grueling six and a half hours. John declared that if the board didn't side with him, he would resign as CEO.

Exhausted, the board backed John. Though they criticized him for hesitating to assert his leadership, they needed him more than they needed Steve, whom they saw as an immature agent of chaos.

The board's clear message to Steve: Let John run the company. The board allowed Steve to keep his title as chairman of the board, but they removed him from his post leading the Mac team—a crushing blow.

Steve left the room and broke down in tears once again.

"I can't believe this is happening," he told Nanette Buckhout after the meeting. Nanette worked as the assistant to—of all people—John. Steve's famed "reality distortion field"—his ability to convince anyone (including himself) that almost anything was possible—made him unafraid to express his emotions to anyone, even the assistant of his nemesis. Apple employees half-jokingly called this ability "the world according to Steve."

"Why did John do this to me?" Steve sobbed. "I can't believe he would do this. He betrayed me."

On May 7, 1985, John and Jay landed in Paris. They needed a spiritual replacement for Steve to lead the Mac team and hoped to convince the head of Apple France, a debonair executive named Jean-Louis Gassée, to do it.

Like Steve, Jean-Louis had a je ne sais quoi. He was charismatic and handsome. He wore leather jackets, seductive colognes, and a diamond earring. He had appeared in French *Vogue*, where he was lauded as one of France's best-dressed men. Even his descriptions of tech strategy had an edge. "At Apple," he wrote, "one sometimes tends to forget that life is not made of a series of orgasms but also of love."

And like Steve, Jean-Louis came from an unusual background. He had studied math in school, helped manage a strip club in Paris, and spent his early twenties as a door-to-door salesman of elixirs meant to reinvigorate the sex lives of French women. At twenty-four years old, he pivoted from potions to PCs and joined Hewlett-Packard's French division as a senior salesman. After hearing about a start-up called Apple, he made the leap and, in 1981, launched Apple's French subsidiary.

Under Jean-Louis's leadership, Apple France became the company's most successful global arm. Impressed by his track record, John tagged Jean-Louis for a promotion—he wanted him to join the Mac Division. But Jean-Louis was hesitant to enter Apple's toxic leadership fray and was put off by the idea of working for Steve. In his book of essays, Jean-Louis had described Steve as "that handsome and tragic character out of some novel, that visionary monster, aesthete, lonely, detestable and fascinating creature."

When John first proposed that Jean-Louis join the Mac Division, Jean-Louis demanded a letter from Steve guaranteeing that he would hand over leadership of the division within a year. At the time, Steve was outraged at the affront. But now, with Steve on his way out, John could promise Jean-Louis that the division would eventually be his. Until then, he would run Macintosh marketing.

When Steve found out about the arrangement, he was livid. He angrily told Jay that he didn't want Jean-Louis around. Steve wasn't going to stand by as a charming French interloper commandeered his team.

Steve was thoroughly fed up with John. He wanted control of his company once again, so he decided to put a coup in motion. After Apple secured the rights to sell personal computers in China, Steve accepted an invitation to travel to Beijing to speak at the Great Hall of the People. He anticipated that John would want to come too and invited

John on the trip. Then, once John signed on, Steve bailed, leaving John to travel to Beijing by himself.

With John out of the country, Steve planned to go to the board and convince them to make him the CEO. Upon John's return, Steve would go to him and triumphantly demand John's resignation. He could see it all so clearly.

The week before John's trip, Steve informally polled Apple executives about his plot. Most derided it as an unworkable fantasy, saying he was going too far. Even Jay, a close confidant, told Steve that he should drop it. Jay believed the board would side with John because he remained the only credible choice for the role.

The people who heard Steve's plan said he was talking irrational nonsense—all the more reason Steve may have made the phenomenally irrational decision to open up about it to Jean-Louis. Perhaps he thought he could win over a surprise ally.

Steve spoke to Jean-Louis in the parking lot the day before John was set to leave for China, telling him everything he planned to do.

"Steve, it's not your company," Jean-Louis replied. "It's our company."

Big mistake. That night, during a dinner at the home of Apple's chief counsel, Al Eisenstat, Jean-Louis pulled John into the living room and revealed Steve's plot. Shocked, John canceled his China trip and joined Apple's executive staff and board members the next day for its 9:00 a.m. board meeting, as he recounted in his memoir, *Odyssey*.

John waited to start the meeting until Steve, who was running late, arrived. It was an ambush—Steve thought John was in China.

When Steve entered the room, John stared at him from across the hardwood table. "It's come to my attention that you'd like to throw me out of the company," he said. "And I'd like to ask you if that's true."

For an intense moment, Steve just glared back at John.

"I think you're bad for Apple and I think you're the wrong person to run this company," Steve replied, heating up. "You really should leave this company. I'm more worried about Apple than I have ever been. I'm afraid of you. You don't know how to operate and never have."

"I made a mistake in treating you with high esteem," John replied, a childhood stammer creeping back into his voice. "I don't trust you, and I won't tolerate a lack of trust. If I left, who would run the company?"

"I think I could run the company," Steve said. "I think I understand the things that need to be done."

"I'd like to go around the room and just ask each of the executive staff members how they feel about what you've just said," John shot back. "Because if they agree with you, it would be very hard for me to run the company."

One by one, Apple's six senior leaders in the room voiced their discontent with the quagmire. Four of them again sided with John, while the other two stayed neutral. Then the board made its decision. Though directors had grievances with John's leadership, their complaints weren't serious enough to justify firing him at this point. And they still felt that Steve was too immature to be a viable alternative—just as many had warned Steve they would.

Steve flopped his head down on the table. Gone was his bravado. Gone were his typical color and confidence. Gone was his driving spirit. Apple's visionary sat deflated before his board after being rejected for a second time.

"Well," he said, voice trembling. "I guess I know where things stand." Then he stood up and left the room. No one followed.

One week later, on May 31, 1985, Steve was formally exiled to his new role as head of a made-up unit. "They leased a little building across the street from most of the other Apple buildings," Steve told *Newsweek*. "I—we—nicknamed it 'Siberia.'"

Steve was allowed to bring only his assistant and a security guard with him. Few coworkers called to check in. Corporate reports stopped flowing to his desk. "Steve was out in the cold everywhere at that point," recalled Macintosh financial controller Susan Barnes who had previously reported to him. "It was amazing to see how ostracized he was in the Valley . . . It was really cruel."

With nothing of substance to do, Steve went into the office for a few hours each day. When even that began to feel unbearable, Steve stopped going altogether. "There was nobody really there to miss me," he later said.

At night, Steve sat outside his home and looked up at the stars. Every waking moment of his adult life had been spent building Apple—long days, longer nights. Now he had no real friends, no other life to turn to. Steve decided to disappear for a while, to step away from his old life and think.

"Suddenly, he was gone," Jay remembered. "Nobody knew where the hell he was. And they didn't know when he would come back."

2

INTO THE WILDERNESS

You've probably had somebody punch you in the stomach and it knocks the wind out of you," Steve told *Newsweek* in 1985. "If you relax you'll start breathing again. That's how I felt all summer long."

Throughout the summer of 1985, Steve did his best to both relax and breathe. Gone were the frenzied product meetings, the relentless deadlines, and the adoring crowds that had previously defined his life. Instead, he filled his time with reading, long walks in the woods, and travel.

In June, Steve went to Italy with his girlfriend, Tina Redse, a computer consultant with hippie idealist vibes, to explore the majestic churches and rolling vineyards of Tuscany. He drew inspiration from what he saw, down to the gray-blue sandstone that made up the sidewalks of Florence, a local variety called Pietra Serena. He would later use it as flooring in Apple stores.

Then Steve went to Paris. He wondered if it might be time to take his considerable fortune and retire to a quiet life as an American expatriate—reading literature at cafés, studying master painters at museums. Tina wanted to run away with him and settle down there. She later wrote to him:

> We were on a bridge in Paris in the summer of 1985. It was overcast. We leaned against the smooth stone rail and stared at the green water rolling on below. Your world had cleaved and then it paused, waiting to rearrange itself around whatever you chose next. I wanted to run away from what had come before. I tried to convince you to begin a new life with me in Paris, to shed our former selves and let something else course through us. I wanted us to crawl through that black chasm of your broken world and emerge, anonymous and new, in simple lives where I could cook you simple dinners and we could be together every day, like children playing a sweet game with no purpose save the game itself.

But Steve couldn't stay away from work for long. He still wanted to build and create. In early July 1985, he visited the Soviet Union, where he met with Communist Party apparatchiks to discuss the possibility of opening a Macintosh factory there.

Two days later, Steve abandoned his European future and returned to California, where he pondered entering politics—he liked the idea of becoming a larger-than-life historical figure à la John F. Kennedy or Ronald Reagan. He even talked with two political operatives, Pat Caddell and Scott Miller, about the possibility of running for the Senate.

But Steve had a problem: He couldn't figure out whether to run as a Democrat or a Republican. He had never even registered to vote. Ultimately, he decided against it. "I've got too much hair left for politics," he said.

Steve occasionally returned to Apple's headquarters, where he spent time trading barbs with Jean-Louis in the parking lot. In Steve's absence, Jean-Louis had been promoted to VP of product development, where he now oversaw all Apple products—an even more influential position than Steve had held before his ouster.

Jean-Louis's elevation vexed Steve. And Steve's practice of parking in a handicapped space grated on Jean-Louis. He once pointedly asked Steve if the spot was designated for emotionally handicapped people too.

But Jean-Louis also seemed to relish the back-and-forth. He baited Steve by buying a silver Mercedes-Benz 500SEL that looked nearly identical to Steve's. On it, Jean-Louis installed vanity license plates that read OPEN MAC, a reference to his new initiative to transform the Macintosh product.

His Open Mac plan departed dramatically from Steve's philosophy. Jean-Louis, with John's backing, wanted to make the Mac more expandable—adding slots for third-party cards, more ports for peripherals, and greater flexibility for users who wanted to customize their machines. Steve had always opposed such changes. He believed that by controlling every aspect of the system, Apple could offer users a more elegant experience. But that control came at a cost: The Mac remained limited in what it could do and expensive compared with alternatives.

Meanwhile, IBM—whose PCs cost less than the Mac and could be expanded and customized in ways the Mac couldn't—was eating Apple's lunch. "We obviously recognize that IBM dominates the office, particularly with the higher-end products," John admitted in an interview, conceding that many companies were "so true-blue IBM that they're just not going to want to work with us."

Third-party companies built everything from memory cards to specialized software for IBM machines, knowing they'd reach a massive installed base. For business customers especially, the IBM ecosystem offered practical advantages the closed Mac simply couldn't match.

With one eye on IBM and the other on collapsing sales, plunging profits, and Apple's depressed stock price, John and Jean-Louis pressed forward with their Open Mac vision.

In his quietude, Steve embarked on a more structured process of reflection to decide on his next steps. He began listing out, in bullet points, his favorite projects from the last ten years at Apple. As he did so, a clear trend emerged: He felt drawn to education-related initiatives. Helping schools and students made him feel connected to his own happy youth.

One memory stood out: the Apple University Consortium. Launched prior to the Mac's release, the Consortium was a plan to secure large-volume Mac purchases from universities at discounted prices, all while encouraging professors to develop the software library that Apple needed. The program was the brainchild of Dan'l Lewin, a charming, well-spoken salesman with chiseled looks.

Dan'l and Steve worked well together. The two shared an obsession with technology and with Bob Dylan. Dan'l had even written a political-science paper on the Bard as a Princeton undergraduate. Dan'l was the product of a childhood that he called a "circus": His father and uncles were professional wrestlers, and the family kept wild animals, including an African lion and a chimp, which roamed the house. When the chaos became too much, Dan'l would escape to the curb outside, flipping stones into the street.

Despite the mayhem, Dan'l had a gift for learning. He became a serious swimmer and excelled at math. After graduating from Princeton, he went to work for Sony as a salesman of sound recorders made for businesses—and the Sony office just so happened to be next door to Apple's first real headquarters. One day in 1977, Dan'l bumped into Steve for the first time. He recalled him as "stinky, with holes in the jeans."

They remained in touch. When Sony invented the 3.5-inch floppy disk three years later—which would become the storage standard for the next two decades—Steve called Dan'l and asked for a demonstration at Apple's office on Bandley Drive. Impressed with the pitch, Steve recruited Dan'l to join Apple, where he quickly established a reputation as a top-performing salesman.

In 1983, Dan'l was asked to solve a big problem for the company. Apple needed to crack the university market, but it had no direct distribution into universities. Dan'l examined Apple's approach and delivered his verdict: "I need to undo everything you're doing." He laid out his terms to Steve, demanding complete control. "Stay out of my way unless I ask for help, and pay me when I'm done," Dan'l said. Steve agreed.

Dan'l built the University Consortium virtually single-handedly, establishing relationships with twenty-four universities, including Harvard, Stanford, Yale, Carnegie Mellon, and the University of Michigan.

As he traveled, Dan'l kept hearing the same demand: Professors wanted 3M machines. The term *3M* referred to workstations with a megabyte of memory, a million-pixel display, and enough processing power to handle a million instructions per second—instructions being the tiny steps a computer takes to get anything done, from adding two numbers to moving a pixel on the screen.

The leading laboratories of the day, including Xerox PARC, had released a handful of 3M computers to Stanford and Carnegie Mellon. But the devices were so expensive they had to be donated. Meanwhile, the everyday PCs housed at university departments had one eighth to one third of the 3M's power—not enough to enable meaningful research advancements.

Scientists and researchers were eager to see who would produce the first commercial 3M machine. They wanted to buy them in large numbers and for the price of no more than $10,000 each (about $33,000 in 2026 money). In essence, they hoped to put supercomputer capabilities on individual desks.

Despite the lack of a 3M machine, the Apple University Consortium became a massive success, moving nearly fifty thousand units of inventory while Mac retail sales stalled.

Over the ensuing years, the quest for a 3M machine haunted Steve. It led him to begin developing something called the BigMac, which he planned as a powerful 3M successor to the Mac. In the hands of Nobel laureates and National Medal of Science winners, Steve believed the BigMac could be a tool of epic scientific change. It would help him fulfill his lifelong dream of shaping the course of history.

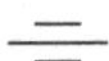

But during the summer of 1985, Steve and his BigMac were nowhere to be seen at Apple. Rather than building futuristic computers, John was busy slashing budgets. On June 14, Apple employees booted up their computers to find a devastating announcement: Apple was laying off 1,200 employees, more than one fifth of its workforce. The company's plants in Texas, California, and Ireland would all be shuttered.

Then, four days later, Apple announced its first-ever quarterly loss, of $17.2 million.

Amid the doldrums, John lauded one division for posting strong sales: Dan'l's education division. The education market had become Apple's most lucrative, with long-term growth potential. Apple also saw it as a means of turning young people into lifelong Apple customers.

But their success didn't save Dan'l's team from John's sweeping layoffs. Dan'l recounted that John asked him to whittle the department down to ten people from his staff of about sixty. When Dan'l pushed back, reminding John that the education market was Apple's most successful business, John pointed out that the snack-chip manufacturer Frito-Lay had managed to build a successful brand with only ten people in the marketing department.

Dan'l chafed at the cuts—and at John's defense of them. Steve would never have drawn such a soulless analogy. More than that, Dan'l found the cuts to be dangerously shortsighted. "The research showed that two thirds of Apple's business was in education," Dan'l recalled. Why clamp down on a key, growing market?

Steve, still pondering, couldn't shake the idea of a 3M machine. When he later told the founding story of NeXT, he would bedazzle the press with the perfect tale. But it was largely a myth. It went like this.

Steve first met Paul Berg, a tall, gregarious biochemist, at a Stanford luncheon in 1984. Paul, fifty-nine and the winner of a Nobel Prize for creating the first recombinant DNA molecule, was teeming with bleeding-edge insights about the creation of life.

In late August 1985, Steve and Paul sat for lunch in Palo Alto. Steve began grilling Paul about how researchers used computers—and why they didn't more often. Specifically, he wanted Paul to explain why biologists weren't using computers to model DNA experiments. In theory, computers would speed them up exponentially.

Over two and a half hours, Paul described to Steve the level of complication involved in conducting biology experiments. With each trial, Paul's team had to choose different temperatures, enzymes, and other variables and then wait to see what worked via trial and error. The 3M machines capable of handling all of these factors were prohibitively expensive, even for well-funded laboratories.

Steve left the lunch in awe. And Paul reciprocated Steve's respect. He loved the Silicon Valley start-up culture that Steve had helped forge and he insisted that his own Nobel-winning research could only have been possible in the cooperative, entrepreneurial environment of the Bay Area.

Steve came away from the meeting feeling confident that he could offer scientists and researchers the product they clearly needed: a more affordable 3M machine.

"And gradually," Steve said, "my spirits started to come back little by little."

This story Steve told about his lunch with Paul was far more elegant than the real story. As Dan'l later recalled, Steve understood the power of being able to say, "I met with Paul Berg, and there was an epiphany." He knew that name-dropping Nobel Prize winners carried weight.

Not long after, Rich Page called Steve, distraught. Rich was one of Apple's star hardware engineers—a six-foot-four, 270-pound Hewlett-Packard veteran who could design cutting-edge computers and wasn't intimidated by Steve's legendary tantrums. If Rich was upset, it was serious.

Jean-Louis had just canceled the BigMac, Rich said. According to him, Jean-Louis's new regime operated on a simple principle: If Steve's name was anywhere near a project, it was dead on arrival. Rich wasn't the only one feeling suddenly homeless. Dan'l, too, saw Jean-Louis's reign as a regime purge more than a corporate reorganization. It brought to mind the French phrase "The king is dead. Long live the king!"

While Steve's loyalists were put out to pasture, their projects canceled, in swept the new court of Jean-Louis.

Steve decided to found a new company to build a 3M computer. His decision came together gradually, inspired by conversations that proved influential over time.

One debate stuck with him. Two years earlier, before the Mac's commercial release, Steve had visited Andy van Dam, Computer Science Department chairman at Brown University, to demonstrate the Mac. Instead, Andy showed Steve an auditorium filled with forty Apollo workstations, networked together and costing around $50,000 each. He was blunt about the Mac's comparative limitations.

"Steve, look at these machines in our auditorium," he said, gesturing at the powerful workstations. "They all have hard drives. They're networked together. This is proven technology. I love the idea of an affordable, little computer, but nobody's going to be satisfied with the amount of memory you have."

Steve dismissed him; the argument grew into a "big fight," Andy recalled. But the confrontation planted something. Now, with Steve sidelined, the professor's words carried new weight.

Steve would need a world-class team to build the machine researchers actually wanted, so he began reaching out to the Apple colleagues he knew and trusted best. Winning them over wouldn't be an easy task—Apple, for all its troubles, was still a successful brand name. By contrast, Steve was at the nadir of his power. Betting on him and his vision would be risky.

Staying at Apple had downsides too. Like Dan'l, many Apple employees resented John's staid leadership style and Jean-Louis's overreach. They missed Steve's vision, his passion for technology, and his panache. Some even took to wearing T-shirts around the office that read "We want our Jobs back."

Steve first pitched the idea of starting a new company to Rich, asking him to join the unnamed start-up as VP of digital hardware engineering. Rich—still deeply frustrated with Jean-Louis—accepted.

Susan Barnes was another key target. A Wharton MBA originally hired to be Apple's general accounting manager, she had been elevated to controller of the Macintosh Division, where she was one of four people who had reported directly to Steve. Her financial expertise would be crucial to raising funds at the new company.

When Steve called with his offer, Susan mentioned that she would have to stay at Apple through September 30 in order qualify for her annual bonus.

"Too bad," he told her.

She was inclined to accept regardless. Life at Apple under John had become a chaotic grind, forcing Susan and her team to work until two or three in the morning frantically revising budgets and financial models.

But Susan was a package deal. "He knew [Bud and I] were dating at the time," she explained. Bud Tribble, Susan's partner, had joined Apple in 1981 while studying medicine and researching neurological disorders as a dual MD/PhD student at the University of Washington. He had also learned technology from some of the greatest software minds of his day. He opted to abandon a stable future in medicine to join Apple, where he helped design the Mac's user interface.

Bud liked Steve. And he admired his ability to incorporate art into technology. Unhappy with Apple's direction under John, Bud and Susan decided to sign on to Steve's next venture as a pair.

George Crow, the analog engineer who designed the Mac's video system and power supply, didn't wait to be recruited. Unhappy with Jean-Louis's leadership and the "very uncomfortable environment" at Apple, he picked up the phone and called Steve directly.

"Are you planning to do anything?" George asked.

"Well, yes, as a matter of fact, I am," Steve replied. Before the call ended, Steve had asked George to join as VP of analog hardware engineering.

On the Tuesday after Labor Day weekend, Dan'l's phone rang while he was in the shower. It was Steve, asking him to meet at his house in Woodside that evening for a walk. As they strolled side by side, Steve laid out his vision: a new computer company focused on universities, the market Dan'l knew better than anyone.

Dan'l was interested but had conditions. His wife, Susan, was still recovering from a surgery, and he wasn't about to gamble his family's future on Steve's latest inspiration. "I told Steve I wasn't interested in saying yes until I knew who was going to run software," Dan'l recalled. Two days later, when Steve said it would be Bud, Dan'l's resistance cracked. He respected Bud's technical brilliance and trusted his judgment. That sealed the deal.

Dan'l rounded out Steve's coterie of cofounders.

By phone, Steve delivered the news to everyone that would make their conspiracy real. He was resigning from Apple the next week, on Thursday, September 12. He proposed that the five cofounders would follow the day after, as recommended by Apple's own outside counsel, Larry Sonsini, who advised Steve on the proper way to handle the departures. "Apple wasn't going to be directly competitive, not necessarily," Larry recounted as to why he helped Steve. If they were still in with the plan, they were to meet Steve at his home the evening after he resigned.

For Dan'l, Susan, Bud, Rich, and George, a realization dawned: They had just hatched a mutiny. They couldn't back out now. If they had made the wrong choice, it could devastate their careers and upend their lives.

3

JUMPING SHIP

Before Steve and the five submitted their resignations from Apple, Steve planned to address the board. He wanted to tell them about his departure himself and offer a proposal to cushion the blow.

"I've been thinking a lot and it's time for me to get on with my life," Steve began at the September 12 board meeting. "It's obvious that I've got to do something. I'm thirty years old." He slid into a soliloquy about how meaningful it had been to bring computers to schools and universities at Apple and how passionately he felt about helping the next generation discover computing, John recounted in his memoir, *Odyssey.*

Then, his big announcement: He was going to leave Apple to design a computer for the university market. At first, the board members appeared puzzled, unsure of what Steve was really saying. He reassured them that his new company wouldn't compete with Apple. But, he said, holding up his hand with five fingers outstretched, he would need to take a few "low-level" Apple employees with him.

He offered Apple the chance to buy distribution rights to his forthcoming product, though he wasn't completely sure what the product would be. Heck, he'd even give Apple the opportunity to license Macintosh software for his new device. He reassured them that however it turned out, it would be a great deal for Apple.

As Steve spoke, the board members grew visibly annoyed. Steve was overplaying his hand, a recurring annoyance they had about him. By framing his departure as a favor to them, he glossed over the fact that he was abandoning his company in a moment of challenge, poaching its employees, and pitching a start-up with long odds of success.

"Why would you take anyone at all?" asked Mike Markkula, Apple's original investor and mentor to Steve.

"Don't get upset," Steve replied. "These are very low-level people that you won't miss, and they will be leaving anyway." Both assertions were untrue.

Despite their irritation, the board recognized Steve's talent and the upside of maintaining a positive relationship with him. They asked Steve to leave the room so they could discuss his offer. Then they called Steve back in: Apple would agree to purchase up to a 10 percent stake in Steve's new company on the condition that its products would complement, and not compete with, Apple's.

Steve asked for time to think about it. He didn't want to commit to anything concrete yet—he still had to secure the departures of his five cofounders.

That night, Steve returned home to his historic mansion, the Jackling House, a thirty-minute drive from Apple's Cupertino headquarters. Located in a quiet, forested neighborhood, the home featured thirty rooms spread across two floors. There he met his cofounders to help them plan their exits, which were to happen the next day. They had to be strategic. Any missteps could get them fired before they had a chance to quit or, worse, ostracized from the tight-knit world of Silicon Valley.

Also there: Larry, Apple's outside counsel who was helping Steve structure his new company. Steve recounted the board's uncomfortable reaction. "I did what you recommended, Larry," Dan'l recalled Steve saying. Then Larry left. But he stayed involved in the new venture, "ever present, very sincere," Dan'l recalled.

That evening, the five set their split of the company ownership: Steve would take 70 percent of the shares, 20 percent would go to future employees, and the five cofounders would split the final 10 percent, at 2 percent each.

Steve's hired cook, Mark, served the kind of meal that had become Steve's signature: a salad course, followed by pasta with fresh vegetables from the garden, topped off with another salad for dessert.

Steve himself ate mostly Medjool dates, part of his latest diet.

Early the next morning, as John wrote in his memoir, Steve called John's office and asked for five minutes with him at 7:25 a.m. It was Friday the thirteenth and John had a foreboding feeling.

At 7:25, Steve entered John's office and handed him an envelope. John opened it and unfolded a typewritten note listing the five Apple employees who would resign that day: Rich Page, Dan'l Lewin, Bud Tribble, Susan Barnes, and George Crow.

John looked up, shocked.

These were not "low-level" employees, as Steve had claimed. Susan was financial controller of the company's important Macintosh Division. Rich was a senior engineer with access to projects across Apple. Bud had worked on the Mac's user interface and was revered by his teammates for his technical brilliance. George had salvaged the entire Macintosh launch by designing a new floppy drive when the original disk failed just months before shipping.

Dan'l, meanwhile, had built Apple's most profitable business from the ground up and was running all of the company's education sales. Its continued success rested on his relationships with university buyers. Now Dan'l would be taking his skills, knowledge, and relationships with him.

John panicked. He feared not only the loss of talent but also the loss of secrets. The defectors carried Apple's schedules, costs, and product plans in their heads—knowledge that could give Steve's new company an instant advantage. Steve asked John to ensure that the departures would be "as smooth and unharassed" as possible.

At 7:30, John delivered the news to his top six executives gathered in the boardroom. As he read off the names of the departing leaders one by one, the meeting devolved into chaos. Jean-Louis and Jay accused John of failing to assert leadership. He had let this happen, they said, by failing to advocate more fiercely for Apple's interests.

Then they turned their ire toward Steve, who was not in the room. This team had been working late nights and losing sleep through the company's hardest year yet—only for Steve to pick up and leave with their most talented staff. It was more than a slap in the face. Steve had just launched an attack against Apple. And he was still chairman of the board, making it a dereliction of his fiduciary duty. They feared his departure could send Apple over the edge.

As they discussed what to do next, a consensus quickly emerged. Apple, they told John, needed to move decisively against Steve.

One and a half hours later, around 9:00 a.m., the five cofounders submitted their resignation letters. Apple's response was swift: Security guards escorted them out of the building. The five felt upset at the treatment—after years of hard work building Apple, they had become pariahs.

They retreated once again to the Jackling House.

Fortunately for his coconspirators, Steve had progressed past the forced austerity of his younger days, when his furniture consisted of little more than a mattress in his bedroom, folding chairs for guests, and a picture of Albert Einstein on the wall. Now Steve told *Newsweek*, "I bought a few Eames chairs, so I have a place to sit down and read a book other than the floor."

Everyone gathered in Steve's living room. But rather than celebrating their exit, they faced an awkward question: "Now what?" Dan'l asked. Their new company had no name. No business plan. No product. Only a vague vision of building computers for universities. Steve and the team huddled for days to figure out how to get it off the ground.

As they worked through possibilities, Steve's confidence began to falter. He wondered aloud whether he had become washed up, an impostor, yesterday's visionary. He asked if he was doomed to spend the rest of his life wandering aimlessly.

Compounding his insecurity, hostile board members were speaking to *The Wall Street Journal*, tearing Steve to shreds anonymously. The trash talk became a regular occurrence. Steve complained to Apple board member Mike Markkula that the reports were both "misleading to the public" and "unfair to me" and that Apple was "adopting a hostile posture towards me and the new venture."

At the same time, Steve shot back. "I think it is fair to say that the people running Apple are not from the valley at this point in time," Steve told *Newsweek*. "If the culture of the valley and some of the principles and practices of the valley are truncated, then I think it is pretty likely that the innovation will stop."

Reporters camped outside Steve's house to get his reaction to the conflict. "I'm not bitter. I'm not bitter," he said. But he wasn't convincing anyone. "He was not a happy camper," Dan'l recalled.

To move forward, Steve urgently needed two things: money and a name. Ten days into the new endeavor, Steve announced he would sell off $21.4 million of Apple stock; he then invested $7 million of his own money in the new company.

It was the fifth time he had filed with the Securities and Exchange

Commission (SEC) to sell shares that summer and a financial disaster for Steve—Apple's stock was hovering around its lowest-ever price, down from its highs following the release of the Mac nearly two years earlier. Within five months, he'd sold the last of his stock; he kept one share so he would receive corporate reports. In order to get the new company off the ground, Steve ate the loss.

Dan'l was appointed the intermediary for the stock sales and made calls to Morgan Stanley on behalf of Steve. "Are you serious?" the brokers asked. The severity of the losses sounded ludicrous to them.

"Yes, he wants it gone," Dan'l said.

For help with the company's name, Steve turned to a friend named Tom Suiter. Tom was a gregarious and highly creative graphic artist who had designed the Mac's packaging. Plus, he was an independent consultant, leaving him free from Apple, where much of the rest of Steve's network remained stuck. "Hey," a voice said when Tom picked up the phone, "I'm starting a new company."

"What are you going to call it?" Tom asked.

"Two," Steve replied. "For my second company."

Two? Seriously? Tom thought it was a terrible name, making it sound like Steve's new company was going to be second best to Apple. "Everybody's going to ask what happened to number one," he panned.

Steve wanted Tom's suggestion for a name. Tom said he'd get back to him. He was about to attend a Microsoft conference in Seattle where Bill Gates was set to speak about a novel technology known as the CD-ROM.

From the stage, Bill extolled the virtues of the CD. He said it would displace the floppy disk and transform how we watch media, listen to music, and access our information. As Bill spoke, he kept saying the word *next.* The *next* big thing, the *next* device, the *next* standard, all coming in the *next* year. "I had my little journal," Tom said, "and I wrote down the word *next* probably twenty-five times."

Listening to Steve's greatest rival, Tom experienced an epiphany. He hopped on an airplane back to San Francisco and called Steve.

"I got it," Tom said, heart pounding, "Next."

Silence on the other end. Then: "I *love* it!"

The name Next imbued a sense of agency, suggesting that Steve had leapt onward to his next great endeavor where he would make cooler and more advanced technology than he had at Apple. Steve didn't seem at all bothered that the name was inspired by the words of a frenemy. On September 19, 1985, he registered the name Next Inc. with the state of California.

Apple's lawyers watched Steve's every move. Once he filed a name, it was time to strike. On September 23, John sent a memo to all Apple employees. "After long and careful deliberation, Apple's board of directors and officers have decided to file a lawsuit against Steve," he wrote. "The matter is now in the hands of our lawyers."

That day, when John announced the news in the company auditorium, staff members broke into tears. Steve, the spiritual father of Apple, had turned into a nemesis.

Later that afternoon, at 3:35 p.m., a process server wound through Woodside's forested hills to Steve's estate. Reading through the documents, the team saw that Apple had singled out two codefendants: Steve and Rich. Steve, for supposedly running off with valuable proprietary information as a board member. And Rich, for allegedly handing Apple's 3M technology to Next.

As Rich was the hardware engineer who could actually build the machine, without him, Next would effectively just be Steve talking. "[Apple] was hoping they could discourage me and scare me off," Rich said.

But the team quickly found a hole in Apple's lawsuit. Next had no hardware yet—nothing beyond the vague idea of building a 3M machine for university science departments. What could they possibly have stolen from Apple? And how could a no-name company like Next—six people in Steve's living room—present a threat to a decade-old tech titan like Apple?

But Apple meant business. One day, Steve took a phone call from Apple's lawyers and the Phoenix-based firm representing them called Brown & Bain. Rich remembered them as "gunslingers." He said that lead attorney Jack Brown had two rules: He didn't lose and he didn't give up.

After the call, Steve turned to Susan, his closest confidante. "They said they're going to have me arrested!" he told her.

4

THE CRUCIBLE OF DREAMS AND DEPOSITIONS

On October 2, Dan'l received a certified envelope from Brown & Bain. It contained a letter reminding him that he had never officially completed an exit interview before leaving Apple. Now the company's lawyers were asking him to complete one in writing.

They asked him to confirm whether or not he had knowledge of eight Apple "trade secrets," starting with the existence of the BigMac, the prototype Apple had canceled the previous summer.

Dan'l refused. "In viewing the pending litigation, I do not believe it would be appropriate for me to comment on 'the list' included in your letter," he wrote back, "which I assume you drafted for purposes of the lawsuit."

Dan'l was going into the legal fight with Apple nearly broke. He had a mortgage, college loans, two kids, and a wife who'd just suffered a medical issue. His involvement in the lawsuit could destroy not just

Next but his ability to work anywhere in the Valley—no employer wanted to hire a troublemaker.

And his association with Steve wouldn't save him. At this point, Steve wasn't yet regarded as an undisputed genius in the industry. Instead, people saw him as "the terrible infant," as Dan'l put it. He could sell anything, but his reputation was poison. When Steve tried to poach other great Apple engineers, they had refused to follow him.

More thick envelopes landed at Next every few days. They contained deposition notices and document demands with tight deadlines. For counsel, Steve turned to the firm McCutchen, Doyle, Brown & Enersen and its intellectual property expert Gary Moore, a litigator with a gentle smile and a law degree from Harvard. Gary had a crisp courtroom style and plenty of experience defending fledgling start-ups.

But finding him hadn't been easy. Apple had retained almost every major law firm in Silicon Valley, conflicting them out of representing Steve and Rich. Larry Sonsini's firm was among them; he had to temporarily stop advising Steve since his firm was already on retainer to Apple.

Gary's firm had adopted a policy of never representing Apple. "We found it was good business," Gary recalled, "because we could then defend people when Apple was on the other side." McCutchen Doyle became Silicon Valley's designated Apple opposition firm.

When Steve came calling, Gary jumped at the chance to represent him. "Steve Jobs was obviously even then Steve Jobs," Gary said. "We just thought this was an interesting case for an interesting defendant."

Gary understood Apple's strategy. He knew the company didn't have a real case against Next—Apple's lawyers couldn't say which secrets Next had stolen because it didn't know what Next was doing. But they could strangle the company by keeping the Next team tied up in depositions and forcing it to spend countless dollars in legal fees. That would be time and money not spent building computers.

Apple also believed that Steve and Rich amounted to trade secret time bombs, ready to deploy everything they'd learned about Apple's advanced projects at Next. The concern wasn't entirely paranoid; Rich and George's knowledge about Apple's forthcoming projects could jump-start Next's development by years.

But Gary had seen this movie before. California courts had spent decades sorting out when departing employees crossed the line from legitimate competition into corporate theft. The classic case involved milkmen who left one dairy and immediately started delivering for a competitor. They won their cases when they found customers through public directories. They lost when they stole their former employer's customer lists and hijacked their routes.

The courts had distilled this into a simple test: Did you steal your old boss's secret customer list, or did you just look everyone up in the phone book? Did you target the old boss's customers *with the intent of screwing over your old boss*?

Apple hoped to paint Dan'l as the thief of the customer list, acting on Steve's orders. "They wanted to pin me as the milkman," he said.

In the lawsuit, Apple's lawyers kept calling it a "nefarious scheme." They alleged that Dan'l would use confidential customer information to unfairly compete against Apple. But in higher education, there was no secret customer list to steal.

Dan'l could prove it. At University of Texas at Austin, academic computing director Charlie Warlick published a reference book every year, titled the *Directory of Computing Facilities in Higher Education*. It contained entries on 1,700 institutions, including information about their computing infrastructure, contact names, and phone numbers. All of it was public—essentially, the yellow pages of academic computing. Dan'l had referenced the book at Apple and wanted to use it at Next, though he already knew many of the key people in the university market.

Where the law was concerned, Next was on solid ground. But if a Next employee admitted to using Apple contacts or files, Apple's weak case would suddenly have teeth. So Next team members walked a tightrope. One verbal stumble in a deposition could turn the dream of Next into one very expensive legal bill. Gary made a rule for any new Next recruits leaving Apple: "Don't bring anything. Don't bring your Rolodex. Don't bring your files."

In public, Steve put on his game face—all Zen composure and confidence. "I wasn't aware that Apple owned me, you know," Steve said to *Newsweek*. "It is hard to think that a $2 billion company with 4,300-plus people couldn't compete with six people in blue jeans."

Privately, the suit hit him hard.

"We had no idea that Apple would take this action," Dan'l recalled. "It just didn't really make any sense to us." Overnight, the start-up went from an idealistic dream to legal combat zone. Meetings blurred into late nights as the six founders huddled around tables and sofas, parsing legal memos that seemed to multiply by the day. The question no one dared to ask: What if Next was over before it even began?

"It was stressful," Rich recalled. But the siege forced the team to take a practical approach. Next's document retention policy, Dan'l explained with a slight grin, was elegantly simple: They didn't retain documents. There was, as it happened, nothing much to keep anyway.

Legal warfare had the unexpected side effect of welding the team together like combat veterans. And Steve, displaying the single-minded determination that had made him famous at Apple, refused to let anything slow him down.

"Now, you might say we're all crazy," he told *Newsweek*. "We have a general direction. We want to find out what higher education needs. We plan to visit a lot of colleges in October and just listen. Then we want to build it for them, whatever it is."

The team scattered into the field like corporate anthropologists. They haunted electronics shops like ComputerLand and Businessland, lurking in the aisles to watch which machines made people stop and stare and which ones they walked right past. The team made a careful study of product bundles and packaging choices.

Then they visited universities. In a fluorescent-lit office at Harvard, the entire team interviewed Harry Lewis, a professor of computer science who had been a friend of Apple for years. He laid it out plainly: The software available on the market simply wasn't ready. It suffered from clumsy interfaces. Faculty didn't want to waste time learning to contend with clunky software. They also didn't want to have to learn to code, though they did want to develop their own applications. Finally, the price would have to be right. "It has to be under $3,000," Harry said.

Harry had watched Steve operate before. He'd toured the Mac assembly line in early 1984 and recognized something about Steve's approach: "Jobs's uncompromising insistence on simplicity sometimes got the better of him," Harry wrote. In other words, his refusal to compromise could be shortsighted.

At Brown, Andy van Dam, the professor who had first told Steve about the 3M concept, was even more blunt. "Courseware is at the Wright brothers stage," he said. And unless Next's hardware came in under $2,500 at volume, he was "exceedingly skeptical" any machine they built would ever work.

Michael Carter, who directed Stanford's academic computing strategy, told the team that professors needed tools simple enough to build simulations and tutorials on their own—"as easy to use as MacPaint," he said, referring to the dead-simple painting app for Mac. Institutions would buy the computer if it was priced between $3,000 and $5,000, Michael said. But if Next wanted to reach students directly, the price would have to come in below $2,000.

A 3M machine had long been higher ed's holy grail, but no one had managed to deliver it affordably. Now, after conversations with the Next team, universities believed someone might succeed. "He had a ready-made audience in higher ed for his product," Michael said.

But first, Steve had to survive the depositions.

At Steve's house, Gary gathered the team around stacks of legal briefs and sample deposition questions. He outlined two rules for them. "First of all, tell the truth," he said. "And second, answer the question—and all you have to do is answer the question. Don't tell them everything you know about a topic."

On the chilly morning of December 3, Steve walked into Brown & Bain's Palo Alto office for his deposition. Everyone expected it to be brutal and, sure enough, Apple's lawyers came out swinging. "[They] did absolutely everything they could to piss him off," remembered George. "I was sitting there just waiting for him to blow."

But remarkably, Steve kept his cool. "I was really impressed," George said.

After Steve finished, Rich took his turn in the hot seat. Apple's lawyers flashed BigMac schematics in front of him. The intricate technical blueprints were Rich's own handiwork.

"Did you use this at Next?"

"No, because we don't even have a product yet," Rich replied.

During the deposition, the Next lawyers kept objecting to the Apple team's questions and framing. So the lawyers had to keep calling the assigned judge for the case, Peter Stone, for rulings. After one too many calls, Judge Stone got in his car and drove down to the deposition site himself.

At fifty-eight, Judge Stone was a seasoned jurist, known in San Jose legal circles for his long hair, muttonchops, and a mustache that curled down at the ends like commas. Once in the room, he watched the proceedings with bemusement, apparently unsure whether the drama was primarily legal or theatrical. But the technological aspects of the case left him adrift. During a break, the judge turned to Rich and asked, "Unix—is that hardware or software?"

Over the next three weeks, George, Bud, Susan, and Dan'l endured depositions of their own.

"How much do you all get paid?" Apple's lawyers asked Susan.

"We don't know yet," she said. "We haven't done any of that."

The Apple lawyers tried to pin Dan'l to an admission about stealing Apple's distribution list, but Dan'l had come prepared. He dropped the directory of academic computing departments by Charlie Warlick on the conference table.

"Here's my Rolodex," he told Apple's lawyers. "Call Charlie if you want a copy."

That killed Apple's milkman theory, but the lawyers kept pushing, producing more than six thousand pages of documents and criticizing Next for providing "virtually nothing" in return. For Judge Stone, the disparity only seemed to underscore how little Next had actually built.

In their motions, Gary and the defense team laid out their logic: "Apple can't have discovery into Next until they identify the stolen trade secrets."

Apple's lawyer Jack Brown shot back with a circular argument: "But Apple can't identify the stolen trade secrets until we get discovery into Next."

Judge Stone watched the ping-pong match with growing bewilderment. "The judge clearly thought the whole thing was ridiculous," Rich said. "I remember him shaking his head during hearings, like, 'Why am I even dealing with this?'"

After five weeks, Judge Stone had seen enough. When Apple tried to overwhelm Next with sweeping, ill-defined trade secret claims, he pushed back hard. In the end, he tossed out whole portions of Apple's case for being too broad.

Amid the fighting, the Next team began to wonder if Apple's all-out lawsuit was making Next seem like a bigger deal than it really was. Steve sensed an opening. If Apple wanted to cast Next as the villain, he would take advantage of the spotlight.

Steve hoped to win the narrative—as much for the future of the company as public perception. He believed strong teams needed a visionary story to believe in. So he called John Nathan, a filmmaker he knew.

John had previously made *In Search of Excellence*, a series of vignettes about successful companies that included a glowing portrait of the Mac team. Steve had been difficult during that earlier shoot—a "full blossomed pain in the ass," John said—but Steve liked the resulting film. When John secured funding from Merrill Lynch to make his second film, Steve agreed to participate.

Now Steve wanted him to make a war documentary about Next. "I'm going to disobey my lawyer," Steve told John. "They're telling me I shouldn't get near this with a ten-foot pole because I'm being sued by Apple. But we're going to let you in."

John loved exploring the human currents underlying commerce. The chance to embed with Steve once again sounded too good to pass up. Steve asked John to come and film Next's first team retreat, a landmark event for the new company. The footage would air on prime-time PBS as part of *Entrepreneurs*, a documentary about four emerging businesses.

In December 1985, the Next team caravanned to the resort town of Pebble Beach, whose windswept cypresses, coastal fog, and crashing surf invited rest and introspection. The group, which now included five additional hires poached from Apple, checked in to a cluster of rooms and gathered in a grand conference room with ocean views.

Steve stood before his team—and John's cameras—in a crisp white shirt, red suspenders, and a black turtleneck. He was deliberate and composed. "More important than building a product," Steve said, "we are in the process of architecting a company that will hopefully be much, much more incredible. The total will be much more incredible than the sum of its parts."

Apple, he added, "was built from the heart. Unfortunately, we didn't always use our heads and we can do better in many respects, because we are wiser, and smarter, and know more, and those kinds of things."

Over the next two days, the team debated two of Steve's proposed parameters for the project: first, that the machine cost no more than $3,000 as per their conversations with university officials. And second, that the computer would have to launch by spring 1987. Universities acquired new computers during summer break, and if the team missed that window, a year of momentum would be lost.

The latter point was particularly controversial. A new marketing contractor, Joanna Hoffman, who had recently joined Next from Apple, wasn't afraid to tell Steve so.

Joanna knew that Steve's reality distortion field could motivate people, but she worried it could also get them into trouble. Set an unrealistic date, she cautioned, and the team would be forced into flawed design decisions. She reminded Steve that when they had been at Apple, this exact dynamic had led them to put out an unrealistic list of fifteen software packages that would be released in one year, only to make bad design decisions under pressure, and then be forced to tear up their work and start over.

Steve cut in. Next needed to plant a stake in the ground, he said. If they missed the spring 1987 window, sales would fall short, they'd fail to cover operating costs, and word would spread that Next was flailing. "A lot of the credibility starts to erode," he warned.

But, George asked, would any customers take the 1987 deadline seriously in the first place? He also doubted the team's ability to finish software in that time, pointing out they'd been burned at Apple when they'd tried to create a word processor that was supposed to take six months but remained unfinished three years later. "That's what I'm worried about," he said.

"Well, George," Steve snapped, "I can't change the world!" Steve rejected the idea that past failures guaranteed future ones. "If we don't do this," Steve said, "we will not be able to attract great people, we will not be able to retain some of the ones we have, and it just won't be us."

Ultimately, Steve ended the debate. The team would have eighteen months to build an entire computer—along with its operating system—

from scratch, and that would be that. They knew the ambitious timeline reflected one of Steve's core mantras: *Great artists ship*.

Some, including Joanna, still felt uneasy about the timeline. She had come to Next from Apple partly out of loyalty to Steve, marveling at his ability to "pick up and run again and get all excited" after everything he'd been through. Yet something felt different this time. For the first time in her years of working with Steve, she felt jaded.

As Next's goals began to come into focus, so did its culture.

Susan described the initial team dynamic as a circle: everyone facing each other, absorbing the mission in unison. Soon, each cofounder would have to turn outward and build his or her respective wedge of the company: marketing, finance, hardware, and software. But it would only work if they trusted one another.

Accordingly, Steve set a high bar for new recruits—"Zero is better than a negative," he said. He sought both brilliance and breadth: champion swimmers, musicians, surfers—people with edge. In interviews, he posed each candidate a trick question. He might say, "Are you the best hardware designer in your field?"

If the candidate said no, he would reply, "Then I'd rather talk to them!"

Steve was obsessed with finding and keeping the best people. And he had witnessed what happened when leaders failed to do it.

In late 1985, Steve decided he wanted in to the advancements happening in the computer graphics industry. Susan accompanied him to George Lucas's ranch in Marin County to evaluate the Lucasfilm Computer Division, which owned the unit that would later become Pixar, for a potential acquisition. There, Steve watched its owner, George Lucas, operate with a different philosophy.

George, cash-strapped from a $35 million divorce settlement, was threatening to fire the division's entire team if no buyer emerged. His approach to creative work seemed to be to assemble the world's best team, complete the movie, and then "blow them out," Susan said—dissolve the group and start fresh next time.

According to Susan, Steve found this approach revolting. At Next, he was determined to build the opposite: a permanent ensemble of brilliant people who would stay for the next impossible project and the next one after that. Steve wanted grokking from team members—full-body absorption of the company's DNA.

Negotiations with George stalled almost immediately. He wanted too much money. Besides, Ed Catmull—the computer scientist who had cofounded the Lucasfilm Computer Division and built its technical foundation—made it clear that even if Steve purchased the company, it wouldn't be his sandbox to control.

But George soon folded, under financial pressure from his divorce. In February 1986, Steve bought the company for $5 million and renamed it Pixar Animation Studios. The sale price was a sixth of George's original ask, but it would prove to be just the beginning of Steve's financial commitment. More importantly, he set terms that respected Ed's authority while assembling an anti-Lucas model: a permanent team of brilliant people, not a disposable crew. "We have to be loyal to each other," Steve told Ed.

Pixar worked with technology Steve didn't understand—computer graphics and animation—and he was forced to trust his team's expertise. Ed observed that Steve "didn't know anything about graphics or the direction it was going. He just believed it was going to become important." Ed even asked Steve to stay out of creative meetings because his presence was so overpowering that he could derail discussions simply by speaking.

Where Ed handled the Pixar team, at Next, Steve would become his own biggest obstacle to keeping great people. He was determined to manage everything, from the exact shades of color used in the logo down to the angle of robots on the factory floor—decisions that often brought him into conflict with his team. As Susan liked to remind him about Silicon Valley talent, "your assets have feet" and could walk out anytime.

Sticking with Steve demanded a certain temperament. Steve respected talented people who could fight. "Next was a very intellectually contentious environment," recalled Leo Hourvitz, a software developer who joined Next in December 1985. You had to be willing to push back against Steve. Your ideas would survive only if you could "evangelize . . . and convince all the smart people around that this was the best option," Leo said.

The culture was so intensely combative that when Next veterans moved on to other companies, their new colleagues would tell them to dial it back. They'd been conditioned for a kind of intellectual warfare that didn't exist elsewhere.

At the same time, Steve attempted to impose order. For example, through radical pay transparency. Everyone knew exactly what everyone else made: $75,000 for senior staff and $50,000 for everyone else. He didn't tolerate salary politics.

Steve cultivated a feverish culture where everyone felt they were holding the levers of history—charged by Steve's ability to bend reality itself. "We thought we had more power than we really had," recalled a finance executive.

The illusion was intoxicating. The question was whether Steve, having built this arena of genius, could resist playing god and listen when his champions fought back.

Though Apple's lawsuit still loomed, the team left Pebble Beach renewed and united. Toward the beginning of 1986, Next moved from Steve's living room into its first real office in the Stanford Research Park at the foot of the Palo Alto hills, where the wind rustled the trees and horses wandered in the distance.

At the same time, Apple began to weary of its extended legal siege.

Throughout the ordeal, Steve, Rich, and their defense lawyers had met with Apple's general counsel, Al Eisenstat, every five or six weeks. It was the legal equivalent of divorced parents meeting over coffee—painful but necessary. By the fifth month, Al complained to them that a single set of depositions had blown past his entire annual budget.

Even something as seemingly simple as searching for Rich's name in the pre-web LexisNexis database turned into a money pit. One search produced a thirty-inch stack of printouts, which Apple divided among ten teams to comb through by hand. It took them three months to emerge with nothing. All told, the lawsuit's cost surpassed $20 million.

"You could stop," Steve told him.

Four months into the lawsuit, Apple showed up with a proposed settlement. Among other things, it would dictate the kind of computer Next would be allowed to build. Apple wanted to force Steve into building premium, high-performance computers exclusively.

For Steve, this was perfect—this was, after all, exactly what he had started Next to do. Bud watched Apple's own goal with disbelief. "I felt like Br'er Rabbit," he said. In the African American folktale, Br'er Rabbit tricks Br'er Fox into throwing him into a briar patch—the one place he most wants to be—by begging not to be thrown there.

According to Apple's terms, Next's machine would have to include a chip at 20 megahertz or faster, an intimidatingly powerful processor when Apple's lawyers wrote it down. The computer would need to have at least 4 megabytes of RAM, a luxury for 1986. And it had to have a high-resolution display with more pixels than Apple's—meaning crisper, clearer graphics that would make Apple's screens look fuzzy by comparison. The monitor also couldn't sit on top of the computer. Finally, the computer couldn't use Apple's floppy disk format or chipsets.

As Gary put it, the whole arrangement was essentially "an eyewash," a way for Apple to claim they'd gotten something out of their expensive legal crusade.

Finally, on January 17, 1986, Apple and Next settled. Though there was no admission of wrongdoing, the Next team knew who had won.

The settlement allowed Apple to inspect Next's future prototype computer to determine if any trade secrets had been stolen. If Apple suspected theft of its intellectual property, it could take the question to a court-appointed arbitrator, who would make a final ruling.

As Steve later recounted to Dan'l, when he and Al signed the settlement, Al looked at him, shook his head, and said, "Shame on us."

Steve came away with an unexpected gift: freedom. Apple's attempt to shackle him to a ruthless legal fight had failed, and now he was free to build the computer he had envisioned all along.

5

THE HERO-SHITHEAD ROLLERCOASTER

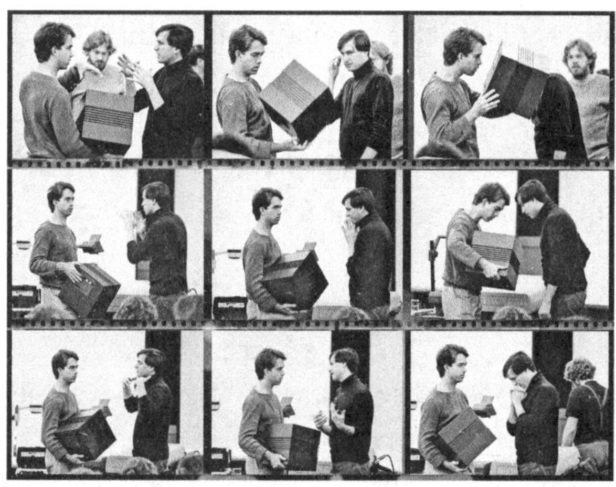

After the team's legal victory, Dan'l and his wife, Susan, went to dinner at Stanford computing director Michael Carter's house. It was supposed to be a small, quiet Friday evening. Then, as dinner was being prepared, Steve called Dan'l on his cell phone to celebrate the end of the lawsuit.

When Steve heard that Dan'l was at Michael's house, he invited himself and his girlfriend, Tina Redse, to the cozy gathering. Then he called back and asked if his Zen Buddhist monk, Kobun Otogawa, could join them as well.

Michael spun toward his then-wife. "The monk. What does he eat?" he asked. She was making pâté. Steve's monk was a member of the Japanese Zen tradition, which is generally vegetarian. "Oh, shit," Michael said, yanking open the refrigerator.

Michael worried that the night would be over before it even began. As he scurried to make a vegetable paella, he glanced outside his window. Under the stars, the Buddhist monk had arrived in flowing ocher-brown robes. He held a cigarette in one hand and a champagne glass in the other as he stood laughing with the small crowd.

Monks from most Buddhist traditions were expected to abstain from life's excesses—smoking, drinking—and to live austerely and separate from the laypeople who revered them. But Steve's monk followed his own code of enlightenment, refusing to be called by religious honorifics such as "Venerable" and not letting traditions get in the way of a good party.

Michael served what they had frantically prepared—paella with vegetables, the chicken and shellfish removed.

Steve's dedication to Japanese Zen, with its emphasis on simplicity and minimalism, informed his approach to design as well as to life. At meetings, Steve was already beginning to sketch out the form of the company's computer with his hands in the air. He kept making the same shape: a cube.

Steve had been inspired by a five-foot black cube called the Connection Machine, unveiled in 1985. It stood like the black monolith from the opening scene of *2001: A Space Odyssey*, its translucent panels revealing thousands of red LEDs blinking like synapses in a giant brain.

The machine was the brainchild of MIT computer scientist Danny Hillis, who wanted to build artificial intelligence by connecting sixty-four thousand processors in what he called a "20-dimensional hypercube." "Someday, perhaps soon, we will build a machine that will be able to perform the function of a human mind, a thinking machine," he wrote about his idea. Working with designer Tamiko Thiel, he transformed this mathematical concept into a striking physical form: eight smaller cubes fused into one large cube. Though it looked like a museum piece, and was later shown at the Museum of Modern Art in New York, the Connection Machine actually functioned as a supercomputer for scientific experiments.

Steve discovered the Connection Machine through Joanna Hoffman and became obsessed—here was proof that a computer's form could deliver emotional satisfaction alongside raw functionality. The cube shape also solved a legal problem: Apple's lawsuit settlement forbade Next from putting a monitor on top of the computer box. This pushed Steve toward designing a perfect cube that would sit next to, rather than under, the display.

Steve asked Joanna to find out who designed the Connection Machine. He wanted her to design the Next computer. By the time Joanna tracked down Tamiko, she had left for Germany to become an artist.

Instead, Steve hired a European design firm and tasked it with designing a perfect cube. "They called us and said, 'You've got to get on the next plane to Europe and see what we've come up with. We've done the obligatory cube,'" Steve recounted. "'But we have something far better that's going to change the shape of computing forever!'"

Steve flew to Europe and sat through "a really fantastic buildup." Every computer was going to look like this in five years, the designers promised.

"And they pulled off the curtain," Steve said. "And it was in the shape of a human head."

Aghast, Steve fired the designers.

For his third try, he called a designer who worked with Apple by the name of Hartmut Esslinger. Hartmut—tall with a mop of curly hair and a bold mustache—ran the iconoclastic firm frog design. In the cold, technical world of early computing, Hartmut was a renegade. His mantra: *Form follows emotion.* He thought computers should feel human, intuitive, even sensual.

Hartmut had moved to California from his native Germany in 1982 to work with Apple. The collaboration began with a design contest. "We chose six designers, gave them $100,000 each, and asked them to design five products," Steve told the *San Jose Mercury News*. Hartmut and his twelve-person team at frog design won the contest and were awarded a contract with Apple.

Hartmut began by sharing his assessment that Apple's existing products were clunky and uninspired. In response, Steve gave him carte blanche to experiment with a new direction. Hartmut's first triumph was the Apple IIc, which featured a crisp white aesthetic dubbed "Snow White." The look became a visual blueprint for Apple's next generation of tech. "Hartmut rescued us, and I think he's the best product designer in the world," Steve said about his work at Next.

By 1986, Hartmut had become disenchanted with John's soulless approach to building computers. After resolving his contractual obligations with Apple, he signed a new contract with Next and got to work on his kitchen table. He felt free to finally pursue a design with philosophical depth.

Hartmut was taken with Steve's idea of designing a cube. "It's a mystical shape that never exists in nature," Hartmut said. It was pure, unblemished, abstract. As much as any industrial product could, Hartmut hoped that a cube would challenge the user and invite contemplation.

Hartmut drew inspiration from ancient geometry—the Greek cubic form, which was later echoed in Islamic architecture through the Kaaba, the sacred black stone structure in Mecca that Muslims face during prayer.

The cube had other, more practical advantages too. Steve later explained that, after examining several shapes, the cube was "by far the most efficient in terms of packaging stuff in here," such as the motherboard, chips, and hardware features. "We can fit up to 1.3 gigabytes in here now, up to 3 next year, so what you can fit in a one-foot cube, which is a smaller footprint than a PC . . . is quite remarkable."

Hartmut and Steve decided to make the cube black, like the Kaaba and the Connection Machine. As a machine designed for scholars, they felt black would imbue it with a sense of seriousness, power, and mystery. It also marked a deliberate departure from Apple's cheerful white.

Steve called the new computer "The Scholar's Workstation," and wrote in his business plan that it would "help revolutionize learning in the next five years."

Steve also needed a world-class logo. Four graphic designers had pitched Steve, but he found their work generic and forgettable. Then Creative Director Susan Kare—Next employee number ten, who had previously designed desktop icons at Apple—handed Steve a stack of books and articles by a designer she admired: Paul Rand. "He's one of the most articulate, excellent writers and designers," she later recounted.

Paul was one of the most respected figures in American design. He firmly believed, as did Steve, that a logo should convey something essential about a company's values. "Simplicity implies not only an aesthetic ideal, but a meaningful idea, either of content or form, that can be easily recalled," he wrote in his acclaimed 1985 book *A Designer's Art*.

At seventy-two, Paul was stout and bespectacled, with a Brooklyn accent, an encyclopedic knowledge of art history, and eccentric habits like putting ketchup on spaghetti. He had created iconic logos for IBM, UPS, Westinghouse, and ABC. He taught at Yale (he had also designed the Yale University Press logo) and worked out of a modernist home of his own design in nearby Weston, Connecticut, which overflowed with books and mock-ups made from colored paper and tape.

And though he created some of the computer industry's best-known logos, he never used a computer for his designs. When Steve later sent him a Next machine, Paul opened the box and said to his assistant, "What do I do with this thing? Take it to the garage."

Paul did not suffer fools gladly. As a teacher at Yale, his critiques were so brutal that one student, pushed past his limit, punched him in the ear. When Ford Motor Company invited Paul to redesign its logo, he walked into a conference room with fifty executives and immediately asked, "Who makes the decisions here?" Then he presented only to that person while the other forty-nine people sat watching.

At IBM, where he worked as a design consultant, Paul believed the UK team's output was "the worst work shown in IBM. Poorly conceived and implemented. Disorganized, cheap appearing," as a colleague wrote. One time, finishing up a portfolio review with one of IBM's graphic designers, Paul asked the designer how old he was. Thirty-two, came the reply.

"You still have time to be good," Paul said.

After the designer left, Paul turned to his colleague Tom Hardy and asked, "Was I too hard on that guy?"

"He believed criticism was how you got to excellence," Tom explained. In Paul's mind, brutal honesty was a form of kindness.

Steve thought Paul's designs were "phenomenal." And it matched his own aspirations. "[Paul's] work for me is very emotional and yet, when you study it, it's very intellectual," Steve recounted. "If you scratch the surface on any of his work, you find out the depth of the intellectual problem solving that's taken place."

When Steve spoke to Paul for the first time, he asked if Paul could present him with a few options for Next's logo. "No," Paul said. "I will solve your problem, and you will pay me."

Paul's price: $100,000, whether or not Next ended up using the logo. It was a monumental sum, but Steve agreed.

"Our challenge was that it usually takes ten years and $100 million to associate a symbol with the name of the company," he said. Steve wanted to choose an iconic logo off the bat and skip the waiting period.

Paul told his own design team in Connecticut that he found the Next project appealing. He thought Steve would be a good client—one who understood the value of great design and was willing to pay for it. But there was one potential snag: Paul would need permission from IBM to work with Steve since he was locked into an exclusive contract.

Steve called IBM CEO John Akers directly to ask for an exception.

When those calls went unanswered, he kept pushing until he reached Vice Chairman Paul Rizzo. After days of relentless pursuit, Paul Rizzo made a pragmatic calculation: Resisting Steve was a waste of time. That hurdle cleared, Steve could sign Paul Rand.

Paul flew out to meet Steve at Next's office in Palo Alto, where Steve walked Paul through his vision for the company and how its first product—the Cube—would look.

Paul listened carefully, took it all in, and left.

Steve's big logo spend sparked worry inside Next. Apple's lawsuit had already drained time and considerable resources. Now, though the company still lacked investors or a product to sell, Steve had dropped six figures on a logo. Even by twenty-first-century standards, that was a lot of money for a new start-up to spend.

Because Steve had seeded Next with $7 million of his own personal money, the company's finance team had assumed he'd be more frugal than he had been at Apple. He even spoke to the staff about the need for discipline and control.

"But he still had the champagne taste he'd gotten used to," said CFO Susan Barnes. The company's burn rate climbed as old habits resurfaced: lavish spending, obsessive detail, uncompromising taste. Steve wanted every facet of Next's image to be perfect. He wanted a New York ad agency. A top-tier public relations firm. A full marketing staff. A receptionist with a prestigious college degree who could remember the names, faces, and positions of every visitor who walked in the door.

But the $100,000 logo fee topped it all. It even spawned an inside joke on Next's staff—a new unit of financial measurement called the milli-logo. One milli-logo was one hundred dollars. A high-end computer monitor might run twenty milli-logos. A designer sofa? Seventy or eighty. Steve overheard the joke once. He didn't laugh.

When the tile grout in the office bathroom was installed in the wrong color, Steve had the brand-new tiles ripped out and replaced at a cost of about $20,000. The episode gave rise to another unit: the milli-grout, otherwise known as twenty dollars.

Steve's extravagance wasn't pure recklessness: He knew exactly how much money he was burning. He understood business mechanics in ways few people recognized. At Apple, he had mastered cash flow—getting paid by customers quickly while taking time to pay suppliers. "I can do a balance sheet better than anyone," he once told Susan, "but I'll never get credit for building on a shoestring."

At Next, he was playing a different game. One of Susan's financial analysts captured the shift: "We in finance are all looking at segments of an orange, and Steve keeps seeing the whole orange." Rather than bootstrap again, Steve was making calculated bets on an expensive foundation. According to Susan, he believed so strongly in Next's potential that he saw cheaper alternatives as false economy, like trying to turn a Volkswagen into a Mercedes instead of just buying a Mercedes from the start.

And Steve's openness to financial oversight had limits. What Susan considered responsible stewardship, he saw as nagging—it was his money after all.

His spending priorities also sent a clear message to the team: Even something as quotidian as the office tile work needed to reflect the company's soul.

Up the road in San Francisco, Paul holed up at the Stanford Court Hotel and got to work on the logo. Steve further described his vision to Paul over the phone, and Paul doodled as he listened. He moved quickly. He spent the next few days sketching ideas on hotel pads and napkins.

Paul started by stylizing "NEXT" inside a circle, once in black and then again in white. He emphasized the *X*, making it bleed into the *E* and the *T*. He even tried filling the spaces around the *X* to resemble a bowtie.

Then, on the backside of a Hertz rental car brochure, Paul placed the word "NEXT" in all caps diagonally inside a cube. It looked like progress to Paul. He liked the idea of playing with the cube graphic—and so did Steve. But he quickly saw a problem: At a glance, "NEXT" in all caps could easily be mistaken for the word "EXIT." Not ideal.

He turned his attention to the letter *E*, scribbling out associated concepts: *education*, *expertise*, *excellence*, *enlightenment*, even $e = mc^2$. He eventually opted to lowercase it, creating "NeXT."

"Lower case 'e' is good contrast and more unusual," he later noted.

Paul could feel himself getting closer to a solution. It was time to pick the right typeface and colors. "It is preferable to keep the type rather neutral and let the message be conveyed by some meaningful concept," he wrote. He chose vivid colors, one per letter—vermilion, yellow, green, and a striking cherry-pink shade called cerise—to capture the company's youthful energy.

He described the resulting design as a "study in contrasts." The colorful letters inside the cube, he wrote, brimmed "with the informality, friendliness, and spontaneity of a Christmas seal and the authority of a rubber stamp."

Paul sent proofs to his printer, Mossberg & Co., in South Bend, Indiana. When he visited Mossberg, a crucial final change happened almost by accident. As Paul's assistant Bob Burns remembered, Paul had casually turned the cube logo to a 28-degree tilt as a stamp on the back of an envelope. The printer's son noticed and liked it. Paul agreed, and the subtle angle became one of the logo's most distinctive elements.

What Paul saw as a happy accident, Hartmut Esslinger saw as cosmic destiny. The logo's 28-degree tilt was, Hartmut insisted, rooted in mystical harmony. In Pythagorean philosophy, twenty-eight was a "perfect number," equal to the sum of its divisors. The ancient Greeks believed such numbers held the keys to the cosmic order.

A few weeks later, Paul flew back to California to present the logo to Steve. After eating dinner at the Jackling House, Paul handed Steve a carefully prepared booklet that traced his creative journey to reach the final design. Steve sat on the floor and read each page slowly.

The booklet contained discarded options and each evolution that led to the final design. As Steve turned the pages, his smile grew. When he finally arrived at the black cube, tilted at exactly 28 degrees with "NeXT" split across two lines, he jumped to his feet and gave Paul a bear hug. Paul looked surprised.

Paul liked Steve and valued their partnership. But he still had reservations. He told Bob, "You wouldn't want to work for this guy. He's a taskmaster." Bob thought: "Pot, meet kettle."

Paul had the right idea. When he worked up the final proofs for Steve, he had trouble matching the exact shade of yellow he had shown Steve in the booklet, Pantone 115. The change was hardly perceptible. But Steve noticed it immediately. "Steve *hates* the yellow," Susan Kare wrote to Paul. "Which he says looks orange. He wants a 'real yellow,' similar to the yellow you used in the logo book. (Be thankful for small favors: he likes the red, green, and cerise.)"

Steve's meticulousness extended to NeXT's slide decks, brochures, and the sign at the office driveway. He wanted the phone and fax numbers on the company's letterhead to align precisely. He felt that the company's business cards, printed on cardstock from the legendary papermaker Crane, weren't thick enough. "However, SJ wants them heavier," Susan wrote Paul. "Maybe something from Mohawk Superfine?"

The NeXT team kept its aesthetic standards high too, in anticipation of Steve walking by. Graphic designers called it the most painstaking work of their careers, obsessing over the slope of a single line or the shape of a caption. They would even rewrite internal documents to avoid awkward line breaks or jagged margins.

Whether through his intensity, his taste, or his insistence on discipline, Steve created a design culture that employees never forgot. Many loved the high standards and the pride that came from producing excellent work. Even years later, a number said that NeXT was the most magical place they'd ever worked. Nowhere else came close.

Still, Steve's feedback was hard to predict or plan for—and could be searing.

Partway through an ad agency pitch meeting, Steve cut off the already nervous executives with a request. He wanted a phone book brought to him. Once it arrived, he leafed through a few pages. Then, looking up, Steve said, "This makes for more interesting reading than this shit I'm hearing from you guys." The room froze.

He was mercurial too. NeXT team members referred to this as the "hero-shithead rollercoaster"—a phrase they'd inherited from Apple veterans who'd ridden it before them. He could lavish praise on your work one moment, then turn around and tear you apart in front of a room the next. You never knew where you stood.

Paul saw the danger in Steve's volatility. After listening to Steve rant about graphic design, the logo designer cut him off: "Between now and when you have a product, you are the product, my friend, and so you better be nice to people."

Steve, caught off guard, responded weakly. "Well, I'll try."

From across the room, NeXT's receptionist chimed in. "There is no try, Steve," she said. "There is only do."

In March 1986, four months after the team's first retreat, the NeXT staff boarded buses back to Pebble Beach for a second gathering. Steve once again stood in front of a conference room overlooking the surf, this time wearing a checkered button-down over his black turtleneck. A slide projector lit up a screen behind him. He clicked to the first slide, which read "The Honeymoon is Over."

"We've been a company now for six months," he said. "And yes, you could say that, well, we had a lawsuit for four of those months . . . but the bottom line is the world doesn't really care. What the world cares about is what we produce . . . and how timely we bring it to market."

With fifteen months until launch, the team still hadn't coalesced around a concrete product vision—all they had was a loose prototype of a workstation they'd lugged along with them in a locked box. As the company's arduous design process began to butt up against hard deadlines, frustration bubbled to the surface. "I'm not getting a clear idea from anybody, really, what the features are and what is this thing that we're talking about doing," Bud, the head software developer, said at one point in the retreat.

Steve snapped during team presentations. "And boy, that just makes me smoke," he said, waving his hands as the team discussed the go-to-market timeline. Steve foresaw a vision of futility: Another month would pass, he worried, and still nothing of interest would be in development. Then another month and another after that.

When Susan suggested pushing back the shipment date, Steve erupted: "No, forget about slipping the time . . . Just look to shipment!" When he got frustrated, he turned ugly, NeXT employees recalled.

The real battle, he said, was simple: Don't run out of money before the product ships. The irony was that Steve's profligate spending was leading NeXT down a precarious path. Because they talked a big game in public, Susan told the room that vendors assumed NeXT had $20 or $30 million in the bank. In reality, it had far less.

At the retreat, Susan addressed the spending problem: Somehow $100,000 had become the company's standard spending unit—as if Steve's logo had set the baseline for what constituted normal expenses. Steve, ironically enough, criticized the team for buying new equipment instead of scrounging for deals. "We've stopped nickel-and-diming for that stuff, and it all adds up . . . I don't see that start-up hustle," he told them.

Two months later, Steve's commitment to fiscal discipline hit a very personal speed bump. He'd learned that Apple had fired Chiat/Day—the same ad agency that had helped make Steve a household name. John

Sculley had handed Apple's $50 million ad budget over to BBDO, the button-down agency he'd long admired.

"Steve felt very personally involved in the way Chiat was treated," Susan recalled. To take advantage of the opening, he spent $22,000 of his own money on a full-page ad in *The Wall Street Journal*, roughly the annual salary of the typical worker.

Steve's full-page ad began sarcastically: "Congratulations, Chiat/Day. Seriously." It then pivoted to pure provocation. "The personal computer industry is now being handed over from the 'builders' to the 'caretakers,'" the copy read. "That is, from the individuals who created and grew a multi-billion-dollar American industry to those who will maintain the industry as it is and work to achieve marginal future growth." It closed on a personal note: "I can guarantee you: there is life after Apple."

As always, Steve's spending reflected his priorities. "So much of Steve's motivation at NeXT was about sticking it to Apple—basically, to stick it to Sculley," Dan'l reflected.

While Steve blew his own money settling personal scores, Steve's $7 million seed funding for NeXT was disappearing fast. In Susan's view, it was time to raise money from investors, and she wanted to act fast. By hammering out funding deals before desperation set in, the cofounders could avoid being forced into a bad deal, maybe even giving up control of the company. "You always want to raise money when you don't need it," Susan explained. "You don't want to put your back against the wall."

When Steve and Susan finally hit the investor circuit, they had plenty to promise. Their investment proposal touted an "unusually talented and experienced" team, breakthrough technology, and a $40 million valuation. But they didn't have much concrete to offer. They didn't have a developed product or any revenue to speak of.

They faced consistent rejections. "One [Wall Street firm] even ripped into us, accusing Steve of being a felon because Apple had sued him," Susan recalled.

6

THE MAGICAL MONITOR STAND

In Pittsburgh, Steve and Dan'l stood at the head of a long table and pitched an investment in NeXT. Their target: Carnegie Mellon University's (CMU) investment subcommittee of the board of trustees. Steve declared that, with NeXT's forthcoming Scholar's Workstation, the company would transform higher education. The machine would outperform anything in its class, he said—powerful enough to perform research simulations, yet affordable enough for university departments to buy.

He sketched out the massive market opportunity: higher education was a $60 billion sector with more than 3,200 institutions, 45,000 departments, 600,000 faculty, and 12 million students. Top universities like Harvard, Stanford, and the University of Michigan dipped into the same total budgets as Fortune 500 companies. And NeXT, as the only computer maker dedicated to serving them exclusively, had a chance to corner the market.

Steve concluded his presentation and asked for CMU's buy-in.

Pat Crecine, the university's provost, flipped through the investment pitch and financial statements. He liked what he saw, but Dick Cyert, CMU's president, who controlled the purse strings, didn't. "The $40,000,000 valuation seems a little high," Pat wrote to Steve, reflecting his superior's concerns about Steve's proposed valuation.

Pat was a heavyweight in the world of academic administration and would go on to become the president of Georgia Tech the next year. Pat and Dan'l had become close friends three years earlier, when Dan'l was building Apple's University Consortium and Pat was purchasing Apple machines for CMU's campus. They'd initially bonded over swimming—Pat had been a competitive swimmer himself—and their friendship deepened over time. When Dan'l's son was born, Pat sent a Speedo as a baby gift.

Though Pat wanted to invest in NeXT, the terms of the deal gave the investment subcommittee pause. In addition to NeXT's high valuation, Steve specified that he did not want to pursue a public offering—the dream exit for early investors. Instead, Steve proposed that NeXT would buy back investor shares using future revenue. It was a growth workaround to avoid losing control and repeating his fate at Apple.

That meant investors would only see a return if NeXT hit Steve's sky-high sales targets. If the company pulled in $100 million in revenue within two and a half years, as Steve promised, CMU could more than double the $1 million investment that Steve was seeking. But if sales fell short, or if NeXT didn't turn out to be worth as much as Steve claimed, the university might never get its money out.

Pat ultimately convinced CMU's leadership to make the investment, successfully arguing for Steve's vision and personality. "Based on the track record of you and your team," he wrote to Steve, "how can you miss??"

CMU split the investment with Stanford—whose president, Donald Kennedy, was a friend of Steve's—making a total investment of $1.3 million in NeXT in exchange for 1 percent of the company. While $1.3 million wasn't going to save the company's fortunes on its own, it was a critical vote of confidence from two respected institutions.

Steve had another interest in CMU. He had heard about a software revolution taking place within its computer science labs led by a pioneering PhD student named Avie Tevanian.

Avie, the son of an Armenian machinist and a bookkeeper, grew up in New England and went to college at the University of Rochester, where he had spent his time coding computer games. As a doctoral student at CMU, he began building something far more ambitious—a tool that could change software development forever.

Avie's breakthrough lay deep in the machine. He was rethinking the computer's kernel—its software heart. The kernel instructs the machine on how to complete basic functions like managing memory, juggling tasks, and keeping everything running. At the time, kernels were sprawling beasts jammed with functions. Among other things, kernel code typically instructed computers on file management, networking, and drivers.

Avie and his colleagues wanted to simplify the kernel by stripping it down to the bare essentials, while pushing everything superfluous outside. Avie's stripped-down model was called the "microkernel." It was more flexible and easier to port to different machines than a traditional kernel design.

Crucially, its clean architecture made it well suited for juggling multiple processors—accommodating the latest advances in hardware design. On a muddy walk to lunch, Avie's fellow researchers joked about naming the microkernel "muck." A faculty member misheard it as "Mach" and the name stuck.

In 1986, Avie was riding high at CMU as the gatekeeper of the Mach kernel. "I've got all these computers to myself," he told the Computer

History Museum. "Because I'm writing the OS, no one else can use them." That's when he heard Steve was interested.

Steve wanted to build a powerful operating system called NeXTSTEP—and he wanted Avie's kernel at the heart of it. Avie flew out to meet with Steve. There, Steve told him about his vision for NeXT and the Mach kernel. He also tried to hire Avie on the spot, but Avie remained committed to finishing his PhD. They stayed in touch, and NeXT began folding in his ideas.

Meanwhile, Steve and Bud recruited two key developers to build NeXT's software. One of these hires, William Parkhurst, a surfer and record-breaking Stanford weight lifter, joined NeXT in January 1986 as its nineteenth employee. He was also the first who hadn't been poached from Apple.

He arrived to find a start-up with nothing concrete, only a vague decision to build on Unix, the text-based operating system that engineers loved. William got to work right away solving problems.

He required extensive quiet time to think, so he started coming into the office in the middle of the night. Though Steve initially worried that William was isolating himself, he adapted to his style. "Steve rented the building next door," William said. From then on, NeXT's work was split across two hubs: hardware in one building, software in the other.

William was tasked with building the core development environment from scratch. His first assignment was to test an existing software package that NeXT was considering buying—one that contained the basic tools every programmer needs: text editors, compilers, debuggers, and file utilities. But William came to feel that the software was "junk" and pitched starting over from scratch.

William, Steve, and Bud chose to work in the language Objective-C, which was little known at the time. Because of the way it leveraged something called object-oriented programming, it offered engineers simplicity and flexibility that the alternative C++ lacked, allowing them to execute and update applications more quickly and easily. Bigger companies like AT&T and Bell Labs were throwing their weight behind

C++, which meant they, not NeXT, would have far more control over the programming language. Steve also wanted a language that could be unique for his platform. "That was simply not possible with C++," Bud recounted.

At the time, software development was a painstaking process. Engineers had to write out every program line by line. Each and every application was a one-off, built from the ground up. As a result, designing software was frustrating, expensive, and slow.

Most of the industry followed the "waterfall technique," a rigid process that locked developers into monthslong cycles. "You'd start by writing a design, then draw flowcharts, then code everything in C," Bud explained, "compile it, debug it, and finally hand it to users, only to hear, 'This is terrible, I can't figure this out.' So you'd go back to the top of the waterfall and start again."

The process was so time-consuming, Bud said, that teams would often give up early. "They'd just say, 'This is taking forever. It's good enough.'"

The waterfall technique started to break down as hardware advanced. Manufacturers were releasing new computers with four or eight processors—up from the old single-processor standard. And new power brought new software expectations.

What if, developers began to ask, you could build software like Legos? Instead of starting from scratch, what if you could develop reusable, modular components and snap them together to perform various tasks?

It would all be enabled by object-oriented programming. Traditional programming was like writing a recipe in which every step had to be spelled out from scratch each time—dice the onions, heat the pan, add oil, wait thirty seconds, add onions, stir every minute. Object-oriented programming was different. Developers could create smart building blocks called "objects" that knew how to handle themselves.

An "onion" object would already know how to dice itself, how long it needed to cook, when it was done. A "pan" object would know its own temperature and when it was ready. Instead of writing out every tedious instruction, programmers could just tell these objects to work together: "Onion, cook yourself in that pan." The objects would figure out the rest.

The result would be a faster, more flexible development process. And the resulting programs would be harder to break—each object protected its own inner workings from being accidentally scrambled by other parts of the program.

Within a month, William had the first application up and running. He called it AppKit, a collection of prebuilt software components that handled common tasks every application needs, such as windows, buttons, menus, text fields, and user interactions. It became the backbone of NeXTSTEP.

AppKit let developers work with clean, reusable building blocks instead of having to write and dig through chaotic, low-level code. If object-oriented programming allowed for the use of Lego blocks, AppKit made the actual box of Lego blocks ready to use.

Before, brilliant ideas weren't getting built because writing software was just too hard. But NeXT would enable small teams to build powerful apps without an army of engineers, thanks to AppKit coupled with a program called Interface Builder. Interface Builder was a visual tool that let developers drag and drop AppKit's components to design their applications in real time.

"Just sitting down and watching Interface Builder operate," Bud said, "was such a vivid way to demonstrate that you didn't have to be a programmer." It unlocked creativity. People looked at it and thought, "Gee, I could try that."

Steve immediately saw the power of AppKit and Interface Builder. Though he didn't write code, he had a relentless eye for design and a need to shape the user experience. The team's new tools gave him control over the software development process—just as he had hovered over foam mock-ups during the Mac's development, he could now do the same with software.

He'd sit next to Bud, point at the screen, and say, "Move this menu here. Put that dialog box there." And it would happen immediately. Steve could now direct software development the way a filmmaker cuts a scene—intuitively, visually—refining the feel and flow frame by frame.

Still, the breakthroughs came with a major risk. NeXT was building these tools on a new, proprietary platform. The company couldn't lean on Apple's market share or Microsoft's developer base to achieve wide distribution. If NeXT's elegant computers didn't catch on, NeXTSTEP might turn into a masterpiece that no one ever got to use.

At this point, NeXT wasn't using its own computers. Those weren't finished yet. So all of the software was being built on Sun workstations.

One day, at an industry party, a NeXT developer casually mentioned that they were using Sun workstations. Word traveled fast through the Valley's gossip network, and competitors heard that NeXT had no functional hardware.

The perception created a serious problem and demanded a response. "We had to show that we have some vision," Dan'l, who ran marketing and PR in addition to sales, later recalled, "because we were just doing smoke and mirrors."

So Dan'l crafted a draconian PR policy that authorized NeXT employees to say exactly one thing about their work: "I work at NeXT." On a wall in the office was a vintage military poster about the importance of secrecy. It read: "WARNING. The sharp ears of Enemy Agents are always listening for scraps of information."

Journalists were carefully vetted for interviews with Steve. "Choreograph, don't chase," Dan'l wrote of the media strategy. *BusinessWeek* was tagged as starry-eyed but sympathetic. *Newsweek* was "somewhat sensational" but reliably pro-Steve. *Time* was expected to play it down the middle.

But where the media was concerned, Steve could be an open book.

One day in summer 1986, he got in his car with *Esquire* journalist Joe Nocera and veered into a reflective mode as they drove toward San Francisco.

"Whenever you do any one thing intensely over a period of time," Steve told him, "you have to give up other lives you could be living." He gave a small shrug. "You have to have a real single-minded kind of tunnel vision if you want to get anything significant accomplished."

Then, after a pause: "Especially if the desire is not to be a businessman, but to be a creative person."

But, Joe asked, wasn't the CEO of NeXT the very definition of a businessman?

"My self-identity does not revolve around being a businessman, though I recognize that is what I do. I think of myself more as a person who builds neat things."

As 1986 drew to a close, NeXT prepared for its most audacious gambit yet. Steve had decided to manufacture computers in-house. It would all take place at a new manufacturing facility in Fremont, California, using cutting-edge robotics and automation.

Steve thought that building a NeXT-operated facility thirty minutes away would give him tighter control over manufacturing. And it would all be automated. He loved the idea that the manufacturing tech could stamp out human error and variability.

He envisioned the facility enabling an elaborate buying experience. Just like Ferrari customers fly to Maranello, Italy, to pick out their cars straight off the assembly line, so would NeXT's customers with their computers. "If you're going to buy a great sports car, what's the best way to do it?" he reportedly asked employees. "You fly to Europe, go to the factory, and buy it there."

The facility was slated to be Steve's most expensive endeavor yet. Its six-and-a-half-year lease would cover 41,250 square feet, with monthly costs of almost $30,000. The full commitment, including rent, renovations, and maintenance, would top $2.7 million, a staggering sum for the nascent company.

At the same time, NeXT's cash reserves were rapidly dwindling. As they did, the chasm between Steve's sports-car vision and reality grew. NeXT had burned considerable funds designing the logo, the software, and the Cube itself. Now it would have to pay for the Fremont factory too.

Worse, revenue was nowhere on the horizon. The team now knew for certain that the targeted spring 1987 launch—just six months away—was no way in hell going to happen. Yet again, Steve, Susan, and the team needed a lifeline. And they needed one fast.

Then, on November 5, 1986, the Texas businessman H. Ross Perot happened to tune into PBS. On came *Entrepreneurs*, the documentary about NeXT that John Nathan had filmed earlier that year.

Watching Steve in action, Ross remembered the spark he'd felt when meeting Steve years earlier at Apple. Back then, he was assessing the company for a possible acquisition by his client GE. Steve was "Mr. Electricity. Smart, modest, and not on any kind of an ego trip," Ross later told *Life*. "This young man went up against IBM . . . and ate 'em alive."

The next morning, Ross left Steve a voicemail in his high-pitched, rapid-fire Texas drawl. "If you ever need an investor, call me," he said. Steve didn't want to look desperate. So he waited a week, then picked up the phone.

Ross dispatched a trusted adviser, Morton Meyerson, chief technology officer of General Motors (which, two years earlier, had acquired Ross's technology services company, Electronic Data Systems), to meet with Steve to vet the opportunity. But Morton didn't get a product pitch. Instead, Steve fed him a vegetarian meal at the Jackling House, showed off his motorcycle, and treated him to a design lecture on the Cube's monitor stand. Steve was proud of the stand's invisible torsion bars—a feat of engineering that would make the monitor appear to float.

"He spent two hours on the stand," Morton said, still dumbfounded. "What the hell's he talking about? What about the machine?" He never saw one.

After his visit, Morton advised Ross to walk away. But Ross couldn't give up the idea—the prospect of building an all-American computer from the ground up captured his imagination, appealing to his patriotism as much as his investor's instinct.

He also couldn't shake the fear of missing out. Seven years earlier, Ross had passed on the chance to buy Microsoft for what he remembered as $40 to $60 million—a decision he deeply regretted.

Above all, Steve had Ross spellbound. "He's so articulate," Ross kept saying.

It hardly made for an intuitive pairing: Steve, a California mystic in sandals. Ross, a military man turned conservative billionaire. "Ross was not a Birkenstocks kind of guy," Morton said. "But he looked at Steve and fell for it." Steve reminded Ross of a less button-down version of himself—relentless, locked in. "He's a lot smarter than I am," Ross said.

He decided to invest $20 million in NeXT in exchange for a 16 percent stake, becoming the company's largest outside shareholder. "I bet on the jockeys, not the horses, and you're the right jockeys," Ross told Steve. But Ross required that Steve also put more skin in the game—Steve had to contribute another $5 million of his own money to the funding round.

Steve invited Ross to join NeXT's board, and in November 1986, Steve recruited Pat Crecine as well. He liked that Pat had influence in NeXT's target university market.

But Ross's $20 million wasn't just about building a better computer for college students. He saw another, highly lucrative application for NeXT's powerful machines: national security.

Unbeknownst to most in the company, Steve and Ross had struck a second, secret deal. It would never appear in any press release or regulatory filing. They didn't even write the terms down: To sell the NeXT computer, Ross was willing to mobilize his high-level government networks and his sales force from the company he was planning to start, Perot Systems. It would build on his past success selling technology to the military, intelligence agencies, and the federal government.

Even as Steve pitched NeXT's educational mission, he allowed technologists from Ross's military contracting business inside the company, giving them "early and meaningful access in anticipation of going into the government," Dan'l explained.

Steve had been preparing to sell computers to the American security establishment longer than anyone realized. Just months earlier, when he acquired Pixar, the press focused on the company's potential in film, animation, and medical imaging. But they missed the hidden story.

The Pixar Image Computer had been released four months earlier at a list price of $135,000—priced for an elite market that needed the very best hardware available. Pixar cofounder Ed Catmull explained that the machine's processing power was orders of magnitude beyond existing workstations. It sold fewer than three hundred units, but a handful of those units went to government intelligence agencies. It gave them the ability to process classified satellite feeds with unprecedented clarity.

Dan'l gathered information from Pixar's engineers about their confidential work. They were "taking satellite imagery and distilling it using Pixar software so that you could see things on Earth, right from 200 miles in space."

Steve was building the future of American surveillance while snacking on Medjool dates and sipping at his favorite drink, carrot juice.

NeXT had pulled off a remarkable feat: securing capital without showing a real product. Now the company had backers, a board, and a bankroll. To skeptics, it still looked like vaporware masked by charisma. But to the true believers, including Ross, Pat, and the early team, something deeper was taking shape. They believed they were building the future.

"I can *feel* it," Steve declared that November from the stage at EDUCOM, a major academic tech conference in Cincinnati. He was laying out his new vision for learning through technology. He proposed that NeXT computers would allow students to drop into the worlds they were studying: physics problems, a DNA strand, even the court of King Louis XIV. The court would have had courtiers with powdered faces bowing to the king in his heels; Steve didn't explain how his computer would simulate this world, but his audience believed him.

Onstage, Steve promised a machine ten to twenty times more powerful than anything currently for sale—raising the bar from his earlier NeXT pitches. He also quietly acknowledged that the $3,000 price tag was slipping away. But no one seemed to notice, and no one seemed to care. By the time Steve stepped offstage, the room was electrified.

"I just stood in one place, and people kept coming up to me saying, 'What do you guys do?'" remembered Dan'l.

Steve mesmerized audiences in ways that every start-up founder envied. But it was never enough for him. Dan'l, who watched Steve up close during these triumphant moments, saw that Steve "was always searching for something else," he said.

That search became more urgent after November 1986, when Clara Jobs—the woman who had adopted Steve as an infant—died. Eventually, Paul, her widower and Steve's adoptive father, remarried. His new wife, Marilyn Chovanec, had a daughter who, by pure suburban coincidence, lived across the street from Dan'l.

Steve kept showing up at Dan'l and his wife Susan's house. He had no family of his own and was fighting constantly with his girlfriend, Tina. The visits followed a pattern: Steve would visit his father and new stepmother when they were at the house across the street, then drift over to the Lewins' home. "He came because we had little kids around," Dan'l recalled. Steve's constant dropping by created an unexpected intimacy between NeXT's chairman and his cofounder. Steve became just the guy who kept coming over, searching for something he couldn't quite name.

At the same time, Steve felt he was running out of time to make his mark. The feeling would surface in conversations with colleagues, when Steve told them about his intuition that he wouldn't live a long life. He couldn't explain where it came from, but at thirty-one, he believed his time was limited.

7

DEEP SHIT LIST

In early 1987, Steve, Ross, Pat, the NeXT team, and a few special guests gathered in a wood-paneled dining room at the Stanford Faculty Club. They were there to celebrate Ross's massive investment in the company.

Steve rose first to toast John Nathan, whose PBS documentary *Entrepreneurs* had brought Steve and Ross together in the first place.

Then Ross stood. He told those assembled that he viewed himself as a grain of sand that enters an oyster and, by causing irritation within the shell, creates a pearl. He laughed wryly and said, "This is going to be hell on the oyster."

The NeXT team chuckled nervously. Behind the scenes, the oyster was already in hell. Steve had declared his intent to achieve perfection—the black cube that looked like modern sculpture, boasting a blazing-fast processor, pristine audio, software years ahead of anyone else's, and a screen so precise that what you saw would match exactly what the laser printer produced. "What You See Is What You Get," or WYSI-WYG, was an advancement in an era when everyday PCs showed crude green text that looked nothing like the final printed page. But some high-end computers had already adopted the approach.

NeXT's strategy was to run font software called Adobe PostScript, which made the screen font look like the printed page. This meant they could bundle a simple, inexpensive printer at a high profit margin that didn't need expensive PostScript processing built in—though it had the side effect of making the display painfully slow.

Steve encapsulated the philosophy behind those technical decisions with the phrase "If you want to make a revolution, raise the lowest common denominator"—meaning NeXT would drag the entire industry upward with innovation rather than merely match existing machines.

His employees were fired up to be a part of this vision, but they were often tired too. Even as they raced to finish the computer, he calmly told his team about their product's inevitable death and demise. Every computer platform peaked after five years, he explained, then declined slowly as its own software became its prison.

"An interesting thing happens at the peak," he told his employees. For five years, developers write thousands of programs for your computer. Spreadsheets, games, word processors—this growing app library becomes your platform's greatest selling point. But then it becomes a trap. "All of the application software that has been painfully built up becomes the architecture's greatest liability, because it can't change or break [make unusable] all those applications."

If you upgrade the screen size, old programs might malfunction. If you upgrade the memory system, existing software might crash. If you add new capabilities like sound and a color display, none of the existing software would be able to use them. Every improvement risked destroying the very ecosystem that made you successful in the first place.

So you freeze. You ship the same basic machine year after year with incremental upgrades. Your competitors, unburdened by success, build something better. Your developers, locked into old constraints, can't compete with fresh platforms.

The Apple II, the IBM PC, and soon the Mac—all followed this pattern, he said. NeXT would peak sometime in the next decade, in 1993 or 1994. He predicted they would have five good years, maybe six.

Knowing this, most CEOs would cut costs and ship quickly. Steve did the opposite. This was the reason that he felt NeXT had to start with perfection.

In early 1987, Steve's pursuit of perfection was devouring the timeline. Every revision pushed deadlines further back and every prolonged debate over this or that component drove costs higher. Yet no one could make decisions without Steve, and Steve couldn't stop perfecting. While Steve demanded revolutionary technology, every delay allowed competitors to catch up, rendering the technology less novel.

Steve was caught in his own trap: He believed his vision was perfect and didn't need changing, yet he couldn't stop tinkering with it. Meanwhile, the responsibility for executing his exacting vision at warp speed fell on the fifty people working on the Cube. "The most important thing you're competing with is not another company," Steve declared. "It's our own ability to execute."

Steve's solution to this contradiction was smoke and mirrors—pulling a cloak over investors, journalists, and university buyers until NeXT could pull something together. "I want to continue to be a very, very secretive company, and I think that just makes people all the more interested," he told his employees in a conference room.

NeXT's strategic planning boiled down to what Steve called the "Deep Shit List"—a list of existential threats scrawled out during all-hands meetings. "If we don't solve them," Steve said, "we're going out of business."

First on the Deep Shit List? Choosing a circuit board architecture.

Designing the circuit board, which connected the computer's various internal components, was a foundational decision for the company. And the team was stuck in a bitter debate among options. One side, led by analog hardware chief George Crow, advocated for the use of a through-hole architecture. This was the old-school method, which was slow in operation but sturdy and would be familiar to work with.

Steve, on the other hand, wanted NeXT to go with surface-mount circuit boards. Surface-mount was clearly the future. This new architecture would make manufacturing more efficient and create cleaner-looking circuit boards, but it would also be riskier. The industry was mid-transition, and not all of the new parts were ready for prime time. Rich proposed splitting the difference with a hybrid architecture.

Even as the debate raged on, NeXT's VP of manufacturing, Linda Wilkin, had to begin building the company's Fremont factory. With no firm decision on the circuit board—a choice that would dictate the factory's plan—Linda did the rational thing and prepared for both possibilities.

When NeXT's factory schedule inevitably slipped, rather than blaming his own indecision, Steve took out his frustration on Linda. He fired her in January 1987. And per her employment agreement, he forced her to sell back her NeXT stock at its original price of fifty cents a share, even after Ross's investment had sent NeXT's valuation soaring. She sued for wrongful dismissal, but the case was ultimately thrown out.

The factory descended into chronic chaos before it had produced a single computer. "We had five or six factory managers," Rich observed. When each one was fired, Rich would step in as interim manager—effectively working two jobs at once.

After all the brouhaha, Steve made the call: The team would go with the newer surface-mount architecture. Steve told his board he was "extremely pleased" with the decision. Never mind that the final circuit board turned out instead to be a hybrid of the two architectures. Steve, as Rich later put it, had a habit of turning future possibilities into present facts.

Next on the Deep Shit List? Designing the computer's chips.

Steve made a bet that revealed the forward-looking expanse of his vision. While competitors' computers ran on one megabyte of memory, NeXT machines would ship with eight, which was already overkill for 1987. But Steve predicted they'd need to double it: "Every computer we ship is going to have 16 megabytes within two years," he told his employees.

But building that far into the future meant tortuous complexity in the present. When it came time to deliver, a pair of engineers everyone called Big Dave and Little Dave—nicknamed simply for their contrasting sizes—was tasked with building the gate arrays, custom chips that would do the work of multiple standard chips on a single piece of silicon.

Steve wanted to consolidate everything onto one massive custom chip—partly for looks, partly because he thought it would sound impressive to customers. Using multiple smaller chips would have been easier and faster, but Steve cared about how the inside of the computer looked. Each time the chip designers got close to a final layout, Steve would change his mind. "Add this," he'd say. "Now move that." His perfectionism about the chip's appearance created months of delays.

Each tweak meant rearranging the entire blueprint like a sliding puzzle. One shift triggered another, which triggered another, which often blew up the plan altogether. When Steve asked how long it would take to finish the ever-changing design, the engineers knew the honest answer: about a year, working seven days a week. But they also knew that timeline would never fly. So they lied. "One more month," they'd say each time Steve asked.

The bit worked until it didn't. At the next company retreat, held at Palo Alto's Garden Court Hotel in January 1987, Steve marched Big Dave and Little Dave out in front of the entire company and lit into them. "You guys are gonna make the company fail," Steve raged. The verbal assault was so ruthless that Dan'l and others had to intervene—clearing the room so Steve could cool off.

Big Dave and Little Dave had now made the Deep Shit List.

Then, a week or two later, Big Dave and Little Dave had an announcement: They were ready to ship the master chip design to Fujitsu in Japan, the only manufacturer in the world that could make such an advanced gate array. Steve's mood swung instantly. "Let's give them $25,000 bonuses each," Steve told Dan'l—half a year's salary.

Steve called the pair into the conference room and handed them the checks, presenting himself as the magnanimous leader rewarding his brilliant engineers. The two men packed their belongings, and then, as Dan'l put it, "they walked out the door and never came back."

Ninety days later, the final chip arrived from Fujitsu. The team snapped it into the computer for a test run. Nothing. It didn't work.

As a result, Steve had to push back the release schedule a full year. "Who's going to figure this out and how long is it going to take?" Dan'l wondered. Other engineers had to step in and somehow detangle what they called the unique "jigsaw puzzle" of the chip. Without sophisticated chip design tools—and without the only two people who understood the arcane design—they were stuck with a computer that couldn't function.

Even the Cube's case found its way onto the list.

The moment NeXT started planning to mass-produce it, costs exploded. For a material, the design team settled on magnesium, which is lightweight, rigid, and beautiful, but dangerously flammable. Hartmut, the designer, would later admit that going with magnesium wasn't "the smartest choice." But it felt good in the hand and looked serious. NeXT leaned on the fact that the specific alloy the company went with was hard to ignite under normal conditions.

The team planned for each face of the Cube to measure exactly one foot, except for its vertical sides, which had to be shaved slightly shorter to correct an optical illusion that made them look too tall. Steve also wanted each side to be perfectly vertical, which meant skipping the standard manufacturing shortcut—tapering the sides of the computer slightly so that a mold could release cleanly, like a cake pan. The sharp, vertical faces Steve insisted on would get stuck in conventional molds.

NeXT searched the country to find a machine shop capable of making tooling that could accommodate Steve's design, reported journalist Randall E. Stross. One shop in Chicago could do it. It agreed to make custom tooling for molds that would come apart with all the sides releasing at once, for the price of $650,000.

Even then, the molds would leave faint seams on the edges of the case. Imperfections like that would never fly with Steve, so NeXT bought a $150,000 machine that did nothing but sand mold lines.

But it still wasn't enough. Inspired by a turntable he liked, Steve decided that the magnesium case should be painted a deep matte black. The result looked stunning but wasn't especially practical. The black paint revealed every manufacturing imperfection, and it could be easily damaged. Even a plastic shipping bag would scuff the finish.

One engineer brought up a problem to Steve. The special black paint couldn't be applied by robots, he said; it would have to be done by hand. That would ruin the company's vision for an entirely automated factory.

Steve wasn't hearing it. He kept pushing, kept gesturing, kept finding new angles of attack while the engineer grew more and more unhappy. "It took a while to get the process working," Rich said, "but in the end it was automated."

All told, the Cube wound up costing far more to manufacture at low volumes than the team had planned. The paint job alone cost $50—as much as the team had originally budgeted for the entire exterior of the Cube.

As time went on, the Deep Shit List started to look less like an existential priority list and more like Steve's personal wish list. He kept piling on features, adding costs, and making last-minute demands.

Inspired by his love of music, Steve decided that NeXT's workstation should output the best sound it was possible for a computer to produce. While competitors treated audio as an afterthought, he imagined a future where sound was as fundamental as text or graphics.

"Not a lot of you know what this thing does," he said, holding up an audio chip called a digital signal processor before thirty employees, "but let me tell you, I dream great dreams."

Julius Smith, a Stanford music professor and signal processing expert who consulted for NeXT one day a week, had brought proof to the retreat of what the chip would enable. He played cassettes of music created entirely by computer—no instruments, no musicians, just mathematical code turned into something akin to a MIDI file. With existing technology, it had taken a powerful computer the size of a room hours to generate these few minutes of music.

When the music filled the room through high-end Bose speakers, the employees fell silent.

Steve rose and asked, "Should we do this?" The technology existed. Julius had just proved it. Steve wanted to shrink that power into a desktop machine, making advanced audio as accessible on the Cube as the Macintosh had made computer graphics. Julius said yes.

The chip Julius championed was, by his own estimation, "two or three years" ahead of its time. It could create music mathematically in real time, with no recordings needed. It would be another expensive addition to an already expensive machine. "Only Steve Jobs really thought music was great," Julius later admitted. "The rest of the company thought of it as an optional thing." In the 1980s, computers barely made sounds beyond simple beeps and blips. If you wanted decent audio on your personal computer, you had to buy a separate circuit board called a sound card, crack open your computer case, and plug it into one of the slots inside—assuming you could figure out how and had a slot available.

Next on the Deep Shit List: storage. Instead of going with a floppy disk drive, which was standard fare at the time, Steve wanted to incorporate his latest obsession.

One day in early 1987, an executive from Canon had called Steve with an unusual message: "I want you to come back over to Japan and romp through the laboratories."

Canon wanted Steve walking through its labs, blessing its technology with his attention. He had a track record of building multiple billion-dollar products and making his suppliers rich and famous.

They saw him as someone who could spot magic in components they'd overlooked. Canon executives told Steve they were developing something called an erasable magneto-optical disk that could store 256 megabytes—vastly more than the typical floppy disk, which held about 1.4 megabytes. The technology traded the clunky floppy disks of the day for a rewritable, shimmering glass surface. While Canon could sell the same drive to anyone, an executive told the team: "We know Steve will refine something and make it a part of a computer better than anybody else could." NeXT would handle the engineering needed to make the drive work with their system.

To Steve, the drive sounded like magic. And it was—the drive was so advanced it didn't exist yet in production form. Steve envisioned the optical drive as the primary storage for the entire computer, replacing both floppy disks and traditional hard drives. "Floppies were the seventies storage technology," he explained to his employees in a conference room. "Hard drives don't work for the nineties because they're too expensive and unreliable."

Instead, users could pop out a gleaming 256-megabyte disc containing their entire digital library—dictionaries, software, and personal files—and carry it anywhere.

In April 1987, Steve flew to Japan with his engineers for what he described to the board as a "very secret" mission. For two days, the NeXT and Canon teams huddled in conference rooms, finalizing technical details and hammering out specifications. Steve made his position clear: NeXT couldn't pay more than $500 per drive. Canon's engineers admitted their components were expensive—the drive's electronics alone would cost 60 percent of the total price of each drive.

But they understood the opportunity to get their optical drive to the mass market. As Steve wrote to the board, "NeXT is the only company in the world committed to making an optical drive the main system mass storage device." Canon promised a prototype by July but wasn't sure it could hit Steve's specified price of $500 per drive.

The drive meant another risk. If it worked, NeXT would be at the center of a giant leap forward for computer storage. If it didn't, the company would be stuck with an unproven gamble compromising the core of its workstation.

After returning from Japan, Steve gathered NeXT's academic advisory board on April 30. It was made up of sixteen university presidents, deans, and technologists from across the country, chosen by Dan'l for their clout in the field.

With the advisory board, Steve and Dan'l became a double act. While Steve obsessed over whether the Cube needed handles or not, Dan'l kept university buyers interested. He created an air of mystery by offering limited unveilings of Cube features. NeXT colleagues called Dan'l the "silver-tongued" diplomat who could sell the dream.

Under strict nondisclosure, Steve and Dan'l unveiled their plans for the sleek case, the custom chips, the software stack, and the sound system to the advisory board. Steve strategically held back a few secrets—he didn't mention the unfinished optical disk.

Instead, he gave a demonstration of his beloved audio chip. Steve played Bruce Springsteen's "Born in the USA" on endless repeat on speakers.

"Watch!" he announced. He held up a prototype motherboard like an excited kid.

The advisors stared at the motherboard. Nothing moved. No fans whirred, no lights blinked. Just Bruce Springsteen on a loop.

"Well, gee, that's really great, Steve. What am I not seeing?" asked Michael Carter, Stanford's computing director.

"Nothing's moving!" Steve said, triumphant. The digital signal processor was creating perfect audio while the motherboard sat perfectly still—experiencing no mechanical vibrations that other computers needed to make sound.

"The advisory board was unanimously 'blown away' with the product and its embedded technology," Steve recounted to his other board, the board of directors, "and wants NeXT to win."

But a few members of the advisory board—including Stanford's Michael Carter, Brown administrator Brian Hawkins, and Vassar College administrator Marty Ringle—also reminded Steve of the importance of keeping the price low. The expectation among future customers remained $3,000 per unit, they said. Whatever else the machine became, it couldn't scare off universities with sticker shock.

Steve nodded in tacit agreement. But the truth was already obvious. Steve was building a cutting-edge machine with untested features. The dollar signs were adding up.

On July 14, Steve gathered NeXT's board of directors—made up of Ross, Pat, and Steve himself—for their inaugural meeting. NeXT's corporate bylaws required a small board of three people that would ensure Steve had access to expert advisers while allowing him to keep control, avoiding a repeat of his Apple ouster. After Steve toured them around the Fremont factory, which was still under construction, the board discussed numbers.

The company was now burning through $1 million a month, Steve and Susan reported, substantially more than what the team had projected six months earlier. And it was about to get worse. The factory buildout—already $1 million over budget—and the company's growing head count would push NeXT's burn rate higher through the summer.

Despite the news, NeXT's first board meeting ended on a high. Steve had dazzled the board with his plant, his team, and his cutting-edge technology. Pat told Steve it was a privilege just to be involved. But he also warned Steve about the slipping timeline. A missed launch would delay much-needed revenue, but more dangerously, could break the spell that NeXT had cast on the university market.

Still, Pat and Ross stood behind Steve's judgment. They believed the team was already doing everything it could. "Keep smiling," Pat wrote to Steve, "and keep your troops smiling."

Smiling? Ha.

Inside NeXT, team members were exhausted by Steve's frequent verbal tirades and his personalized leadership style. Instead of formal systems or performance reviews, Steve imposed a de facto hierarchy based on what he saw as technological importance. Software engineers were his favored inner circle—they created the user experience that would dazzle customers. The digital hardware team came second, designing the custom chips that would give NeXT its competitive edge. Analog teams, like George's hardware team, were barely acknowledged at all. To Steve, analog hardware was essentially plumbing, the power supplies, voltage regulators, and basic circuitry that kept the machine running.

Every company process was ad hoc. Getting things done meant persevering through endless internal politics until Steve finally made a decision. Every raise, every hire, and every stock grant went through him.

And NeXT was falling even more behind schedule. "The bad news is we're late," Steve admitted to the board at the next board meeting in September 1987. The chips were supposed to have been finished two months earlier. His beloved optical drive had been due then too, but NeXT was still awaiting prototypes with no firm commitment from Canon on pricing or mass production. The factory was meant to be fully operational by October. Now the team aimed for a November or December opening.

In autumn 1987, Steve gathered NeXT's academic advisory board once again to reassure them.

To prepare for the meeting, NeXT engineers had stayed up for days trying to get a Cube prototype to perform basic functions, like booting up without crashing, and opening and closing files. At four in the morning on the day of the presentation, they finally turned on the machine to a miracle: One line of text for running commands appeared on the screen.

At the meeting that day, NeXT's academic advisers stared at the screen, unsure why Steve was so excited. "What's that?" an adviser asked, confused. The system worked, but it clearly still had a long way to go.

The main event for the advisory board meeting was a field trip: a tour of NeXT's Fremont factory, just like the board of directors had taken that summer. Though unfinished, the factory was breathtaking. It featured sleek white walls, bright gallery lighting, designer fixtures, a custom-built staircase, and a twice-rebuilt lobby (Steve didn't like the colors of the first two iterations) with $20,000 black leather chairs.

The equipment on the factory floor was cutting edge, striking, and all repainted a matching shade of gray. When one arrived in a slightly off-color shade, Rich had stopped the installation cold. "That's not the right color!" he said, and had it repainted.

Steve choreographed the tour perfectly. The advisory board watched as NeXT's very first motherboard made at the factory—serial number one—was assembled by robotic arms and then emerged complete at the end of the line. "This is going to be historic," Steve declared. Everyone applauded. Then dinner was served right there on the factory floor, white tablecloths next to the conveyor belt.

The demonstration was a success, but Steve still had one final obligation to fulfill. As part of his legal settlement with Apple, he shipped them the first working NeXT prototype for inspection in early December 1987. Apple had until December 31 to examine the machine and clear it of any intellectual property violations—forcing them to work through Christmas and deliver their verdict by New Year's Eve. It was a final jab against his former company.

A purely rational CEO might have focused all his energy on fixing what wasn't working. But Steve had a different instinct: When in trouble, think bigger. While NeXT burned through cash and missed every deadline, Steve conducted secret negotiations that had the power to reshape the entire computer industry.

They began at *Washington Post* publisher Katharine Graham's seventieth birthday party on June 30, 1987, otherwise known as the *Post* publisher's gala. It was the kind of Washington power pageant that Steve both desperately wanted to be a part of and scorned—six hundred luminaries gathered to pay homage to the woman who had helped bring down a president.

At the party, Steve found himself face-to-face with John Akers, IBM's CEO. John, the archetypal IBM company man, had spent twenty-seven years marching up the Big Blue ladder wearing dark gray suits. He embodied everything Steve had positioned Apple against.

Now John needed a boost. While IBM had once looked untouchable in the computer market, the company was now hemorrhaging billions of dollars in value. John had promised shareholders a return to greatness and Steve spotted an opening. "I couldn't resist telling him I thought IBM was taking a giant gamble betting its entire software strategy on Microsoft," Steve said to *Fortune*, "because I didn't think its software was very good." He was referring to the fact that every IBM PC ran on Microsoft's DOS operating system.

Steve explained to John that Microsoft was just grafting Macintosh features onto Windows, creating a crude imitation of what Apple had already perfected. John thought for a moment then asked a question that made Steve's pulse quicken: "How would you like to help us?"

He could hardly believe it. An alliance between NeXT and IBM—which sold computers by the millions—would rock the industry. It could give NeXT the broad distribution it would otherwise struggle to achieve. And it could offer the company a needed cash infusion.

As an added bonus, any deal would edge Bill Gates toward the sidelines.

Five years earlier, Bill had become enchanted by Steve and the still-under-development Mac. So much so that he'd created an entire division within Microsoft to write software for it. Steve and Bill had talked regularly, and Microsoft became the premier maker of Mac software—earning hundreds of millions along the way.

Then, in 1983, the partnership crumbled. Steve felt that Bill had stolen the Mac's graphical user interface for his operating system that was still in development, Windows 1.0. He dragged Bill into an Apple conference room and accused him of committing a grievous betrayal.

Now Steve was on the cusp of edging Bill out. If IBM made NeXTSTEP the standard for its workstations, Bill would lose both money and power.

And that's exactly what NeXT proposed to IBM, audaciously suggesting that IBM adopt NeXTSTEP for its new workstation computers under development. To prevent conflicts of interest, the proposed deal stipulated that IBM would remain focused on the business market while NeXT stayed confined to the education market.

If IBM agreed to the terms, the deal would put NeXT's software on millions of machines worldwide and keep IBM out of its academic market.

As the deal was negotiated, things began to grow cozy between NeXT and IBM. The NeXT team started referring to their IBM counterparts as family. "Cousin Bill" was Bill Lowe, the head of IBM's PC operations. "Cousin Frank"—Dr. Frank King—ran the PC unit under Cousin Bill. "Cousin Andy" was Andy Heller, who was president of IBM's workstation unit and named his newborn son after Steve.

Over the course of eleven meetings from August to November, the two teams hammered out the details of their partnership. Steve seemed as volatile as ever, but he told his executives that it was part of a plan.

Todd Rulon-Miller, Dan'l's vice president of sales, told employees that Steve wanted to "play a game of chicken" with IBM. A logo design Steve found unattractive would set him off. An inapt product name would send him storming from the room.

But it was unclear how much of the behavior was intentional, versus Steve just being Steve. "It's IBM, and I fucking hate IBM," Steve exclaimed after their counterparts left one day. This was the same man who had once posed flipping off an IBM sign in New York City, wearing a leather jacket and jeans.

But whether consciously or not, Steve had perfected the art of projecting strength from weakness. Here he was, the CEO of NeXT—a start-up with no shipped products and a rapidly dwindling bank account—lecturing IBM about the terms of a potential deal. In reality, IBM had other options for software. But this was probably NeXT's one best shot at gaining distribution and escaping Silicon Valley obscurity.

In September, Steve pushed his luck even further. He hosted the IBM executives at his Woodside home and laid out ambitious financial terms for the deal. IBM would have to pay NeXT royalties for its operating system, starting at a breathtaking $500 per copy. Meanwhile, IBM's flagship personal computer, the Personal System/2, cost about $2,000 for the entry-level version.

The terms were negotiated down, but the talks soon stalled. Steve grew impatient and decided to lay down the law to IBM's executives. Any workable deal would have to be quick and simple, he told them over the phone.

IBM's interpretation of quick and simple arrived at ten o'clock the night before IBM's negotiating team would arrive again from headquarters in Armonk, New York. The NeXT team gathered around the fax machine, watching impatiently as page after page spewed out. "When's it gonna stop? When's it gonna stop?" they wondered aloud. "Typical IBM," Dan'l joked.

Finally, the fax machine fell silent. Sitting in the spool was a 125-page contract thick enough to choke a lawyer.

Steve opened it that night and made it to page ten. "This is not going to work," he told NeXT counsel Gary Moore, who had represented Steve and Rich in the Apple lawsuit and then joined NeXT as its top lawyer. An internal memo described it as "brain-damaged," Silicon Valley–speak for hopelessly bureaucratic. Steve wanted a deal that favored NeXT. And he understood a fundamental law of negotiation: Whoever writes the first draft controls the conversation. "If we start from this document, we're not going to end up in a place that makes sense," he told Gary.

Four IBM cousins arrived the next morning in their Armonk uniforms—dark suits. They settled into NeXT's conference room. Dan'l and Gary were already waiting when Steve walked in. Without a word, Steve dramatically tossed the 125-page document onto the conference table. "Sorry you came all this way," Steve said, "but this agreement just really isn't going to do it for us."

Then he left.

The door clicked shut. The IBM men looked at each other, then at Gary and Dan'l, then at each other again. "Is he serious?"

"He's serious," Gary said. "How about this? What if we take the first stab at an agreement?"

The IBM men looked at each other again. They'd flown all this way. "Okay," they replied.

Gary worked on a new contract to replace their 125-page document. The document was a couple dozen pages. It demanded $100 million in royalties paid by IBM over three years.

The negotiations dragged on for another 103 days until NeXT's patience snapped completely. Then, in April 1988, Steve and the IBM executives gathered at Ross's suburban Dallas office for one last negotiating session. When the smoke cleared, they had a deal, executed days later by fax machine. It gave IBM the right to evaluate NeXTSTEP and set the terms if it opted to pull the trigger.

It was only an option, not a commitment, and the final terms were a far cry from the aggressive ones NeXT had proposed. But it was still a deal. And it meant that NeXT would get some badly needed cash.

Steve gathered his employees in a conference room and told them to keep the secret: IBM agreed to "$30 million on signing the contract, another $30 million on shipping, and then royalties on every copy they ship," he said. It was three times Ross's investment—a windfall that "bought them years of runway," Gary recounted.

Against Steve's wishes, Cousin Bill flew to Seattle to inform Microsoft about IBM's new partnership with NeXT as a courtesy call, *Fortune* reported. IBM and Microsoft were developing their own operating system together, but Microsoft had recently violated their tacit agreement not to poach each other's executives. Now Microsoft was nervous about IBM's intentions because they damaged their goodwill, and Cousin Bill felt that Bill Gates deserved to know IBM was hedging its bets with NeXT.

When he learned about the deal, Bill Gates erupted, pulling out every stop to kill it. In his telling, IBM already had access to Microsoft's superior software—why would the team go looking for anything else? "NeXTSTEP isn't compatible with anything," he fumed. But the deal also made him wonder, if IBM was interested in Steve's software, how good was it really?

He called Steve.

"I hear you guys are doing really good things," Bill said, all casual friendliness. "Maybe we should take a look at what you're up to. Maybe we'll write some software for you guys."

Steve, sitting next to Dan'l in the open office, started smiling.

"Bill [Gates], I know you just talked to Bill Lowe."

"Bill who?" Gates replied, playing dumb.

"Bill Lowe," Steve said.

There was a pause. "Oh yeah, he did come by," Gates admitted.

Bill Gates suggested he fly down from the Microsoft headquarters in Redmond, Washington, the following Monday. After hanging up, his assistant called back requesting NeXT send all its technical documentation to Bill. Steve was in another building, and so Dan'l took the call and refused. That wasn't how NeXT did business—it asked for signed NDAs first, then talked.

Bill called back and someone handed the phone to Dan'l. "I don't want to meet with you, and I don't want to meet with Steve," Bill said. "I just want to find out what you guys are doing technically."

Dan'l kept his cool. "I don't think that approach will work for us," he replied, "but I'll talk to Steve and we'll get back to you."

Steve immediately called Bill back with a masterstroke of manipulation. He told Bill that Dan'l was one of the most mild-mannered, reasonable people he knew—whatever Bill had said must have been truly insulting to upset him. Dan'l was a cofounder, Steve reminded him, and they couldn't have the meeting unless Bill apologized.

Minutes later, Dan'l's phone rang. Bill, the richest man in tech, called to apologize. Clearly, he didn't want to miss out on seeing what NeXT was up to.

When Bill showed up at NeXT—alone, doing his characteristic rocking motion when he was thinking—he listened to the company's pitch without signing an NDA. Days later, he sent a thanks-but-no-thanks note that he didn't want to write software for NeXT.

That left NeXT and IBM with a signed deal and Bill nowhere to be found. For the first time in Microsoft's partnership with IBM, Big Blue had made a major software decision without asking Bill for permission. Dan'l was ecstatic about what this meant.

To understand the magnitude of what IBM was offering, consider the computing landscape at that moment: The entire industry was up for grabs. Businesses and institutions were still deciding what operating system would run their computers for the next decade.

If IBM, as the undisputed king of computing, threw its weight behind NeXTSTEP—with its elegant interface, object-oriented programming, and groundbreaking technology—Steve's software could become the standard that every office worker booted up each morning. NeXTSTEP could have been what Windows eventually became.

The deal could put Steve Jobs back on the map.

8

"YOU SHOULD KNOW EVERYTHING'S BROKEN"

One late evening in April 1988, NeXT's chief scientist, Richard Crandall, was toiling alone at the office. The building was dark except for a pool of lamplight on his desk and his blinking terminal casting shadows on the walls.

Into this scene wandered Avie Tevanian, the young software developer Steve had first courted two years earlier. He had finally graduated with his PhD from CMU and was slated to start at NeXT the following day. But his curiosity couldn't wait.

"I'm brand new," Avie explained to Richard. "I start tomorrow."

Richard barely looked up. "Well, you should know everything's broken," he said. Officially, Richard wrote educational software. Unofficially, he was NeXT's designated pessimist.

Avie wondered if he had made the right decision to take the job. He could have gone anywhere. Bill had personally interviewed him for a role at Microsoft, he told the Computer History Museum. But there, he'd have been a cog in a vast machine. NeXT offered him the chance to develop his Mach kernel into a real-world product from the ground up.

As Avie settled into NeXT that spring, the company was entering the frantic final sprint toward its first product release. After repeated delays, Steve had decreed a new deadline of July 1988, which was more than a year after his original release date. But NeXTSTEP still wasn't ready, nor was the company's hardware. It really was all broken.

It wasn't surprising to many on the team. The company was attempting to build an entire computer from scratch. Twenty-five young software engineers were building an operating system, development tools, graphics, audio, and a file management system from the ground up—all at the same time. They had the support of about eighty employees total, many of them in hardware engineering. Something was certain to go wrong. Yet time and again, Steve planned for perfection instead of preparing for inevitable setbacks.

That spring, a series of cascading crises exposed the error.

Because Big Dave and Little Dave's gate array chip had failed—taking with it Steve's dream of integrating multiple chips into one—NeXT had to redesign its motherboard with conventional components. NeXT had been counting on Motorola's much-hyped 68040 chip to provide the Cube's speedy brain. But Motorola delayed it. Left with no choice, NeXT fell back on the previous generation chip, the 68030, which was still respectable but now six months behind the cutting edge.

Worse, NeXT had to bolt on an additional, separate chip to allow its customers to perform advanced math calculations. The improvised solution worked, but it wasn't fast, and it made the whole system feel a step behind.

In better news, Canon had finally delivered its optical disk. "Revolutionary," Steve said when NeXT finally received it. By using this optical disk instead of a traditional hard drive for storage, the computer wouldn't emit any pesky mechanical noise. Instead, the futuristic cube would whisper to life.

But NeXT's engineers weren't so sure about Canon's drive. When Rich bolted it into the Cube and powered it up for a test run, minutes passed. No boot. Unix—the operating system that was built to constantly swap data with storage—hit a wall. The optical drive couldn't keep up. "It was slower than expected," said Rich.

To fix the speed problem, NeXT decided to offer customers traditional hard drives as optional add-ons—another unplanned, inelegant, and expensive concession.

It wouldn't be the last compromise. As the team trudged along, competitors Sun Microsystems and Apple had begun transitioning their high-end workstations to color displays. Now customers in scientific labs, medical imaging facilities, and academic publishing houses were all asking for them.

But color monitors generated lower-definition images than those of the grayscale monitors they replaced. Steve wasn't on board with the muddier image quality, demanding WYSIWYG—that the display resolution match a laser printer's output with perfect fidelity.

Steve made the call that NeXT should stick with the older, higher-resolution grayscale monitors. Better to ship a machine that looked outdated than one stuck with what Steve called "baby color." Besides, megapixel color would have doubled the price, creating an impossible burden for a start-up already bleeding cash.

The technological retreats were piling up. Steve had promised a groundbreaking computer in every respect. Now there was a growing feeling within NeXT that the team was preparing to ship yesterday's technology.

By May 1988, NeXT's financial outlook was also looking seriously gray. The company had $25 million in the bank but needed $27.5 million to survive the year. To make it work, they'd need to sell sixteen thousand machines by year-end. But the team could barely get one to boot properly.

The situation didn't stop Steve from planning another grand, expensive gesture. As the company approached a hundred employees, Steve told Pat and Ross that the company's footprint needed to grow. He had found an opportunity for NeXT to move to a brand-new office park, Seaport Centre in Redwood City, overlooking a creek and a marina.

Ross and Pat reviewed the lease, which covered six buildings and would cost nearly $2.5 million in first-year rent, with millions more committed to tenant improvements and campus upgrades. The figures were shocking—NeXT was proposing to spend more on office space than most start-ups raised in total funding. But the board approved it. Steve had sold them on his vision for growth.

As the first tenant at Seaport Centre, NeXT got a generous allowance from the developer to build out its empty office spaces. Even though the job didn't require any demolition, Steve quickly blew through the allowance.

According to Randall E. Stross, Steve opted to scrap the already built elevators (this was before the passage of the Americans with Disabilities Act), never mind that their absence would make moving equipment a nightmare. He commissioned a grand, gravity-defying entrance staircase from I. M. Pei's firm that appeared to float in space. He selected gray, black, and white marble for the dining area. He decided that common spaces would be outfitted with $2,200 chairs and $10,000 sofas. Every desk would bear the highest-quality phone Steve could find—priced at $450 each.

The complicated build-out was scheduled to take a year. The NeXT building itself was designed to generate breakthroughs: corridors arranged to force engineers to collide, creating what one called "organized serendipity." Steve saw every process, from how people moved through hallways to how they sorted email, as a layout to be optimized.

Steve would patrol these spaces himself, ambushing employees with questions about their work, turning hallway encounters into impromptu design reviews. The opulent chairs created comfortable spaces where these spontaneous collaborations could flourish.

In the meantime, NeXT brought in select outside experts to test its troubled machine. One was Jonathan Seybold, who published one of the most influential newsletters in the computer industry. Jonathan loved the computer, and he especially appreciated the elegant software. But a neat machine alone, he warned, "doesn't mean as much as it used to."

Jonathan hammered away at the core question: "How does a small company win market acceptance?" Sure, NeXTSTEP was powerful, he acknowledged. But without a library of tools and applications built by third-party developers, he believed that NeXT would struggle to gain traction.

Steve got the concern. He had been working hard to pursue software partnerships. He started by going after Improv—Cambridge, Massachusetts–based Lotus's experimental spreadsheet software—which could do things Excel couldn't touch.

Before Improv, every spreadsheet was a house of cards—thousands of brittle formulas where one human mistake could break everything. Lotus programmer Pito Salas had an elegant breakthrough: Instead of building separate spreadsheets to see your data different ways (sales by month, by region, by product), Improv stored everything in one smart structure. With a click, you could instantly reorganize the same data—view sales by region, then flip to see them by month, then pivot to compare products. Steve wanted it, and he wanted it before all his competitors.

In exchange for discounted development machines from NeXT, Lotus had to promise that NeXT users would get Improv before anyone else. Steve knew a killer app you couldn't get anywhere else would sell more black Cubes than a thousand advertisements.

And he won.

"It was the glamour of Steve Jobs, as much as anything," recalled Pito. "Everybody wanted to play with Steve Jobs." Across the Valley, others were beginning to make similar bets on NeXT, including Adobe, Frame Technology Corporation (the creator of FrameMaker), and university computing departments.

Like Lotus, the players were drawn by the man in charge as much as the machine he was building. Adobe brought the technology called Display PostScript (which would later evolve into the format called the Portable Document Format, or PDF), making NeXT the first computer in which screen and printer spoke the same language—what you saw on your monitor was exactly what would print on paper, pixel-perfect at 400 dots per inch. FrameMaker, professional publishing software (similar to Adobe InDesign) for companies, would now be in student hands thanks to NeXTSTEP. Even *William Shakespeare: The Complete Works,* published by Oxford University Press, would come built in to the software bundle alongside *Webster's Dictionary.* Most students still cranked out papers on their typewriters and basic word processors, but Steve wanted NeXT users to have access to a complete creative studio.

Steve had even bigger ambitions too. He wanted NeXT computers to crack open a field that most considered dead: artificial intelligence. The grand promises of the early '80s—computers that would diagnose cancer or argue legal cases—had crashed and burned in what they called "AI winter."

Yet when Steve visited labs at Stanford and Carnegie Mellon, he saw researchers hunched over $50,000 workstations, stubbornly teaching machines baby steps like understanding sentences or solving puzzles. They wrote in Lisp, an exotic programming language that lets programmers manipulate ideas the way other languages manipulated numbers.

Steve made a decision that would have sounded insane to other executives: bundle Allegro Common Lisp—software that cost thousands per license—for free with every NeXT machine. While IBM and Sun treated AI tools as exotic luxuries, Steve was intent on putting them in university computer labs.

In June 1988, Dan'l wrote a blunt memo to Steve: "We are over a year late. The competition has progressed more than we expected. Our product is twice as expensive as we imagined." He warned Steve that the computer still wasn't working and pushed him to reset expectations. An October 1988 release was now the best they could hope for.

Just over two years earlier, at the Pebble Beach retreat, the team had warned Steve that setting an impossible deadline would force them into bad decisions and flawed designs. Now they were living in the worst of all worlds. The ambitious release timeline had forced them to compromise on design, and they had missed their target date by more than a year.

Steve woke up to the reality after spending a week with the workstation on his desk. "The computer takes several minutes (my guess is five plus) to boot," he wrote to his senior team. "My computer crashes once every hour or two. With the current state of our software, the industry will laugh us into bankruptcy. We are running out of time. It's all up to you."

For months, when Dan'l had tried to raise these exact concerns, Steve had dismissed him, saying his marketing team wasn't "spending enough time with the product." Now Steve was seeing the problem for himself.

The sales team had a name for this Steve phenomenon: "Go North." The joke went like this: Steve hires a salesman and tells him to "Go North." Sacramento. "Keep going." Oregon. "Go North." Washington. "Go North." Finally, the guy's calling from the Arctic Circle. "What the hell are you doing up there?" Steve explodes.

Bob Fraik, a software manager, offered a solution to the lagging timeline. He proposed releasing what was essentially alpha software—an early, unfinished version full of bugs and missing features—by calling it NeXTSTEP "0.8 release." It would give developers something to experiment with while NeXT worked toward a more stable beta version (0.9) and eventually the complete, market-ready 1.0 release.

Steve agreed to go along with the plan. He wanted to launch NeXTSTEP at the launch event for the Cube, even though they were giving themselves nine months to deliver the finished operating system—until the end of June the following year.

"That was probably not the smartest thing to do," Susan later said.

Then, on June 20, *Time* magazine hit newsstands with a blistering exposé on NeXT. "Unfortunately, the NeXT computer does not perform flawlessly," it read. "Industry sources familiar with the machine have told *Time* that the most recent delay is directly related to the computer's all-important video display," a reference to the team's dithering on whether to use a color or grayscale display.

Someone inside NeXT was talking. The article recounted details like rising chip costs and a new price range for the machine—somewhere between $4,000 and $8,000.

The article also mentioned that Steve was driven by "childish pique to show [Apple CEO John] Sculley what he can do," reinforcing a perception that irritated Steve. The kicker was a quote from an anonymous industry source: "This is the reason Jobs is being so low key. He is embarrassed." Steve was having his aura stripped in the press.

If Steve thought the *Time* article was embarrassing, worse was on the horizon: His top patron, Ross, was losing patience. In the company's next board meeting, after hearing about NeXTSTEP's alpha release plan, the Texas billionaire leaned forward.

"You shouldn't introduce a product before you can ship it," he said, cutting through Steve's reality distortion field. "What is it going to take to get the sales? How are you going to build the rest of the company?"

Until now, Ross had held back and let Steve run the show, despite presenting himself publicly as a tough mentor. Ross's newfound skepticism worried the team. He was NeXT's main benefactor—the company's largest investor and source of outside credibility. A satirical poem, circulated at a company party, described their relationship with Ross this way:

"Rossy Perot-Man is a very wealthy guy. If he looks at you and says, 'You jump,' always say, 'Yes sir, how high?'"

The delays rippled across the company. With no product to sell and therefore no possibility of earning commissions, NeXT's salespeople were dying on the vine. Dan'l recruited heavy hitters who had been making $400,000 to $600,000 a year at companies like IBM. Now they were pulling down a $75,000 base salary, waiting to move a product whose release timeline kept slipping.

Dan'l did everything possible to keep his twenty-person sales force from evaporating. He drove to a department store and bought twenty luxury Motorola cell phones at a price of $2,500 each—$50,000 worth of cellular phones. The phones cost $500 a month just for the service plan, with calls costing an additional $4 a minute.

At a company retreat, Dan'l handed them out ceremonially. "We recognize you're making $75,000 a year with no commissions coming in," he told them. "At least you'll be able to phone your family with these."

To prepare for the launch, Todd Rulon-Miller had to recruit more world-class salespeople without being able to say anything about the product they'd be selling or when it would ship.

Todd had joined NeXT two years earlier, walking away from a six-figure salary at Tandem Computers, a major manufacturer of machines for banks and telecommunications companies. Now he made a $75,000 base salary with stock options at NeXT. He'd bet his career on Steve's vision, and he was asking others to do the same.

Another challenge: Sales were certain to be an uphill challenge even when they had a finished computer to sell. NeXT's target customers—university professors and researchers—had what Todd's planning documents called a "zero BS quotient." They had deep technical expertise and were fiercely skeptical. They would see through the machine's flaws instantly: its sluggish optical drive, outdated processor, and inflated price. "You're talking to people who think small, and then you've got Steve Jobs who's bigger than the world," Todd said.

Meanwhile, Steve continued to play chicken with IBM, risking the partnership that had the potential to save the company. If Steve lost IBM, it could quickly become a competitor. Dan'l warned Steve: "The longer we take to get to market, the sooner we will have to directly compete with our cousins, and they will have a less expensive box with the same tools."

As deadlines slipped and commitments blurred, IBM began to grow impatient too. And Steve made matters worse, refusing to give even an inch of control or take feedback over NeXTSTEP's development—causing consternation for IBM, which wanted to shape the operating system for the needs of its customers. Steve told everyone that he feared IBM would take NeXTSTEP for its own computers and then use it to eat into sales of his beloved Cube.

While Steve stalled, others advanced. Sun, which commanded the business workstation market, was already beginning to encroach on the university lab budgets NeXT desperately needed. The longer NeXT took, the more Sun computers landed in universities, and the less likely it was that university administrators would want to rip out their Sun workstations for NeXT. The first company to achieve market dominance would run the table for the foreseeable future.

In August, Steve walked into The Lodge at Pebble Beach to face IBM president Andrew Heller, aka "Cousin Andy"—with a computer that still crashed every couple of hours.

It turned into an eight-hour showdown to iron out the last details of their agreement from the previous April. IBM needed an opportunity to train its developers before launch. IBM accused Steve of agreeing to those terms previously but now changing his mind.

But Steve remained unyielding. With two months until the NeXT-STEP 0.8 release, IBM wouldn't get a developer camp, Steve insisted. No observers. NeXTSTEP was all too confidential. IBM would just have to solve the problem itself.

The software's name, NeXTSTEP, became another battle. IBM's lawyers found trademark conflicts everywhere—Siemens owned "STEP" in the UK, Sweden, and Norway; Sony held "NEXT" in Japan. Steve was unmoved. We're keeping NeXTSTEP, he told them. Figure it out.

Despite the friction, Steve radiated confidence in his report back to the team about the meeting with Cousin Andy. IBM was talking about using NeXTSTEP "everywhere," he told them. The cousins were "getting into the spirit."

His confidence turned out to be well founded. On September 13, a report in *The New York Times* made it official: Steve had sealed his IBM deal, unchanged from the previous April but now formally announced to drum up excitement a month before the Cube's launch event.

NeXT's machine still didn't work, but now IBM was committed to backing it. From IBM's perspective, NeXT offered an escape hatch from irrelevance. The company feared becoming a boring, commodity PC maker. And despite all of NeXT's troubles, IBM hoped NeXTSTEP could offer excitement again.

Steve declared victory. He'd played chicken with the world's largest computer company and won. Or, at least, he convinced himself he had. Whether or not it would save NeXT was another question.

9

WHEN REALITY DISTORTS BACK

One group had always been adamant about the Cube hitting its target price: NeXT's advisory board. As representatives of top universities, they knew what was in academic budgets and what wasn't. They made clear, over and over again, that in order to achieve high-volume sales, the computer couldn't exceed $3,000.

So when Steve told Burt Cummings, NeXT's director of sales programs, that he was going to have to break the news about the Cube's new, higher price to the advisory board at an upcoming dinner meeting, he blanched. The Cube's expensive components had driven the price up to $6,500. That was more than double what Steve had initially promised—and light years from the $1,000 that had made the Macintosh a campus sensation.

To make matters worse, $6,500 was only the base price. Choose to buy NeXT's "breakthrough" laser printer too? That would cost you another $2,000. Want a real hard drive instead of Canon's lethargic optical disc? That was going to be $2,000 for 330 megabytes or $4,000 for 660 megabytes. With add-ons, a usable NeXT system would cost a whopping $10,500, or $12,500 for the bigger hard drive. In 1988, that was more than an average year of tuition at a private university.

Burt agreed to present the proposed pricing to the advisory board on one condition: "You're gonna be right there when they start throwing the tomatoes," he told Steve. Sure enough, Burt recalled the board "howling in dismay and anger" when he broke the news.

The dinner meeting wound up running until the wee hours of the night. "You need to drop the price," Marty Ringle from Vassar told Steve. "You have to build your footprint in higher ed. Otherwise you're not going to exist."

Brian Hawkins from Brown University stood up to say that at the new price, Brown wouldn't be able to buy anything close to the number of units it had originally planned to purchase. In response, Steve questioned Brian's integrity and berated him in front of the entire board. During the break, Brian told colleagues he was done. He wrote his resignation letter the next day.

In addition to the unpalatable price, advisory board members told Steve that NeXT had become too inwardly focused, too obsessed with elegance at the expense of usability. "Where were the applications?" they wanted to know. "What made NeXT different?" Then the board members reminded the team they had five months, at most, to fix everything.

NeXT executives defended their high price using Wall Street logic: They had bills to pay, they said. They had investors to satisfy and margins to earn. The team pressured the prestigious names in the room to commit to ordering the Cube, its new price notwithstanding. But they could barely muster orders for a handful of machines. NeXT would have to offer deep discounts to get them on board.

Steve's handpicked cheerleaders were fast becoming critics.

Steve turned his focus to winning new converts. He planned for the launch of NeXTSTEP 0.8 and the far-from-production-ready Cube to be a blowout theatrical event. For a venue, the team selected Davies Symphony Hall—the grand, 2,700-seat home of the San Francisco Symphony. Steve hoped to use its excellent acoustics to showcase the Cube's audio capabilities.

To direct the presentation, Steve didn't want a staid corporate event specialist. He wanted to hire someone special. He had heard about George Coates, a postmodern theater director who had just completed a work involving performers suspended inside a giant spinning circle with projections swirling all around them.

Steve loved the piece. But even more, Steve loved George's cachet. When approached about staging the NeXT launch, the director was skeptical. "Why do you need me?" George asked Steve, "You could get anyone to do that."

"We want someone with a name," Steve insisted to NeXT designer Eddie Lee, his liaison with George. "We want to work with the best."

George agreed to stage the event. He hoped to ditch the mores of stuffy corporate presentations, instead pitching Steve on an immersive experience with projections on the floor—and even some spinning elements from his installations.

In the end, though, the team settled on something more conventional: a man (Steve) sitting onstage clicking through computer applications projected onto a screen behind him, with a vase of flowers on a black-clothed table. George was reduced to a very expensive stagehand for a live demo.

With three days to go before the event, audio engineer Julius Smith was in serious trouble. He had spent the summer playing Whac-A-Mole with low-level glitches in NeXT's audio software. Now, days before demo, the software still wasn't working.

At one in the morning, bleary-eyed and desperate, Julius bumped into Steve and Bud in the NeXT hallway. "How bad would it be if we just played a CD?" he asked, regretting it immediately.

Steve fixed him with a lethal stare. "If you can't get this together," he said, "you will not have descendants."

For Steve, music wasn't just another computer feature; it had become the soul of the machine. He was determined that NeXT's computer would make live music and had placed a donated Steinway grand piano in the NeXT lab as a hulking monument to that commitment.

Steve's aspirations were put to the test at the team's pre-presentation software meeting. Julius had grim news: The Music Kit, which was the live-band application that NeXT was developing—a proto-GarageBand—was technically complete but nagged with bugs. Julius wrote to the team that he'd need three weeks to squash the bugs and couldn't even start working until after the launch event because he had so many other pressing problems.

He reported that he had created thirty-nine digital instruments for the app but only ten worked reliably. Worse, NeXT's orchestral software, which was supposed to make the instruments harmonize into a symphony, had yet to produce a single note.

Across various projects, problems were cascading. The team complained about constant bugs cropping up—and the fact that no one at NeXT had developed tools to track them, a basic quality control practice at most companies. It was like trying to repair a car engine in pitch darkness.

Making everything more difficult, Steve would regularly stand behind the software engineers as they worked, reaching past them to point at code on their screens to demand adjustments. One time, as the engineers worked on NeXT's system for organizing and storing files for the 0.8 release, Steve started rearranging how the computer organized and accessed data. The problem was that customers expected NeXT to work like other workstation computers they were familiar with. With his changes, Steve had created a file system that confused users into rejecting the operating system.

Steve spent the two days before his launch event rehearsing at a high school gymnasium in Berkeley. To combat buggy software and frequent crashes, the team constructed an elaborate digital illusion. As Steve demonstrated software on an onstage computer, a hidden machine in the wings would actually handle all the music and audio demos. This division of labor reduced the chances of a crash during the show. The team rehearsed dozens of times, secretly switching the presentation display between the onstage computer and the hidden audio machine to make it look seamless. The backstage operator followed a scripted sequence with predetermined cue points rather than mirroring Steve's mouse movements in real time. They even had a plan to jam blue ice packs inside the machines to prevent them from overheating.

The night before the launch, Steve and his presentation team stayed up arguing until two in the morning about the exact shade of green that would be used on the projector. The color they settled on would be only one among many background colors used during the presentation. But Steve insisted on getting it exactly right. So there they sat, cycling through a parade of barely distinguishable RGB values in a dark conference room as the night ticked away.

With only hours to go until showtime, NeXTSTEP's bugs still hadn't been fixed. Onstage crashes were looking inevitable. At the last minute, Bud materialized with a new OS disk, casually instructing Paul Vais, the presentation's executive director, to load it for the software demonstration because "it's more stable." To Paul, it felt like putting a Band-Aid on a leaky submarine. "If it crashed," Paul said, "I would have been dead."

But at least they'd settled on the right shade of green.

On Wednesday, October 12, 1988, the day of the event, grown men wept outside Davies Hall.

Three thousand invitations had gone out for the unveiling, but many of Steve's most devoted followers hadn't been on the list. Some had trekked from across the country to see their hero present, with no invitation in hand, only to be denied entry. Even at his lowest ebb, exiled from Apple and running a struggling computer company, Steve inspired loyalty, fervor, devotion.

Burt, who was six feet tall and two hundred pounds, was stationed at the door to keep them out. One particularly desperate soul caught his attention: "I took a bus all the way here from Kansas City," he pleaded.

"What were you thinking?" Burt thought to himself.

Inside, digital music pulsed as placid men and women in business suits filed to their seats. Backstage, Steve straightened his navy blue jacket. After three years in exile, the prince was ready for his grand return.

Then, at 9:30 a.m., he walked out to thunderous applause.

"I think I speak for everybody at NeXT saying it's great to be back." Beat. "I haven't done this in a few years, so I'm a little nervous today."

It sounded like the man had just admitted weakness to almost three thousand people. But Steve's team, waiting in the wings, knew better. Steve Jobs didn't do nervous.

"I think together, we're going to experience one of those times that occurs once or twice in a decade of computing. A time when a new architecture is rolled out that's really going to change the future of computing."

Every computer architecture had roughly a ten-year life cycle, he now claimed (though he'd told NeXT employees it was only five years). The IBM PC? "Peaked in around 1986." The Macintosh—his own baby? "It's going to peak next year. You can already see cracks in the architectural foundation."

He wasn't done. "You will never see programs for the Macintosh that escape the orbit of working perfectly on that nine-inch electronic screen."

He also said, "Macintosh was a revolution in making it easier for the end user, but the software developer paid the price of that revolution. It is a bear to develop software for these things."

He claimed that NeXT's computer, with its more powerful processor and bigger screen, would shatter these chains. With the Cube, developers could finally build the future.

Never mind that developers would get only operating system version 0.8 to work on.

Then Steve turned to the demos. "For those of you that aren't software developers in the audience, I'd like to remind you of the first two laws of demoing. First law of demos is that demos will always crash. And the second law of demos is that the probability of crashing goes up with the number of people watching." The audience laughed. "So if something goes wrong today, have some compassion for the demo-er."

Steve sat down to demonstrate the NeXT Cube. As if on cue, the computer paused while booting. Backstage, Paul felt his stomach plunge. "Oh shit, it's failing," he thought. Steve turned slowly toward him, eyes like lasers. No compassion there.

Then, mercifully, the display flickered to life as the backstage team executed the most seamless sleight of hand in tech demo history. The two-machine setup, ice packs and all, had just saved the presentation from disaster.

Then Steve did something with few precedents: He built an application live onstage using Interface Builder, dragging and dropping a physics simulation that a graduate student had created. A gas molecule bounced in a cylinder that materialized on screen.

Backstage, the team was sweating. The molecule viewer had been crashing all week. "We were all biting our nails in the back, hoping it doesn't glitch this one time," said systems engineer Gregor Bailar. Miraculously, it didn't.

The audience oohed and aahed.

After finishing his demonstration, Steve introduced Dr. Richard Crandall, NeXT's chief scientist, to show off the computer's sound capabilities. Paul stood in the wings alongside Steve, both watching as Richard demonstrated real-time audio analysis, showing how the computer could capture sounds through its microphone and display visual representations of the audio waves and frequency patterns.

Richard concluded his demo with a flourish. He gently tapped the microphone and watched as the computer's display showed the visual pattern of whatever sound his single hand had produced.

"That," Richard declared, "is the sound of one hand clapping."

As if on cue, the software started glitching, Dan'l recalled. Everyone held their breath. Luckily, no crash.

Then Steve returned to the stage and launched a demo of the computer's dictionary application, an innovation at the time. "A word that's sometimes used to describe me is *mercurial*."

The definition appeared instantly, and Steve read it aloud. "Of, relating to, or born under the planet Mercury," he said, "Characterized by unpredictable changeableness of mood."

The thesaurus entry offered an antonym: *saturnine*. Steve double-clicked on the word. "Cold and steady in mood," he read, frowning slightly. "Slow to act or change, of a gloomy or surly disposition."

Steve grinned. "I don't think *mercurial*'s so bad after all."

The all-important audio demonstration was next. Julius had been up all night fixing it. Steve clicked on it and, just like that, the computer began playing music synthesized live in front of the audience's eyes.

The room went quiet.

Then Steve arrived at the workstation's dreaded price. Burt, watching from the audience, knew what was coming.

"We are going to be charging higher education a single price of $6,500," Steve began.

Burt turned to his marketing colleague and deadpanned. "Get ready to run."

But instead, the audience applauded.

"Our breakthrough printer that everyone seems to want in the office," Steve continued, "we're going to charge, I think, an outstandingly great price: $2,000."

More applause.

The printer was deliberately priced high. More than a year later, HP would release the first mass-market laser printer at less than $1,000. But NeXT was counting on most customers wanting one, and at $2,000 it carried substantial margin to compensate for the razor-thin profits on the $6,500 computer itself.

Then he spelled out the hard drive options to replace that slow optical disc: $2,000 for the smaller one or $4,000 for the bigger one.

For the price, the audience gave him a standing ovation.

Burt sat frozen. Thousands of industry experts had just whooped and hollered for a computer and printer combo that cost more than a Honda Civic. Only Steve Jobs could price a machine out of its market and get adulation in return. As Burt put it, "I just looked at my counterpart and I said, 'I know nothing.'"

Nearly two hours into the presentation, Steve jumped in to interrupt partner testimonials. "Excuse me, I'm going to have to cut this short," he said. "We're running a little late today. And there's another group called the San Francisco Symphony that thinks they need the hall this afternoon."

Steve had saved his biggest gamble for last. The team had planned a duet between Daniel Kobialka, principal second violinist at the San Francisco Symphony, and the Cube, which would calculate its part in real time. Steve said that music was the NeXT feature "that strikes closest to the soul."

The first notes of Bach's Violin Concerto in A Minor emerged from the black Cube, carrying a distinctive digital clarity—not warm, not quite human, but miles beyond the beep-and-buzz of a 1980s computer.

Then Daniel raised his Stradivarius.

The virtuoso's bow touched the strings and ignited something genuinely new: man and machine, trading phrases of a three-hundred-year-old masterpiece. Daniel swept through a passage, his fingers dancing up the neck of his violin. Then the computer would answer, holding the melody, keeping time with one of the world's great violinists through the concerto's most demanding runs.

The hall erupted.

After three years in the wilderness, Steve had just reminded everyone why they'd missed him.

Once the show ended, Ross gushed to the press. "I can't tell you how many hardware announcements I've attended in my life," he said, beaming like his $20 million investment hadn't just vanished into beautiful smoke. "This is the most exciting one and the best presented one I've ever attended."

Steve, he declared, had done things in his twenties that others don't do until they're fifty. He extolled the team's electric energy. He said that anyone who'd seen them work, as he had, wouldn't be surprised by today's show.

This was the same Ross who'd watched Steve spend weeks perfecting the layout of robots on an empty factory floor and who'd sharply questioned why he was launching a computer with an incomplete operating system. But Ross wasn't about to burst the press's bubble.

"Steve Jobs Puts the 'Wow' Back in Computers," *Newsweek* declared. *BusinessWeek* asked, "Can He Do It Again?" *The New York Times* announced, "The Return of a Computer Star." Even *Macworld*—the redoubt of the Apple faithful—proclaimed that "Steve Jobs Is Back."

But the NeXT team knew the truth. "There was kind of an illusion being created about the real state of the company," Paul said.

That night, it didn't matter. Julius came home to a voicemail from Steve: "You really, really blew it away today." For a man who was judicious with praise, this was too much to have hoped for. The hero-shithead rollercoaster had finally rattled its way to the top of the track.

For now, they were heroes.

10

STEVE ON A STICK

"Develop for it? I'll piss on it!"

In the pages of *Newsweek*, Bill Gates dismantled NeXT's Cube piece by piece. "[Steve] put a microprocessor in a box. So what?" he said.

With regard to the futuristic optical drive: "Anyone can write Sony a check." (Never mind that the check actually went to Canon.)

The sleek design? Bill told *Computerworld*: "If you want black, I'll sell you a can of paint."

Though the Cube bore the brunt of his anger, Bill was still feeling rattled by something bigger: the IBM deal. IBM was a crucial partner in Bill's plan to scale up his Windows operating system. If Steve and IBM took things to the next level, Microsoft could find itself facing a major new competitor in the workstation market.

The only other serious contender was Sun, but Sun had already developed its own operating system and it was incompatible with Windows.

Ironically, Bill was holding on to IBM at the exact moment Steve was pursuing Bill. "Steve wanted Microsoft's applications in the worst way," recalled NeXT sales executive Mark Hayes. Steve hoped Microsoft would develop apps similar to Excel, Word, and PowerPoint for the Cube.

But every conversation between the two men ended the same way. "I talked to Gates," Steve would report back to his team. "We're not gonna get it. He just doesn't want to enable us to compete."

The standoff hinted at the opposing philosophies that animated the two titans' rivalry. In the Cube, Steve wanted to build a closed, proprietary system where every developer had to create software that was unique to his machines. Doing so, he believed, would facilitate a better user experience.

In contrast, Bill wanted to scale Windows quickly, selling software that could run on everyone's hardware. Microsoft was "in the business of writing for machines that sell in the millions," Bill later said, "so [NeXT] is not for us."

Meanwhile, at the other major player in town, sales were on fire. "I'm very pleased to announce that fiscal year 1988 was our most successful year ever," John Sculley wrote his employees. Apple, the $4 billion juggernaut, had done the impossible and nearly doubled its profits in just one year. The Mac was thriving in business markets around the world. Even in education—where Sun was gaining ground with university departments—Apple still dominated most campuses.

But success bred its own problems. Apple employees had developed a reputation as "spoiled brats," executives lamented in an internal memo, demanding instant service at Bay Area restaurants and throwing tantrums when they didn't get exactly what they wanted. And John's habitual reorganizations—he was fond of saying that "complexity, unaddressed, breeds bureaucracy"—had become a running joke inside the company. One internal parody newsletter suggested John was planted by Steve to sabotage Apple's success from within.

From the top of the hill, John was eager to mend fences with Steve. "I haven't had a conversation with Steve Jobs in two years since he left," John told Larry King on his radio show. John had sent Steve a copy of his memoir *Odyssey*, which recounted his career at Pepsi and his takeover of Apple.

Steve, who was decidedly less interested in rekindling the friendship—or reliving that episode—said he'd never read it. In fact, he was galled by John's ongoing attempt to cast himself as a technology visionary in Steve's mold. He griped to friends that John's ideas were neither original nor new.

The day before NeXT's launch event, John called Steve to congratulate him. "I thought it was a gentlemanly thing to do," Steve told *Newsweek*. Though Steve insisted there were no hard feelings between them, bitterness leaked through. "I spent 10 years trying to build something," Steve said, "and most of what I built has been dismantled."

In November, the first Cubes finally shipped. By the end of the year, NeXT had shipped a measly 205 computers. Thirty-one more sat in quality testing.

Until NeXT was ready with a fully functioning operating system, Bud's software team asked to limit total shipments to two thousand computers. According to distribution manager Greg Stein, the company sent those first units to "supporters, members of the board, or people who'd been there since the very beginning," along with university departments and software developers who were making custom applications for them.

Even with rock-bottom production targets, the factory couldn't keep up. Burt remembered getting calls from the factory floor with bad news: "You know those twelve machines we promised you today? Well, there's only eight because four of them didn't pass the paint test." The Cube's magnesium casing was prone to microscopic air bubbles in the revealing matte black paint—a problem that engineers had warned Steve about during development.

Meanwhile, customers were returning many of the units that had shipped due to defective parts. NeXT's quality control system consisted of a visual check of the outside of every shipping box. If it was pristinely white, the unit shipped. NeXT also lacked any system for tracking why machines failed and were returned.

The situation with working units wasn't much better. Developers called the unfinished operating system "useless." University clients were unhappy with them. Even at Reed College, Steve's alma mater, sentiment was the same: The college needed a faster and bug-free system. Other schools had taken delivery of the computers but left them languishing in their white boxes, unopened.

Customers were also coming to terms with the machine's lack of basics: no color, no video, no floppy drive. "You said things would be simple," university administrators told sales teams. The incomplete software left users with more complicated demands to code their desired programs from scratch. An internal NeXT report stated that art history professors had been complaining—they didn't want to learn Objective-C.

NeXT's lagging timeline meant that the company was set to run out of runway in a matter of three months. The company's survival fell to Dan'l and Todd, whose sales and marketing team had to somehow sell demanding customers on flawed, expensive hardware running unfinished software. Steve set the ambitious goal of selling twenty-five thousand computers in the coming year and raising more than $120 million in revenue.

Dan'l felt Steve was setting them up for failure. At that moment, the company had almost no revenue, near-zero installed base, and hardly any market feedback to speak of. Its software was six months away from being finished. Tougher still, the university market, underwhelmed with the machine, wasn't showing strong enough demand to move anywhere close to twenty-five thousand units.

When Dan'l told Steve his sales target was unrealistic—and ignored Bud's position that they should only ship two thousand units—Steve didn't want to hear it. "Your position is not acceptable to me," he shot back.

Dan'l decided to lay out the facts in an email to Steve: Bud's software team, under orders from Steve, had redesigned how the computer organized files without documenting the changes. The company was selling to the most technically sophisticated customers on earth while offering "no logical rationale" for fundamental changes to how users could find and access their documents. Even within NeXT, employees were calling each other just to find where basic files were stored.

Dan'l blamed the software team for burning through "$2–3 million per month with no accountability, or written schedule." Todd concurred. The sales team had supported engineering for two years, accepting low salaries and earning no commissions because there was nothing to sell. "To find out we've 'run out of money' when it has finally become our turn to take the baton is a little disillusioning," Todd wrote to Steve.

But Steve wasn't looking for feedback. "I use Release 0.8 every day, and I think it's great!" he replied. Sure, there were "some current deficiencies," but "I truly think that we CURRENTLY have the best product on the market."

As the exchange happened, competitors continued to gain ground. In choosing to do his blockbuster launch event early, Steve had traded mystery for exposure. Now Sun and Apple were preparing "NeXT killer" machines, Dan'l warned him.

As it stood, Sun was moving five thousand machines a month. Apple: more than fifty thousand. Bewilderingly, Steve predicted that NeXT would shortly join their ranks. He was so convinced of it that he worried about the factory's ability to keep up.

One day Steve appeared in Burt's office in a panic: "We're selling everything we can make!" he said.

Burt laughed. NeXT was making eight computers a day.

On a conference call, Steve briefed Ross about the team's efforts to sell the Cube with incomplete software. "So you mean you sent your troops into the trenches, but you forgot to give them ammo?" Ross replied. The veteran and military contractor couldn't resist a war metaphor.

Ross and Steve had shaken hands on selling to government bureaucracies, the military, and intelligence agencies, with the hope of inking $100 million government contracts. But this was foreign territory for Steve. He'd always been about democratizing technology for consumers, not selling to the federal government. And despite the handshake, he told everyone he didn't trust the feds. But Perot Systems, Ross's new company, was ready to hire a seasoned sales force for the federal government from Electronic Data Systems, his former company, to deploy on behalf of NeXT.

Intelligence agencies were drowning in data from satellites, intercepted phone calls, and newspaper reports they couldn't process fast enough. While they'd been using Steve's other product—the $135,000 Pixar Image Computer—to process satellite imagery, the NeXT Cube promised to do similar work for a tenth of the price. It was the perfect spy machine—equipped with specialized chips that could process audio and visual data at lightning speed to analyze reconnaissance imagery in real time, sophisticated enough to model battlefield scenarios, and equipped with optical disks that CIA spies could destroy after reading, leaving no trace of classified material on any hard drive.

"The NeXT Computer has the potential to make significant advances in workstation computing within the Agency," read an internal assessment by the National Security Agency (NSA). "It offers the most integrated system of hardware and the most advanced software environments, all of which are included in the delivered system, in the smallest, cleanest packaging available today." The agency concluded that NeXT could become indispensable for intercepting communications around the world. Its powerful processor could be used for "signals processing"—extracting information from audio and video, visualizing sounds and images that human eyes and ears couldn't capture.

Intelligence agents showed up at NeXT for demonstrations in scruffy civilian clothes. Dan'l remembered them looking just like "the guy next door." They had no business cards and only introduced themselves with first names. "Hi, my name's Bob," said one. Another: "Sally."

These visitors represented the alphabet soup of U.S. intelligence agencies—the NSA, CIA, DIA—brought in through an intelligence contractor named Robert Kohler, who represented a company called ESL that sold technology to three-letter agencies. As the CIA's former director of the Office of Development and Engineering, Robert had been a direct report to former CIA chief George H. W. Bush. His office had overseen the launch of spy satellites with the first cameras that could read a car's license plate from space. Now he worked as a private contractor for intelligence agencies.

After half a dozen meetings in which agents assessed the Cube and asked questions about its security, it was time for the next step. Steve was supposed to join the spooks at a place they called "the fishbowl"—a secure facility near Washington, DC, where the NSA, CIA, and other agencies would gather to see Steve's demonstration. (In intelligence work, the term "fishbowl" refers to the condition of being under constant scrutiny with no privacy.) Robert's staff all waited for Steve in the NeXT parking lot. But he didn't show.

"I don't want to do business with the federal government," Steve told Dan'l.

"Steve," Dan'l said. "You're going to blow up our relationship with Ross Perot."

But Steve refused.

While Ross hadn't arranged this particular meeting, word of Steve's pattern of refusing government work reached him anyway. He wasn't happy.

These weren't ordinary business partners Steve was alienating. Ross's executives included the same men who had broken their colleagues out of an Iranian prison when the government collapsed nine years earlier—former employees at Ross's previous company, Electronic Data Systems, who had flown into hostile territory to rescue their own people. As Dan'l recalled, "You did not mess around with these guys." But Steve was casually blowing them off.

Ross was losing patience with his protégé, so he decided to teach him a public lesson. One night, NeXT assembled its executives and a few key customers at Stars restaurant in San Francisco, a landmark.

Steve stood to speak first, explaining how NeXT would change everything.

Then it was Ross's turn. "I'd like all the customers in the room to stand up," he said. The customers stood. Then Ross turned to everyone still sitting—all the NeXT employees, including Steve—and pointedly said: "Now, everybody who's sitting down, applaud these people who are standing up, because that's why we're here."

The room erupted in applause. Ross wanted Steve to think about the people buying his computers: the people in that room with real problems that needed solving.

NeXT had one more promising lead for helping it build sales volume. Businessland, one of the largest non-franchised computer store chains in the country, was sniffing around, intrigued by reports about the company's partnership with IBM. It was interested in a potential distribution deal.

Talks proceeded slowly until February 1989. That month, Compaq dumped Businessland over a pricing dispute, erasing 15 percent of the store's sales in an instant. Suddenly, the chain needed a new marquee brand.

For NeXT, a partnership with Businessland appeared to be the ideal opportunity. Like other computer stores, Businessland had traditional, physical storefronts. But unlike competitors, it packed behind-the-scenes firepower in the form of a massive corporate sales force. This allowed Businessland to entice manufacturers by offering IBM's reach without IBM's overhead.

As an important bonus, the chain also offered field service. Its 112 stores all had in-house technicians—exactly what NeXT needed to support demanding institutional clients across the country.

From Businessland's perspective, the deal would associate the chain with a buzzy new brand it could charge more for. "We needed computers with margin, because our margin was deteriorating so rapidly on all these commodity products," Businessland VP for Network Systems Kevin Compton explained.

As much as the partnership made sense, Steve had a lingering reservation. "Your stores are ugly," he kept telling Kevin. Where NeXT was a boutique manufacturer obsessed with elegant design and visions of premium retail distribution, Businessland operated mostly through direct sales to corporations. Its typical location was scattered with simple wooden office desks holding an array of Compaq, IBM, and HP computers on top—no beauty in sight. NeXT adopted an internal slur for the Businessland team: mattress salesmen.

After weeks of negotiation, NeXT and Businessland closed a deal at 9:00 p.m. on February 21, 1989. Steve raised a toast. "Let's go kick the shit out of some people," he told the gathered Businessland executives.

"I am pleased (very pleased!!) to report that we 'plucked a BIG one,'" Steve wrote to all of NeXT. "We have just taken a large, bold step in the continuing adventure of building the best computer company in the world."

NeXT had won very favorable terms: Businessland could sell NeXT's computers exclusively for the corporate market, but not for any other clientele, including universities. And Businessland agreed to fix every NeXT machine, whether or not Businessland had sold it. Buried in the fine print: NeXT could, without warning, change prices, warranties, and even software terms.

Dan'l had architected what could have been the deal of the decade. IBM would license NeXTSTEP and put it on computers around the world. Businessland would handle distribution of NeXT's own machines. And Ross's connections would deliver massive government contracts.

As NeXT executives later reflected, this combination should have been the foundation of a counterfactual history in which NeXTSTEP, not Windows, became the world's operating system. The timing was perfect. Windows was still primitive and competitors like Sun were modest and growing. All Steve had to do was not blow it up.

Bill Gates, still pissed about the IBM deal, wrote a missive to Businessland CEO Dave Norman. He said that partnering with NeXT was "the biggest mistake you've ever made," and went on to explain the Cube's myriad technical deficiencies.

Dave, who was not technically oriented, had no idea what any of it meant, so he handed the letter to Kevin. Kevin read Bill's tantrum and wasn't particularly concerned. Bill criticized NeXT's technical choices, but he didn't threaten Businessland or its relationship with Microsoft. Kevin put the letter in a drawer and got back to work.

Dave had committed Businessland to selling $150 million worth of NeXT computers over the coming year, giving Steve his best shot at surpassing the goal he had set against Dan'l's advice, of selling $125 million worth of computers. But Steve's micromanagement made getting started harder than expected. When Kevin sent Steve slides he had prepared for a joint NeXT-Businessland presentation to corporate customers at the Fort Mason Center in San Francisco, Steve called him and said, "These are terrible. [Creative Director] Susan Kare and I are coming over tomorrow at two o'clock. We're going to redo your slides, and you get to have three words and three points on the slide, and that's it."

Businessland's lack of style continued to irk the NeXT team. "Are you buying IBM or are you buying Compaq?" was how NeXT's district sales manager Patrick Wootan thought of his Businessland counterparts' work. "How many do you need? Let's go to lunch."

As had been negotiated in the deal, NeXT was also allowed to hire its own field executives to drum up excitement alongside Businessland's efforts. The idea was that NeXT's salespeople would create buzz for the product while Businessland handled the actual transactions. Quickly, however, NeXT's salespeople began undermining their partners.

"I did work very closely with Businessland," Patrick said, "and I was very successful at not allowing them to sell a single computer."

Because NeXT's machines were for institutions, they required consultative selling—real, technical conversations about software and design. Businessland's reps didn't have the know-how for those conversations. So Patrick would jump in and make sure they never got the chance. When Businessland scheduled demos, he'd show up to "help," and end up doing all the talking.

But even NeXT's one-upping salespeople kept getting one-upped by Steve. When customers were on the fence, they'd bring him in for what sales employees called "Steve on a stick." It was his presentation done the same way every time: black backdrop, minimalist staging, even down to having a single calla lily flower in a vase on a table nearby.

It worked like magic. When Patrick pitched the computer, sales prospects kept delivering the same verdict: beautiful machine, great software, but too slow and expensive. When Steve stepped in, he could execute the sale nearly every time.

It gave him little sympathy for how hard it was to sell the computers. "You don't know how to sell this," Steve would tell Kevin.

"You guys haven't given us anything we can sell," he responded.

So the salespeople had to get creative. Patrick remembers pitching a tanning bed distributor that was secretly selling the same tanning lotion under eight different brand names. They were tracking customers by writing down their names and orders on index cards. Patrick's team built a demo showing how NeXT could digitize the entire operation.

He made the sale.

In May, Steve proclaimed the company was on track to ship seven hundred computers. It wasn't a lot, but at least it would be up from the twenty-one computers NeXT shipped in April.

The team had released the incremental but still incomplete beta upgrade, NeXTSTEP 0.9, in the meantime. But the forthcoming NeXTSTEP 1.0 software upgrade, the complete version, was months behind schedule.

Steve shrugged off the doldrums as "the well-worn path that every new, successful computer company follows."

Once again, he had reason to be optimistic. On June 5, 1989, Hisashi Sakamaki, Canon's chief executive of business systems operations, signed a blockbuster investment deal: putting $100 million into NeXT in exchange for a 16.67 percent stake in the company and the rights to sell the Cube across Asia.

In their negotiations in the NeXT conference room, Steve had leveraged every angle he could, including the fact that Canon's optical drive had turned out slow and expensive, somehow placing the blame on Canon while simultaneously asking for its money. Canon wanted in badly enough to agree.

Canon's executives cut straight to the point: "How much do you need?"

Steve answered: "$50 million."

They pressed further: "How much do you need to guarantee your success?"

Steve replied: "$100 million."

The Canon executives looked at each other. "What do we get for the extra $50 million?"

Without missing a beat, Steve said: "A board seat."

Canon agreed—along with the condition that Steve hire a COO to bring some order to the company.

"The scale of this Canon deal STAGGERS me," Patrick Hickey, a NeXT telecommunications manager, wrote to Steve. In the same email, he casually compared it to his previous career as a marijuana smuggler: "I remember well driving 'keys' from the Michoacan Peninsula into San Diego during the halcyon days of 'traffic' (66–67 . . . or pre-Border Checks) and getting perhaps $100.00 per, after having paid perhaps $25.00 per." The rush of dealmaking at NeXT felt remarkably similar.

Steve played cool about the deal in public, acting as if Canon was chasing him rather than the other way around. "A reasonable fraction of what Canon is investing is going into the bank," he told the Associated Press, as if NeXT was drowning in money.

With Canon's investment, NeXT's valuation soared to $600 million, which was welcome news to both Businessland and IBM, who had staked their reputations on NeXT's success. Steve was convincing the world that he was relevant once again.

Steve's Deep Shit List kept growing. But now when he read it at company meetings, no one listened. If every problem was existential, people thought, then nothing really was.

And they were fed up with shit—especially Steve's. He was making everything so much harder.

Employees revolted at a company retreat in Santa Cruz, promising to resign if he continued his tirades. Steve responded by fostering a new obsession: the Japanese philosophy of total quality management. He announced to the company that he was going to be taking a different approach to management, following in the mold of Japanese business leaders who understood that smart companies reject management in which "bosses do the thinking while workers wield the screwdrivers." Instead, he hoped to mobilize "every ounce of intelligence" from all employees.

But the supposed mindset shift wasn't enough to mollify the NeXT team. Under pressure from Canon and from his employees, Steve agreed to bring in a human resources professional who could impose structure and consistency, alongside their demand that he eventually hire a COO.

Steve pitched the job to Phil Wilson, who was not your typical HR manager. Phil held a PhD in English literature from the University of Chicago, had served as a dean at Princeton, then moved into heavy industry, where he worked in human resources for Cummins Engine. Phil's blend of scholarly polish and industrial know-how caught Steve's eye, though it wound up taking nine months to recruit him.

When Phil arrived at the NeXT office in Redwood City for his interview, he was left waiting in the lobby for an hour. "I thought it was obnoxious," Phil recalled.

Eventually, he was ushered into a conference room to meet the executive team, sans Steve. For nearly an hour, Phil listened as the company's leaders opened up about NeXT's culture issues and their frustrations with Steve. Then, unannounced, the man himself walked in.

Steve perched on a chair at the end of the table, legs crossed underneath him. He said nothing at first, just listening. Then he broke in, "Well, everybody at this table feels very free to tell me everything that's on their mind."

Silence. Phil turned to Bud, sitting next to Steve. "Bud, what's on your mind?"

Bud's eyes dropped.

Phil moved to the next person. "Gary?"

Gary looked down at the table.

One by one, Susan, Dan'l, Rich, George all froze. Seconds ago, they had been griping about Steve. The moment he had entered the room, everyone clammed up.

Next, Phil had an audition in the Fremont factory conference room. He stood at the whiteboard before NeXT's factory team as they began spilling their stories about Steve, the dysfunction, the lack of structure, and the burnout.

Phil got the job.

When he officially started in May 1989, Phil launched a full company diagnostic. He conducted one-on-one interviews, small group sessions, and peer evaluations. He learned that the problems started with basic functions. For example, Steve insisted on personally typing every single offer letter, leading qualified candidates to slip away while their paperwork sat buried on his desk.

His much-hyped, two-tier transparent salary scheme had become a caste system in which a few stars got six figures after sales commissions, while everyone else was left feeling like second-class employees.

When Phil conveyed the team's harsh feedback to Steve, "he was very much taken aback," Phil said.

Over weeks of work, Phil managed to forge consensus on plans to improve NeXT's culture. But just before presenting his proposals to Steve, the conversations would devolve into court politics. One by one, team members would peel off, going straight to the king to renegotiate their stakes privately.

Phil designed a performance review system tailored to NeXT's staff, which he called "light-touch bureaucracy," that aligned compensation with peer feedback rather than top-down judgment. The leadership team agreed with the plan. But this system, like others that Phil tried to put in place, collapsed the moment it made contact with Steve's orbit. Somehow, power at NeXT always snapped back to him.

One day, Steve dropped by Phil's office.

"You're not like other HR guys," he said. "You're smart. I used to think the main function of an HR person is to make sure we have Odwalla in the refrigerator and coffee."

Though Steve may have meant it as a compliment, to Phil, Steve had just disparaged his entire profession. "That's not what you hired me for," he replied.

But Steve had already moved on to his next target.

"We have a problem in sales," Steve announced to Dan'l as he strode into the conference room. "I need you to focus on sales with a hundred percent of your energy while I temporarily take over marketing."

Steve had watched the numbers for nine months now. He had the Businessland distribution network, Ross's government connections, and what he believed was a superior machine. But the reality was that they were only selling machines with unfinished 0.9 software and had agreed to limit shipments to fewer than two thousand units until version 1.0 was ready.

Dan'l had been documenting the problems: Customers were rejecting the incomplete software, the hardware had issues, and the product was overpriced. Yet Steve was convinced that Dan'l's team—which controlled both marketing and sales—was failing to execute, pure and simple.

Dan'l recognized it as a ploy to shift blame and called his bluff. "We're so far away from selling anybody anything right now," he replied. "You don't want to hear it, but this is not a problem in sales."

Steve reminded Dan'l about his plan to sell twenty-five thousand units in the first year, a plan that Dan'l had pushed back on vociferously. The factory was ready, said Steve—ignoring the fact that the factory frequently produced defective machines. Why wasn't Dan'l agreeing to his demand to place an inventory order for twenty-five thousand units?

Dan'l reminded Steve of the team's agreement to limit the initial run to two thousand units until NeXTSTEP 1.0 was finished. He said that the constraint had originally come from Bud's engineering team, which didn't want to flood the market with an unfinished operating system.

Steve kept pushing: The team had to hit twenty-five thousand units or bust, he said.

"I learned from you," Dan'l said, his voice sharp, "the best way to lose money is to build product that people don't want to buy."

Steve wouldn't let it go. He wanted the orders placed.

"I'm not going to authorize that," Dan'l said. "You want it, you own it."

Steve had his answer. If Dan'l wouldn't order the inventory as the marketing chief whose department ran sales, then Dan'l wouldn't be making those decisions anymore. By fiat, the marketing department now belonged to Steve.

At 10:20 p.m. on July 18, 1989, Steve sent an email to the company:

> Dan'l has been consumed in managing our marketing organization, and has not had the time to invest in developing additional sales strategies and channels. Since Dan'l is the most qualified person I know to lead this effort, I have asked Dan'l to focus his time exclusively on NeXT's overall sales strategy.

As for who would replace him? Steve announced that he would personally "assume responsibility for Marketing" until he found a "great person" to fill this position. In other words, Steve would now report to Steve.

More than 250 employees got the message. Patrick, the former marijuana trafficker and current telecoms manager, offered Dan'l sympathy for "such an utterly ridiculous public shitting-upon." Software engineer Bruce Blumberg tried to find the bright side. At least Dan'l could focus on "how we are going to sell this sucker," he wrote.

But Steve's email leaked to the press. Three days later, journalists were calling about Steve having "tapped himself to run marketing," in the words of *The Wall Street Journal.* A *San Francisco Examiner* columnist had a field day: "Picture Steve Jobs, personnel director, interviewing Steve Jobs, job applicant, for a position assisting Steve Jobs."

Dan'l still remained NeXT's primary spokesman, so the man who'd just been stripped of his marketing role now had the unpleasant task of explaining to reporters why it was *actually* a promotion. "I believe that this is a very positive change," he dutifully explained.

Steve had a final gift: After Dan'l finished spinning his own demotion to the press, Steve stripped him of the press job too.

Dan'l surveyed the wreckage. "There were no adults in the room, except for maybe me," he reflected later. Maybe a couple of others, like Phil.

His colleagues heard the rumors about Dan'l's rupture with Steve and asked what really happened in that room. "I will be happy to tell the real tale," he promised supporters. "I am not a gambler, I only bet on myself, and that is exactly what I have done."

11

LAST DAY OF MY LIFE

William Morris, the most revered talent agency in Hollywood, wanted to buy Cubes. The agency had first learned about NeXT when the Pixar short *Tin Toy* won the Academy Award for Best Animated Short Film five months earlier. It had been made using RenderMan, software that came standard on NeXT machines.

Sales manager Mark Hayes knew that Hollywood executives liked star power, so he arranged for Steve to make the pitch himself. On an August morning in 1989, Steve strolled into the conference room at NeXT headquarters—fifteen minutes late. He wore a black turtleneck and jeans, despite Mark having advised him to wear a suit. Across the table sat a team of high-powered agents, along with their accounting consultants from Deloitte & Touche.

"I read your requirements," Steve began, after introductions. "They completely miss the point."

William Morris's consultants had specified that the company should buy standard personal computers with basic hardware and software—whether from NeXT, Apple, or IBM. For Steve, the ask was a non-starter. He was not about to squeeze his product to fit William Morris's specifications.

He started pacing as he sliced into the accountants. "You have no idea what you're talking about!" Mark grew nervous as Steve spoke. Was he about to ruin their best shot at a prestigious deal?

But the agents watched in fascination. "They were so excited," recalled Mark. "They heard the stories, and they got to see him in his glory."

At the time, William Morris was trying to catch up. It had missed the PC revolution, and its agents were drowning in the chaos of Hollywood dealmaking—endless phone calls and negotiations with demanding clients. "In our business, to make one phone call frequently takes four or five phone calls," Walter Zifkin, the agency's chief operating officer, told CNN. "Because whoever you call is busy, whenever they call back, we're busy." Computers could help agents organize the deluge.

Any ordinary Mac or PC would be able to handle the task, though Steve pointed out their screens would be cruder and more pixelated. But William Morris was interested in the Cube, specifically, because of the computer's aesthetic presence. "Those machines looked sexy on somebody's desktop," recalled Allen Denison, a NeXT systems engineer.

NeXT was now selling to corporations through Businessland, not just to universities—the education market alone wasn't big enough. IBM, despite having licensed NeXTSTEP eleven months earlier, still hadn't shipped anything while waiting for the software to mature beyond its incomplete state. In the meantime, NeXT needed every sale it could get. William Morris hoped the computer would impress the directors, actors, and producers who expected their representation to be as cutting-edge as their art. CNN reported that director Tim Burton, a William Morris client, had bought five NeXT machines for his staff and lugged one along to film sets.

Steve was determined to close the deal. An association with the oldest talent agency in Hollywood would inject a shot of credibility and glamour. He bent over backward to make the deal work—offering a specially designed software package that would receive phone calls but also store videos and sound for the celebrities the agency was tracking.

NeXT proposed contracting out the custom software to Adamation, a small Oakland-based firm. Founded by brothers Stephan and William Adams, Adamation had bet everything on developing for the Cube.

Steve sealed the deal with a deep discount. "We used to joke we'd wrap a hundred-dollar bill around every computer because it was literally costing us money to sell product," Mark said. Three weeks later, the two companies made the deal official—NeXT's first major corporate sale. Though the deal was announced at $2.5 million, the real price was far lower. The first thirty computers arrived two months later.

Stephan and William's firm would now be developing a major software package for the most important talent agency in Hollywood. The brothers were Black developers who had discovered something crucial about working on the NeXT platform: Your background mattered less than your product.

"You can't talk about our story without talking about race," said Stephan. To succeed in the overwhelmingly white world of Silicon Valley, the brothers had developed a survival strategy: find platforms so new that race got neutralized by innovation. Get there first, ship brilliant code, and by the time the old-boy networks and venture capital arrived, you'd be too essential to exclude.

But the William Morris deal wasn't all smooth sailing. The agents made big demands of Adamation, changing the software brief despite having a fixed contract. On top of that, the agency's paranoia about its agents defecting to competing agencies created a security nightmare. Every piece of digital information had to be kept in a locked vault with different keys for different people.

The real problem ran deeper than technical specifications. "What they ultimately wanted was the NeXT programmers to be doing their stuff," William recalled. They wanted "that star draw" of Steve again, the glamour of having NeXT itself build the systems.

When Adamation was nearly finished with the software, William Morris called NeXT directly: "We want you guys to do it." NeXT took over the project, but the agency wouldn't receive working software for another three years.

Not that it mattered much. Even though NeXT took over the contract, Steve protected Adamation's reputation. He never blamed them publicly for the failure, and NeXT kept sending them high-profile clients: the Los Angeles County Sheriff's Department and then a luxury real estate broker called Alain Pinel Realtors. William Morris became a reference customer for NeXT, happy to sing the company's praises across Hollywood. The agency had gotten what it really wanted—proximity to Steve's genius. The computers themselves were just very expensive props.

At 10:00 p.m. on Sunday, September 10, 1989, an exhausted Bud announced that his team had spent the weekend fixing a print crash. If nothing else broke by Monday morning, they'd finally ship NeXTSTEP 1.0.

"IT'S SOUP!!!" Director of Marketing Programs Julie Welch emailed everyone on Wednesday—a tongue-in-cheek nod to Lipton's famous "Is it soup yet?" commercials. In other words: *It's ready.*

After nearly a year of delays, product manager Bob Fraik hand-delivered the very first shrink-wrapped copy of NeXT's flagship software to a Businessland executive. Two hundred upgrade packages would follow, rescuing customers who had been struggling with buggy beta software for months. Everyone who bought a NeXT computer would finally have access to a powerful operating system that let developers create applications as easily as sculpting clay.

It had now been four years since NeXT's founding. "There is no looking back," Dan'l told the team.

NeXTSTEP represented a monumental technical achievement. But Steve was most proud of the fact that it was easy to use. An *Alice in Wonderland* text meme that had been making the rounds at NeXT captured the point well. In it, Alice tumbles into a tech conference where animal versions of computer companies—IBM the Elephant, Sun the Bear, and the "Job Sparrow," a reference to Steve—sit passing cups of terrible-tasting custard, each declaring it the "wrong flavor" before handing it on. The custard was labeled "Unix," the powerful but user-hostile software foundation underlying most workstations—a system everyone was trying to tame.

NeXTSTEP was Steve's attempt to make Unix taste sweet.

"Who cares about what operating system it runs?" he told *MacWEEK*. "You've never heard about what operating system the Mac runs because nobody thinks about it . . . We make it usable by mere mortals."

Despite the beautiful operating system and sophisticated development tools, NeXT's developer community was still tiny, meaning that customers had only a small library of applications to choose from. Despite that, Steve described the situation with characteristic bravado. "Every major software developer is writing software [for NeXT]," Steve told *MacWEEK*. "Microsoft's the only one that's not."

Two weeks later, Steve got the chance to express his frustrations to Bill Gates in person. The rivals had been invited to sit on a personal computer industry panel in Carlsbad, California. IBM executive Jim Cannavino had been strategically placed on the dais as a buffer between them.

The panel's topic: font rendering, or how to display typefaces on computer screens. Adobe Systems had kept a tight lock on font technology, angering both Apple and Microsoft. So Microsoft had teamed up with Apple—despite an ongoing legal battle between the two companies—to advance a new font technology. NeXT partnered with Adobe.

From the stage, Bill announced his new alliance with Apple. Steve went on the attack. "Bill, I don't think you could have picked a worse time," he said.

Bill's retort: "We took a font technology that, Steve, you should look at because it's far better."

According to *The Washington Post*, Steve and Bill "rarely missed an opportunity to exchange potshots and indignant glances" over the course of the panel. Jim said he felt like he was in Beirut, caught in the cross fire. At one point during the discussion, conference sponsor Stewart Alsop pleaded: "It's time we stop playing political games and start applying all this technology for the benefit of our users."

The audience applauded, and then the rivals picked right up sparring where they had left off.

Despite his knack for closing sales, Steve hated going on sales junkets. He liked to give his theatrical presentations in the domains he could control—his conference room and his symphony stage. But Regional Sales Manager Deac Manross convinced him that a visit to Ohio State University might be worth the trip.

Steve had a fan, Eric Celeste, in a high place. Eric was the son of Ohio Governor Dick Celeste, and a current undergraduate and president of the NeXT computer user group at Ohio State University and Kent State University. He thought his father should bring the NeXT Cube to Ohio's state universities.

On October 17, the day Steve was set to fly to Ohio, he woke up in Ann Arbor, Michigan, where he'd been attending a conference. While he was at an evening reception at the home of the University of Michigan's president, a magnitude 6.9 earthquake hit Northern California during game three of the World Series in San Francisco. Steve delayed his Ohio trip, spending hours with the NeXT team trying to reach their colleagues in Redwood City, but the phone lines were jammed to allow people in San Francisco to call their loved ones outbound. Though the quake had rattled them, it hadn't caused serious damage to NeXT property.

By the time Steve arrived at the governor's mansion in Columbus, where he'd been invited to stay, it was 2:00 a.m. Eric had been shooting hoops in the driveway all evening, waiting for Steve to show up.

When Steve finally got to bed, it was only to be jolted awake hours later by the Celestes' cat leaping on him.

Steve awoke in the morning in unfamiliar territory: a family breakfast table. The Celeste household was, in Eric's words, "our usual fairly chaotic bunch"—six kids "full of politics, arguments, and inside jokes." The governor's kids were used to famous guests and immune to celebrity. They argued and swore while Eric, the family's lone computer fanatic, sat mute before his hero.

For a man accustomed to controlled client interactions, the situation was revelatory. Here was a family that talked to each other over breakfast, arguing cantankerously as they passed the orange juice. They treated the table as a place for bonding. Steve could feel their love for one another. "He got to see our family be our family," Eric said.

As Steve ate his nuts and fruit, he just took it all in, "eating kind of like a bird," as Eric recalled, following "very strict rules for himself." Then Deac and his boss Bob Longo picked up Steve in a limousine to take him to Ohio State University, where he would give a speech.

As soon as Steve got in the car, he grabbed Bob and said, "Bob, I just had the most incredible experience. I sat with a family who sat around the table and talked about politics and had breakfast. Bob, how did you meet your wife?"

Deac could hear Steve's wheels turning as he pressed for details on how to go about finding a spouse and building a family. "He saw something that he liked and immediately wanted to find out how one does that type of thing," Deac said.

Steve had recently proposed to his girlfriend, Tina Redse, but she had turned him down. Tina and Steve fought constantly. Colleagues described her as "Snow White," beautiful but somehow wrong for him—she was not his future.

Back in California, Stanford Graduate School of Business invited Steve to give a talk as part of its "View from the Top" lecture series. Steve was in high demand, so the too-small lecture hall filled up quickly. When professors asked students sitting in the aisles to clear out, one woman caught Steve's eye as she quickly relocated to an empty seat in the front row that had been reserved for Steve's entourage.

It was Laurene Powell, a twenty-five-year-old MBA student. She later told biographer Walter Isaacson that a friend had dragged her along to the event. "[Steve] was working at NeXT, and he was not that big of a deal to me. I wasn't that enthused, but my friend was, so we went," she said.

Steve got up to speak but lost his train of thought as he looked at her. "I knew something was up when I was staring at her," he remembered, "forgetting what I was talking about mid-sentence."

David Wertheimer, a young NeXT salesman watching from the audience, couldn't believe what he was seeing. "I had never seen Steve lose focus," David said. "He was one of the most focused people ever when he got onstage."

After the talk, Steve found Laurene in the parking lot and asked her to dinner that weekend. She said yes and gave him her phone number. Then Steve walked back to his car and the waiting NeXT team. They had their academic advisory board meeting dinner lined up for the rest of the evening.

But something made him stop. "As I was walking to my car, I asked myself: 'If this was the last day of my life, would I rather have dinner with the important customers or her?'" Steve wrote in an email.

He raced back to Laurene's car and asked, "How about dinner tonight?"

"Sure," she said.

So Steve returned to his team and said, "I'm not gonna go to the meetings."

"Wait, what?" David asked.

"Yeah, I just don't feel like it. I'm just not going." And that was that.

Instead, Steve and Laurene spent four hours talking together at a restaurant called St. Michael's Alley.

Laurene grew up in West Milford, New Jersey, in a home that bordered the forest. When she was just three years old, her father—a Marine aviator—was killed in a midair crash. "I remember being in school and thinking that people don't know this thing about me—that there was a loss inside," she told *Vogue*.

Her mother, a teacher, remarried unhappily, and Laurene learned early to figure things out for herself: how to get financial aid to pay for two Penn degrees, how to make her way to Wall Street. By the time she arrived at Stanford for her MBA, she had already done stints at Merrill Lynch and Goldman Sachs. She was, as a colleague put it to *Vogue*, "a daughter of working-class people, and not afraid to tell you that your idea is not a great one."

Steve later reflected: "You can't plan to meet the people who will change your life."

12

BEAKERS AND BELIEVERS

Cubes were piling up in NeXT's service department. Customers weren't having typical computer problems like user error or software bugs. Instead, the culprit was Steve's futuristic optical drive, the single most common reason for returns.

Canon's drive malfunctioned constantly as a result of dust particles in the air. NeXT engineers determined that 85 percent of returned drives stemmed from what they called "the dust problem."

One day, the service team received a message from a customer whose second optical drive had just died. By talking to other NeXT owners and reading online bulletin board forums—early forums that could be accessed through various internet networks, although the World Wide Web did not exist yet—the customer had discovered that there were "very few [Canon] optical drives which have functioned for more than a few months."

In response, NeXT implemented a strict quality control regime, testing every single drive before installing it. Canon's manufacturing quality could no longer be trusted. The team also decided to ship customers free cleaning kits.

But as far as a long-term fix? The team had no clue what to do. One employee suggested a "subtle disinformation campaign" to keep interest in the drive alive.

For David Wertheimer, who had recently joined the sales team, it was just another problem to solve. He'd been devoted to Steve since he was a kid growing up in Dallas—an engineering setback wasn't going to change that now.

In 1977, when his mother got an invitation to teach at Stanford Law School for a year, young David agreed to make the cross-country trip with her on one condition: He'd get to see Apple. His mom made good on her promise, back-channeling with Apple's lawyer to set up a tour.

In the warehouse that served as Apple's early headquarters, ten-year-old David met Steve and made his hero a declaration: "I'm going to come back and work for you someday."

Twelve years later, when Steve started NeXT, David saw an opening to follow through on that promise. He launched a campaign from his dorm at Duke, sending letters, making phone calls, and badgering NeXT receptionists for any name that might get him closer to a job. "I think they got sick of me at some point," he said.

David's persistence paid off. Dan'l had established a college hire model where his west and east sales directors could each use a slot to hire college talent right after graduation. Max Henry, the western sales director, used his slot to recruit David. He started at NeXT the day after graduation as the youngest employee on the sales force. "I was so excited to get there," David remembered.

Early on, David's job consisted of touring potential customers around the Fremont factory like a museum docent. "This entire circuit board is manufactured without a human ever touching it," he'd announce, watching for the spark of wonder in their eyes.

In November 1989, David worked tirelessly to help close a sale with

Novell, a Utah-based software giant. The company needed fast file transfers between its Mac network and NeXT machines, and NeXT's bundled software wasn't up to the job. David spent what he described to the sales team as "many long nights of sweat and tears," creating workarounds by writing all-new code with a software engineer. (He had been learning to code since childhood.)

Later, a Novell executive told David something chilling: Novell employees were afraid that buying NeXT computers might cost them their jobs.

David relayed that information back to his supervisors, who sent it to Steve, who, well, "didn't want to hear that," David said. Steve mocked David in an email sent to the entire senior staff, suggesting David's months of technical heroics could have been avoided by simply using NeXT software. "It might save [the sales force] 'many long nights of sweat and tears,'" Steve sneered.

Dan'l defended the kid. "I need all the help I can get," he wrote to Steve.

But David didn't take it personally. When Steve called you a "stupid fucking asshole," it just meant "prove me wrong," David said.

Though inking sales wasn't easy when the company kept messing up the basics. When Steve ran an ad in *The Wall Street Journal* offering anyone who wanted one a life-size brochure shaped like the Cube, it turned into a self-defeating blunder. With 5,500 requests waiting, the team realized the brochure didn't fit into any standard envelope. "Millions in advertising spending, no goddamn envelopes," Todd wrote to Dan'l. After rush-ordering custom envelopes, the team then discovered at the post office that special envelope sizes required special postage.

Through it all, low sales persisted. By December, the sales force had figured out how to make ends meet in other, creative ways. Steve had insisted on the unusual practice of resetting sales quotas to zero every quarter against the advice of his sales manager Mark Hayes, who warned him that experienced reps would game the system.

The best salespeople proved him right. Instead of closing deals steadily throughout the year to hit an annual $2 million target, they deliberately stalled their customers, letting deals slip quarter after quarter. Then, in a single quarter, they closed all of their massive deals at once—an entire year's worth of sales.

Because the quarterly quota was only $500,000, everything above that triggered accelerated commissions. That meant, using this scheme, annual commission checks could easily soar into the high six figures.

"I told you so," Mark told Steve. "These guys are smart." Steve quietly switched to an annual commission plan after that.

The sales windfalls presaged further shenanigans: NeXT, desperate to book sales, tried to unload the final shipment of the year of 1,300 Cubes onto Businessland—more than three times what the store had sold all year. Businessland, already drowning in unsold inventory, wanted none of the units. Each side needed to close its books without the machines showing up in the wrong column.

So the two companies played hot potato. NeXT would record the shipment in December, but Businessland wouldn't officially receive it until January. The compromise left the 1,300 computers in accounting limbo, literally riding around on trucks until the new year.

For the NeXT and Businessland managers ordered to carry out this legerdemain, the episode underscored a grim truth: Their companies were in deep trouble.

In January 1990, NeXT held an offsite retreat for executive staff at the Quadrus Conference Center on Sand Hill Road in Menlo Park. The five cofounders gathered around the long conference table for a war council. Steve showed up a couple of hours late, lamenting their situation but not acknowledging the deeper issues.

Then Dan'l reiterated to the cofounders what everyone already knew—the source of endless fighting and pitiful sales. NeXT would not survive, he said definitively, without a $3,000 machine.

Tempers flared. They felt the only choice was to scrap the Cube and start over with a more advanced machine. They looked at the alternatives: lose "only" $54 million over the coming year, retreat, and retrench, or—the words hung menacingly in the air—sell the company.

Dan'l pushed for triage: "The time has come to look at our business proposition." Every operating assumption had been proved wrong: The product wasn't ready, the budget had collapsed, and the strategy kept shifting like sand. He believed that Steve, for all his brilliance, was setting them up for continued failure.

The leadership team posed five urgent questions:

1. How do we match our structure to our original strategy?
2. What budgets do we truly need to execute?
3. How do we keep people motivated when the plan keeps shifting?
4. How do we get accurate information to flow—up and down?
5. When do we admit the strategy isn't working and make course corrections?

To everyone's surprise, Steve agreed.

Susan Barnes, the CFO, suggested that NeXT stop selling the computer nobody wanted, go back to R&D mode, and save cash until a new machine was ready. But Steve didn't want to admit failure. Instead, he declared a new secret project code-named "Warp Nine"—a cheaper, slimmed-down version of the Cube to be built in just nine months.

The problem: Steve insisted on using a magnesium alloy for the chassis, the same aerospace metal that had priced the original Cube out of its market. It looked to everyone like Steve's champagne taste could be on track to doom the new project too. Luckily for them, he ultimately opted for plastic bodywork on the exterior, keeping costs from spiraling out of control.

A month later, Steve pulled yet another rabbit out of his hat, announcing a new, higher-margin IBM deal. Three months earlier, Steve had marched into IBM toting Canon's fresh investment as leverage and convinced Big Blue to pay more for NeXTSTEP. IBM committed to spending another $30 million, licensing not just NeXTSTEP, but buying five years of free rein for NeXT and IBM to use each other's ideas without fear of lawsuits.

It looked like IBM was doubling down on its support of Steve's small company. The press swallowed it whole. "Obviously, I think it's great," Steve told *USA Today*. "There's still a few software developers on the fence, and this will throw them over." Steve hoped the news would devastate Bill Gates.

Why did IBM re-up its commitment to NeXT? IBM was all in. The company's engineers were already deep into porting NeXT's software to its PS/2 computers. It also had plans to convert an old factory in Kentucky into an assembly line for these sophisticated machines running NeXTSTEP software. The deal extended the length of the partnership in order to cover more releases. That meant that if NeXTSTEP took off, IBM would be sitting on a cash cow.

Steve's alliance should have been unstoppable.

Ross Perot's money, IBM's global reach, Businessland's retail empire, and NeXT's revolutionary software—together they would halt Bill Gates's growing stranglehold on computing.

IBM had been trialing NeXTSTEP on its new, blazing-fast computer, the RS/6000 workstation, and its customers were already impressed. Representatives from Shell Oil had seen the NeXT software demos—"screaming fast," they said—and stated their intent to buy thousands of units.

Promising as it was, the IBM deal gave Steve déjà vu. In exchange for another $30 million, he was signing away NeXTSTEP's future royalties and giving IBM exclusive rights to run the software on its business computers for the next eight years. IBM would now own the rights to copy the "look and feel" of NeXTSTEP. It meant realizing Steve's worst fear: losing control.

On their way to Dallas to make a presentation about the IBM deal, NeXT salesman Mark Hayes found Steve at the bookshop at San Francisco International Airport, his face buried in a book, hoping nobody would recognize him. Eight hundred IBM field engineers were waiting in Texas.

The night before, Mark's team had called him at home with bad news: The venue was huge, with projection screens on both sides of the room. They needed two sets of slides, but only one set existed—in Steve's backpack.

Mark had spent the morning agonizing over whether to tell Steve at the airport or let him discover the problem in Dallas. "I've learned from being around him enough he doesn't like surprises," Mark recalled. Since Mark was flying coach and Steve first class, the airport was his only chance to talk.

"Before we get on the plane," Mark said, approaching Steve at the bookstore, "the only slides that we have are in your backpack. And the problem is this room's so big, there's two different projectors, one on the right-hand side, one on the left-hand side."

Mark suggested they skip the slides entirely. Steve could scribble some notes on the flight, then launch straight into the demo.

"So Mark, what you're telling me is I don't have the tools I need to get my job done today," Steve said.

"Steve, come on, there's only one set of slides. I tried to look for a second set, and you have the only set, so we need to think on our feet."

"Mark, you know, I'm just really busy today. And I'm just not going to go."

Steve turned around, walked out of the bookstore, went to the escalator, got in his Porsche, and drove to the office.

After the flight, a limo arrived at Dallas Fort Worth International Airport with its fruit platter and Evian water—and no Steve to consume them. Mark had to face eight hundred IBM engineers alone. "You have to be Steve," his team told him. Without slides, notes, or preparation, Mark improvised desperately. The IBM executives read the no-show as a lack of commitment to the relationship. The deal was effectively dead.

With IBM, Steve had overestimated his power. And he knew it. Years later, he confided in Pixar cofounder Ed Catmull that he had learned a lesson from the collapse of the IBM deal: Never overplay your hand.

Decades after the deal fell through, NeXT executives remained tortured by what could have been. They still believed that a NeXT-IBM partnership could have shifted the entire trajectory of personal computing, preempting the Microsoft Windows monopoly that took hold through the decade.

IBM had committed almost $100 million and would have shipped NeXT-powered computers to its thousands of corporate customers at the same moment that Windows was struggling to find its footing. NeXTSTEP had a real shot at becoming the standard. But Steve flushed it.

After months of negotiations, the deal that could unlock hundreds of millions of dollars in government contracts was finally ready to close. Pat Horner, the CEO of Perot Systems who had flown out on Ross Perot's private plane, sat in NeXT's conference room with the contract spread across the table.

Dan'l went to fetch Steve from the other building. "Pat's here," he told him. "We're going to sign the deal. You coming in?"

Steve looked up from whatever he was working on. "No, I don't want to sign the deal."

Dan'l stared at him. "You know what you're doing, right?"

"Yeah," Steve said.

"You're blowing it up. You're going to blow up the relationship with Ross. You know that's what's going to happen."

Steve had made up his mind. "I don't want to do business with the government."

Dan'l walked back to the conference room where Pat Horner and the Perot Systems executives were waiting with pens ready. The distribution agreement sat unsigned on the table. Dan'l had to deliver the news: Steve wasn't coming. There would be no deal.

Within minutes of Pat leaving and getting back on the plane, Ross called. "Steve is unavailable," his assistant explained. He had ducked out to another building. She handed Dan'l the phone instead.

"Dan'l, this is Ross," came the voice on the other end. "You know, on any given day I can call and speak to the head of the FBI, or the head of the military of Panama, or the White House, and I get through. I'm in business with you. Why can't I talk to Steve?"

Dan'l apologized. He was upset, bitter, repulsed over Steve's behavior. He had seen Steve as a friend who swam laps with him during work visits to universities and who watched TV with his kids. But Steve was blowing up the company's hard-earned relationships one by one. His inexorable compulsion to wrest control was killing NeXT.

Dan'l wasn't the only person who had lost faith. At the company board meeting in February 1990, Ross was done with the magic show. He had studied the company's fundamentals, and he was deeply concerned with what he saw. He demanded that Steve show him a marketing plan to get the company back on track.

Steve was ready with three, gallon-sized chemistry beakers.

"Apple is red," Steve explained, pouring colored liquid into the first beaker, "and they own desktop publishing." He moved to the second beaker. "IBM is blue, and they own spreadsheets."

Then came the finale: "And we are green in this beaker, and we are going to be the owners of interpersonal computing."

"Interpersonal computing" was Steve's latest linguistic invention. It entailed sending video, audio, and files between NeXT machines, which would be the only machines capable of opening the files. With only a few thousand NeXT machines in existence worldwide, "it was crazy," Dan'l said.

"That's not a marketing plan!" Ross screamed, pounding the table. "Monkeys could walk into General Motors and the US government and sell thousands of [Cubes] if you get it done." Ross had already championed NeXT to his friends in the spy agencies and the military. But after all that work—mobilizing his federal sales force, personally vouching for Steve—Steve kept walking away from deals.

Then he asked, "Who's in charge of marketing here?"

Silence. The executives around the table slowly pointed at Steve. It had been six months since he'd stripped Dan'l of the job.

The executives were ordered to clear the room, then they waited outside while Steve and Ross waged all-out war. They listened next to the door.

Ross ripped through the numbers: NeXT had burned $39 million while planning to lose $3 million. Without $56 million from IBM and Ross, the start-up would be long dead. Steve employed sixty-nine manufacturing staff for a company barely shipping product. And, devoid of all reason, Steve forecast sales of eleven thousand computers this year, even though NeXT wasn't scheduled to introduce a new product until October.

Steve's proposed solution? Win the Malcolm Baldrige National Quality Award. A government prize for manufacturing excellence. He wasn't joking. The prize, given to companies that could show they had low levels of defects and strong quality control processes, had become a core part of his strategy.

Ross was fed up. By now, NeXT seemed to him like a lost cause. After hours of fighting, Ross headed for the exit. On his way out, David mentioned he needed to catch a flight to Dallas and Ross offered him a ride on his jet.

Aboard the plane, David sat across from the billionaire, who was reading a newspaper in silence. Then Ross folded it, looked up at the young man, and asked, "Now, David, you know what mistake I made?"

"No, sir."

"I gave Steve too much dang money. When you have too much money, you just don't have that hunger. And you start spending money on floating staircases and $10,000 chairs."

Back in the boardroom, Steve's chemistry beakers sat abandoned on the conference table, the colored liquids settling. Dan'l grabbed one as a souvenir.

"I was at the end of my rope," he said. Back in his office, he pulled every file on the government market—plans, contacts, strategies, all the marketing ammunition Steve had ignored while playing with colored water. He organized them methodically, then composed an email to board members Ross, Pat Crecine, and Canon's Hisashi Sakamaki, laying out the detailed plans they had made to sell their computers and where it went wrong.

Dan'l flew to Pittsburgh the next morning. He felt he owed it to his East Coast team to look them in the eye and tell them: He planned to resign.

Two days later, on Thursday, February 15, Dan'l walked into Steve's office at 1:00 p.m. and handed over his resignation letter. "I'm not fighting with you anymore," he said. "You own this company, and you're going to burn through it."

"Whoa, wow." Steve's voice cracked slightly. "You know, gee, we'll work really hard to make your stock pay off."

Dan'l had barely reached his desk downstairs when one of his own people appeared holding a press release announcing his departure. Dan'l's blood boiled as he read it. "The release was going to bury me," he later said.

He sent the messenger back upstairs: "Tell that pisspot that I built this house, and I know which cards to pull out," he said.

NeXT counsel Gary Moore materialized nearby. "Is that a threat?"

"No. It's a promise," Dan'l said.

The release never ran. When *USA Today* asked if Dan'l had been pushed out, HR Director Phil Wilson delivered the company line: "The answer is a clear and unequivocal no."

The following Friday, Dan'l's last day at NeXT, his calendar showed three final entries: leave the office at 3:00 p.m., get a haircut at 3:30, and then eat dinner at home. His wife, Susan, had once threatened to set up a picnic table in the NeXT lobby if he missed another Friday dinner. After years of Mother's Day meetings that started at 9:00 a.m. (with Steve invariably arriving at eleven), Easter Sundays spent in conference rooms, and the never-ending exhaustion of swimming upstream to build a sales organization for a computer that barely existed, Dan'l, thirty-four, was going home.

He owed NeXT $100,000—a loan he'd taken for his house. He'd find a way to pay it back. GO Corporation had already offered him the role of VP of sales and marketing for a new handheld computer venture.

But first, that haircut. Then dinner with his wife and two kids. Finally.

PART TWO

13

COMMERCE AND ART

Over at Businessland, another of NeXT's tentpole partnerships was coming undone.

Kevin Compton, the Businessland VP, wrote his boss a memo with an ominous observation: "David, these computers are getting really reliable." He wasn't talking about NeXT—those machines still broke down plenty—but about computers across the industry. Businessland's corporate sales depended on the lucrative service contracts that followed each sale. Without a need for constant repairs, Businessland faced an existential threat.

At the same time, Dell and Gateway 2000 were threatening Businessland's model by selling computers directly to customers via the mail. Michael Dell, the founder of Dell, had seen the future, telling Kevin: "Look, Businessland's business model is not going to work."

Businessland was getting squeezed from multiple directions. In addition to the loss of service revenue, the company had become a victim of NeXT's broader sales woes. Fortune 500 companies would buy two or three NeXT machines from Businessland for evaluation, discover their limitations, and never place larger orders. On August 7, 1990, Businessland posted a $21.5 million quarterly loss. Then its stock fell 58 percent in a single day. Within a year, Businessland was acquired in a fire sale and went out of business.

With two out of NeXT's four partnerships down, Steve never stopped playing the optimist. As Creative Director Susan Kare noted, Steve always wanted his team to spread good news about new models on the horizon and lower prices coming soon.

But everyone could see the hard truth: "The company is struggling to sell machines and be perceived as a safe bet," she wrote.

Across the bay in Cupertino, Steve's former rival Jean-Louis Gassée was on his way out at Apple, the victim of another corporate execution.

Steve called Jean-Louis to ask the question he'd been waiting four and a half years to ask: How does it feel to be fired?

Days later, Steve rang again, this time extending an olive branch: "We could do great things together," Jean-Louis recounted in his book *Grateful Geek*. Steve invited him to join NeXT—Steve's hero-shithead rollercoaster on full display. But Jean-Louis demurred, feeling he lacked the emotional strength to work for Steve.

The end at Apple had come over dessert in Palo Alto with John Sculley. When John asked what Jean-Louis really thought of him, he gave the unvarnished truth. "You, John Sculley, don't know enough about the products for me to respect working with you." Just like Steve had told John five years earlier.

Two days later, Jean-Louis was fired.

But when Apple engineers began marching outside the office with signs reading "Jean-Louis Don't Go!" Apple's leadership team panicked, thinking of Steve. What if Jean-Louis's team followed him out the door too? So the company kept him around for eight more months, doing nothing. When HR asked Jean-Louis what would make his stay more comfortable, he said that he would like to take Japanese calligraphy lessons.

John walked into Jean-Louis's office one day to find him painting the character for *heaven* with a tall Japanese instructor. Then Apple gave him the highest executive bonus of the year—a *cadeau de rupture*.

The atmosphere at Apple had changed since Jean-Louis first began at the company. Gone was the start-up informality and creativity. In its place: stifling executive cafeterias, executive washrooms, signing bonuses, and golden parachutes. Where Apple once aspired to change the world, it now seemed content to sell unexciting machines.

In February 1990, Steve Sakoman, one of Apple's star engineers, walked into Jean-Louis's office and announced he was quitting. Jean-Louis's response: "I offered to start a company together."

Free of their employer, the two discussed their frustrations openly. They agreed that the Mac had accumulated "complicated layers of hardware and software silt," Jean-Louis wrote. They thought there was room for a third way—something cleaner than both the Mac and PCs.

Steve Sakoman proposed they start a company and name it "Be."

Jean-Louis pulled out his Oxford dictionary and traced the word through twenty-five pages of etymology. Then he designed the logo himself in MacDraw, carefully adjusting the spacing between the *B* and the *e* until it looked perfect. Their new company, Be Inc., emerged in 1990.

To many people, it looked like a conscious attempt to replicate Steve's moves post-Apple. "Gassée wanted to present himself like the second coming of Steve Jobs," said William Adams, who worked with both NeXT and Be as a software developer, "but he didn't have the vision." Jean-Louis had "Steve Wozniak kind of guys" building clever solutions to problems nobody had asked them to solve, William said.

Starting fresh meant leaving the past behind. At a Silicon Valley charity auction later that year, Jean-Louis put up a memento from his days at Apple for auction: a diamond earring. He'd worn it almost every day at Apple—it was the accessory that had marked him as debonair. Bill Gates won the bidding and immediately approached. "I want my prize now," Bill demanded.

Jean-Louis smiled. "I'd be delighted—on one condition. I install it myself."

Bill caught Jean-Louis's implication. No chance, Bill said. No one would ever see his expensive new acquisition down there.

Steve's Warp Nine project—to build a cheaper computer in just nine months—was nearing completion. The team called it the NeXTstation. True to form, Steve insisted on adding one more thing.

He decided the pizza-box-shaped computer would sit under the monitor and needed an AC connection on the back. The Apple lawsuit settlement from four years earlier required that the box sit alongside, not beneath, the monitor. But that settlement had expired. That way, users could plug their monitors right into the computer, adding convenience and leaving one less cable running to the wall outlet. Steve was obsessed with reducing cable clutter, and years later demanded that the iMac come with only a single cable on the back of the monitor.

"Steve, we're all done," George Crow told him when he brought up the connection. The NeXTstation had cleared the necessary regulatory hurdles. Adding an outlet now would add at least three months to the release timeline.

In response, Steve accused George of being lazy. After working countless hours to get the computer ready, George said he "blew a gasket" at the accusation.

Then something unexpected happened.

"About ten minutes after that," George recalled, "Steve came by and apologized." The NeXTstation shipped without the outlet. George's practical engineering concerns had won out over Steve's aesthetic vision.

In September 1990, Steve returned to Davies Hall to introduce the NeXTstation. In addition to being less expensive, one version of the NeXTstation would also be NeXT's first computer to support color. To show off that new feature, he planned to play a clip from *The Wizard of Oz* for the audience—the moment when Dorothy leaves sepia-toned Kansas and arrives in Technicolor Oz.

Streaming the movie was going to take another demo high-wire act. The team planned to play it from a laser disc through chips with a tendency to overheat. If one processor got too hot, Steve would be standing before a dead computer. In preparation, an engineer hid a chemical spray called a circuit chiller beneath the podium. He would unload it on the chips if they overheated.

"Good morning," Steve began, casual as ever.

Four new products waited behind him—the entry-level NeXTstation, priced at $4,995, roughly half that of the original Cube with the hard drive and printer add-ons; the faster NeXTstation Turbo; the NeXTstation Color with its vibrant display; and the top-tier NeXTstation Turbo Color that combined speed with color graphics. NeXT had also upgraded the original Cube, but the NeXTstations represented the future. Steve introduced the NeXTstation as a "slab" that "sits right underneath the monitor."

More than just a new form factor, the slab design addressed the manufacturing headaches that had plagued the Cube—streamlining the internal electronics from a complex web of parts to a much simpler design.

Each machine had Motorola's latest 68040 processor, which was the chip NeXT had wanted to use in 1988. And Steve had finally surrendered on storage: Out went the temperamental optical drive that made customers curse, in came a simple floppy disk.

He offered to upgrade the Cubes that customers had bought two years earlier. "No one is getting left behind," he promised.

When *The Wizard of Oz* moment arrived, the screen burst from black and white to color at the exact instant Dorothy entered Oz. The audience gasped. Steve pushed further, demonstrating a Ferrari with transparent windows. "You can even see the mountain through the windshield," he declared.

The NeXTstation's video board was revolutionary for 1990—one of the first to render actual video on a computer. Other computers of the day could show flat, opaque images like houses and trees. But they couldn't render transparent objects like windows and glass.

Steve had finally done what everyone begged him to do: listened to the market, cut the price, simplified the product. But by now he was three years late. And the computer's price remained too high—still considerably above the $3,000 price point university buyers had originally demanded.

"No one can say that NeXT doesn't learn from its mistakes," Bruce Webster wrote in *Macworld*, before enumerating familiar problems with the platform, including the "lack of commercial software, high entry cost, and sluggish performance." The $4,995 NeXTstation came with a measly 30 megabytes of free disk space, while most affordable personal computers of the day had between 40 and 200 megabytes.

Yet the NeXTstation's raw speed was undeniable. *Byte* magazine's tests showed the NeXTstation running almost twice as fast as competing IBM machines. But the hardware didn't matter so long as the company didn't have enough outside developers willing to build software for its platform.

As *The New York Times* opined, "In the end, it will all come down to software. For Next Inc. to flourish, Mr. Jobs must find a way to start a software avalanche."

Instead, Steve made the problem worse, actively discouraging developers from porting their existing software to NeXT. When developers tried to create conversion tools that would bring thousands of PC and Mac programs to NeXTSTEP, company executives shut them down. Steve wanted only original creations built specifically for his computers. He was choosing purity over survival.

In late 1990, Steve flew to Burbank on a mission: convince Disney to replace its $100,000 workstations, manufactured by a company called Silicon Graphics, with NeXTstations equipped with Pixar's animation rendering software, RenderMan. If he succeeded, it would validate both his companies at once, giving them the imprimatur of one of the world's most-recognized brands. Steve needed the win: Both companies were seriously struggling.

Disney Chairman Jeffrey Katzenberg sat at the head of a conference table. Ten Disney executives watched as Steve and his team of two people set up the NeXTstation for a demonstration. In the corner sat Roy Disney, Walt Disney's nephew and head of the animation department, chain-smoking in a Hawaiian shirt. The smoke drifted toward Steve—everyone knew he hated cigarettes, but that didn't stop Roy.

To sell his computers to Disney, Steve would have to overcome years of resentment. Under an earlier agreement, Disney had already been using Pixar software to make films like *The Rescuers Down Under*, but it refused to give Pixar credit. Steve felt slighted by having "no marketing credit, no value, nothing," recounted Vice President of Regional Sales Jim Diamond, who was in the meeting.

Thanks to Disney, Pixar was failing in obscurity. Steve had recently off-loaded Pixar's hardware division in a fire sale after moving fewer than three hundred computers in four years. Steve had been reduced to having Pixar and NeXT license technology from each other, signing both sides of the same contract to create the appearance of business activity for employees, customers, and the Silicon Valley community watching both companies struggle.

Now Disney was simultaneously Pixar's most prestigious client and Steve's greatest humiliation. Disney needed the company's technology but pretended like it didn't exist.

Steve turned on the NeXTstation and Donald Duck appeared on the screen in brilliant color. He thought the technology would command respect. But as he demonstrated the machine's capabilities, he couldn't help thinking about his resentment, he later told NeXT employees. Four years of Disney using Pixar's technology in secret, four years of no credit.

Steve brought it up. "That's when things went sideways," Jim recalled. "The argument escalated fast."

Finally, Jeffrey looked at Donald Duck on screen, then back at Steve. "Steve, there's a difference between commerce and art," he lectured. "Commerce is that beautiful computer that your salespeople brought in. Art is that picture of Donald Duck that you have on your computer, illegally, without our permission.

"And if people mess around with our art," Jeffrey continued, "we'll grab them by the balls and squeeze them." He wasn't so mad as to tank a prospective deal completely—Jeffrey eventually agreed to buy twenty workstations. But he would not accept Steve lifting Disney's intellectual property. Pixar, he said, would remain an uncredited partner.

Steve sat there, Roy's cigarette smoke wafting over his face, taking threats over a cartoon duck.

14

THE BLIND SPOT

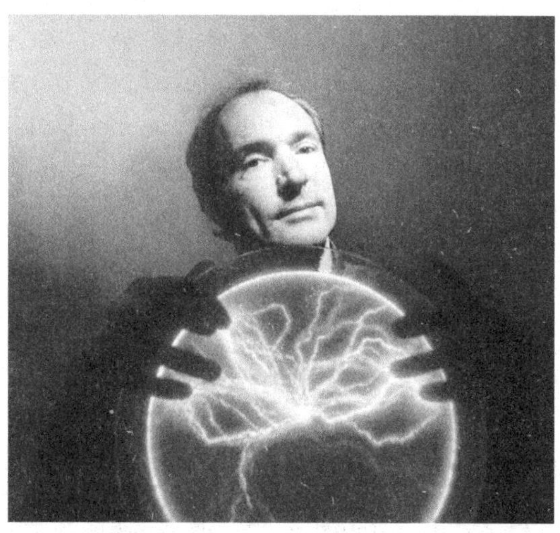

After two years at NeXT's pressure-cooker headquarters, Bob Fraik got Steve's permission to return home to Columbus, Ohio, to manage the company's Midwest sales team. As he tried to ease back into a normal life, he got a call from the corporate mothership.

"There's this guy in Switzerland," the voice on the other end said. "René Ehrenbold. Says he knows you from Sun. Says he can move a lot of machines."

Bob held the phone a little tighter. Europe was forbidden territory for NeXT—Steve had made that crystal clear. "We're not ready for Europe," he'd say. "We're not doing that. No agency approvals. Wrong timing. Infrastructure issues."

On the other hand, a multimillion-dollar lead was a multimillion-dollar lead.

René, the mystery client, offered to pay for Bob's flight to Zurich.

He accepted the flight, telling his coworkers he was going on a short vacation.

When René and Bob met in a small office on the outskirts of Zurich, Bob played it straight. "We're not ready to sell in Europe," he said. "But I would love to sell [Cubes here]."

"You should come with me," René said, grabbing his coat. "Let's go visit some people."

After winding through the streets of Zurich, the pair reached ETH Zurich, otherwise known as the MIT of Europe. René ushered Bob into a conference room where he found himself sitting across from ETH's leadership as well as representatives from other European institutions.

The group explained their computing needs. Then they slid a sales order across the table to Bob. It was for several million dollars' worth of Cubes—one of the largest offers Bob had ever seen.

He was shocked. There had been no haggling, no committee involvement, no approvals, and no phone calls back to a purchasing department. Bob stared in disbelief at the offer in his hands. It would be a boon for his dying company but accepting it would mean breaking Steve's cardinal rule: absolutely no European sales until the regulatory approvals there were complete.

"I'm sitting there going, 'Okay, how do I make this work?'" Bob said. "Because I'm breaking all of the rules."

A few days later, on Monday, Bob walked into NeXT's Redwood City headquarters with the forbidden purchase order in his hand. He strode past Steve's assistant, Susan Weinberger, and straight into a senior meeting. The room turned to look at him.

"What are you doing here?" Steve asked.

"I'm here with a multimillion-dollar purchase order," Bob said. "That's what I'm doing here." Bob passed the document to Steve, who glanced at the ETH Zurich header.

"You know we're not ready for Europe!" Steve said, his anger filling the room.

But Bob had come too far to fold now. "I'm just bringing it to you," he said. "You can turn it down if you want."

The team asked Bob to step outside while they deliberated. Steve had warned everyone at NeXT that they were almost out of runway and would have to close down soon without more cash. The large order was a blessing. In the end, Steve signed off on the deal.

A few months later, in October 1990, on the other side of Switzerland, scientist Tim Berners-Lee was moving offices. He was a visiting software engineer at CERN, a preeminent physics laboratory located on the Swiss-French border. As Tim lugged his belongings down the hallway, he glanced down at the pale gray linoleum that distinguished this level from the red floor below and yellow above.

CERN had a problem. The laboratory employed thousands of scientists from over one hundred countries, most cycling through on temporary assignments. Every time someone departed, critical knowledge walked out the door with them. Other information lived in incompatible silos. And the most crucial details tended only to exist in someone's personal files or memory. Tim wanted to fix that.

Ten years before, he had built a program called Enquire, inspired by a Victorian advice book that promised answers to everything. But Enquire, like all database solutions, required centralized data. CERN's information flows didn't work that way.

The lab needed something that worked like human memory itself—where any piece of information could connect to any other, without requiring permission or centralized control. "The system we need is like a diagram of circles and arrows," Tim wrote, "where circles and arrows can stand for anything."

He called his system "Mesh" in a March 1989 proposal. By the next year, the name evolved to the World Wide Web.

For eighteen months, Tim's proposal gathered dust. Tim had been advocating for a NeXT Cube at CERN, drawn to its advanced development environment. Tim's boss, Mike Sendall, quietly signed off on Tim's project—as an excuse to test the NeXT Cube. "He suggested that I should buy one of these NeXT machines I'd been talking about so enthusiastically," Tim told *Fresh Air*. "And if we needed a sort of test project to run on the NeXT machine . . . 'Why not just do this hypertext thing you're talking about?'"

In autumn 1990, Tim took delivery of a machine unlike any other at CERN: the latest, upgraded NeXT Cube, which had been released alongside the NeXTstations that summer. After its unboxing, it sat like a sculpture on Tim's desk, matte black and aesthetically perfect.

Tim made quick use of it, employing the application builder and taking advantage of the system's ability to display formatted text and images exactly as they would appear in final software with minimal code—crucial for creating the first visual web browser. But the real magic was NeXT's use of object-oriented programming. While other developers in his position might have to build their systems from the ground up, the Cube allowed Tim to focus solely on bringing his innovation to life. "I could do in a couple of months what would take more like a year on other platforms," he wrote, "because on the NeXT, a lot of it was done for me already."

Through October and November, Tim coded in Objective-C, pounding away in his gray-floored office. Before Tim's project, accessing files on remote computers was a clunky, multistep process. Users had to know the exact machine address, log in with specialized software, and type a series of commands to locate what they needed. One wrong keystroke and nothing would work.

But NeXT's visual system let Tim hide these addresses completely. To create a hyperlink—the clickable blue text that would come to define the web—a user simply browsed to something interesting, hit Command-M, selected text in their document, and hit Command-L. The system memorized and managed all those complex addresses invisibly. Command-line programming gave way to pointing and clicking, transforming the internet from a specialists' tool into something your grandmother could use.

The NeXT also came with built-in software for editing text with fonts and styles, which were capabilities most computers wouldn't have for years. Programmers using other systems had to code every visual element from scratch, whereas Tim just had to modify the existing tools to handle clickable links and network connections. "Designing the app's menus was trivial—just drag and drop with InterfaceBuilder," he explained.

In Tim's telling, the NeXT was more than just a computer. It was "a platform: something that allows you to build things which without it would have been possible, but a lot of work."

Because NeXT computers lay beyond most physicists' budgets, Tim encouraged intern Nicola Pellow to create a "line-mode browser" that could run on any machine. He also built a gateway to CERN's phonebook database. "Mundane as it was," he later wrote in his book *Weaving the Web*, "this first presentation of the Web was, in a curious way, a killer application."

Beneath the elegant interface, he was building the plumbing of a new universe: HTTP (the protocol that would let computers request and deliver web pages), HTML (the language that would structure billions of documents with headings, paragraphs, and those revolutionary clickable links), and the server software that would deliver this information to anyone who asked. These three inventions, now invisible to the billions of people who use them daily, would become the fundamental architecture of the web, as essential and unnoticed as plumbing in a house.

By December, info.cern.ch went online. The World Wide Web now existed, running on a single black magnesium cube in CERN's Building 31. Tim scrawled a warning on the Cube in red ink: "This machine is a server. DO NOT POWER IT DOWN!!" If anyone disobeyed, then the entirety of the World Wide Web would disappear from the internet until Tim restarted the machine.

Where Tim saw his project as a leap forward, others weren't so sure. "I didn't find lots of people willing to get excited about the idea of the web," Tim recalled. "They quite reasonably asked to know why it was different from the past."

The skepticism ran deep, even at NeXT. When Tim's CERN colleague showed up at the NeXT headquarters with a demo of the World Wide Web, he couldn't get anyone to pay attention. They were too busy to look at this crude interface that couldn't even demonstrate its key feature. Without a working connection to CERN's servers in Geneva—international internet links were still rare and unstable in 1990—they couldn't see how clicking a link would instantly retrieve a document from across the Atlantic Ocean. Nobody dared bring it to Steve either, scared that he would dismiss it as "shit."

To understand their legitimate doubts, it's helpful to know that the internet and the World Wide Web aren't the same thing. The internet is the underlying network infrastructure—the cables, routers, servers, and protocols that connect computers worldwide. The web is just one application that runs on top of it, a system for sharing and linking documents through clickable hyperlinks. In 1990, many competing systems existed for navigating and organizing information online, including email, FTP for file transfers, and other information retrieval systems.

Tim's web hadn't yet emerged as the standard. Internet projects like Gopher, developed at the University of Minnesota, competed for the same space. NeXT itself was also building automatic internet connectivity for consumers, with modems, IP registration, even billing.

But Steve killed that project. "Several people told [him] that things would go wrong connecting to the internet, and when they did, we would be mostly helpless to support them," recalled the engineer who evaluated the prototype. If NeXT sold consumers a box that connected them to the internet and something broke—a downed server in Europe, a severed cable under the Atlantic—customers would call NeXT for help.

But NeXT couldn't fix problems caused by infrastructure the company didn't control.

The circle was almost complete. NeXT had built the machine that birthed the web and provided the development environment that made it possible. Yet the company was missing what would soon become a revolution. While Tim Berners-Lee's invention spread from one NeXT Cube to millions of screens worldwide, Steve had already moved on to other battles. Nobody—not Steve, not Tim, not anyone at NeXT—could have predicted that this crude interface for sharing physics papers would reshape civilization itself.

15

VISIONARY, TYRANT

"News Flash! Steve Jobs Marries!"

In March 1991, Apple's corporate librarian Monica Ertel sent that announcement ricocheting through the company's email system. Steve's wedding had taken place two days earlier—a low-key, sixty-person Buddhist ceremony at Ahwahnee Hotel in Yosemite—which happened to be the same hotel where many interior scenes from *The Shining* were filmed. Most of Steve's cofounders at NeXT attended. But the bride's identity remained a mystery to everyone outside.

Steve hadn't worked at Apple for six years.

Intelligence about the wedding came by way of a Catholic priest in Yosemite who witnessed the event happening down the road. The priest passed word to an online forum member, who forwarded it to Apple employees two days later. They learned that the alcohol-free celebration featured white roses from France, Tuscan bean soup, wild mushroom lasagna, and "Apple pie that the Bride bought [*sic*] with her."

"I'm wondering if there's any significance to the apple pie," one employee wrote back.

The next day, Monica sent a follow-up email with the subject line "Mrs Jobs Is Revealed!" Laurene Powell, an MBA from Stanford in her twenties. She promised no more messages "unless I get some good honeymoon details! *:-)"

The same year, President George H. W. Bush nominated Steve for a seat on the President's Export Council. The position required an FBI background check, which involved hundreds of hours of interviews with Steve's coworkers.

In these conversations, coworkers struggled to reconcile the visionary with the jerk. "Several individuals questioned Mr. Jobs' honesty, stating that Mr. Jobs will twist the truth and distort reality in order to achieve his goals," an FBI agent wrote. One source told the FBI Steve was both "deceptive" and perfect for a "high level political position," since "honesty and integrity are not required qualities to assume such a position." Another managed to pack the entire Steve paradox into a single breath, describing his personal life as "lacking due to his narcissism and shallowness," then saying, "he has far-reaching vision and can vitalize plans and goals."

Others said he had "integrity as long as he gets his way," was "extremely bright and competent," and "would serve well in a position of trust and confidence"—almost everyone said that, even the people who'd just finished cataloging his sins.

The FBI learned about Steve's daughter, Lisa, whom he'd abandoned and recently started supporting. The agents heard about the LSD he'd dropped in college (mostly taken alone, as Steve himself told the agents).

But even the nation's top law enforcement agency struggled to get time with Steve for phone interviews. His secretary told the agents he couldn't spare an hour for three weeks.

The FBI ultimately determined Steve didn't pose a security concern, and he received a nearly three-year appointment.

No one understood Steve's contradictions better than Susan Barnes. By now, she had been Steve's CFO for six years. She'd helped him raise money from Ross, from Stanford, from Canon. She'd also watched him burn through his own money faster than she'd thought possible.

And now, after all that, she had somehow managed to help Steve eke out a $50 million credit line from J. P. Morgan. He treated it like found money: "If we can't pay it back," he said, "too bad."

"No," Susan told him. "You cannot do that. We're not going to do things that aren't part of the agreements we make with people who helped us build this thing."

If NeXT failed to repay J. P. Morgan on time, the bank could demand immediate repayment of its loan. That meant that if anything went wrong—and things were always going wrong—NeXT would be on the hook for cash it didn't have.

"Is Steve really engaged in listening?" Susan wondered. "Am I adding any value to him? If not, it's time for me to go." The moment came in May 1991, when she delivered her resignation to Steve, unable to keep working for someone who wouldn't honor the financial agreements she'd made.

Susan had been there at the beginning, eating pasta salad with the other cofounders as they slaved away at Steve's dining room table. By the end, she had closed hundreds of millions in deals under challenging circumstances. Despite that history, Steve didn't feel saccharine about Susan's departure.

"I just didn't want to be nagged one more time," he later told Susan.

Susan announced her resignation to the company on May 4, 1991. Her husband, Bud, stayed behind.

As his inner circle began to dissolve, Steve found refuge in an unlikely place: his inbox. By 1991, Steve had become one of the world's first email power users, receiving what Director of Operations Greg Brandeau estimated to be a thousand messages each day at sjobs@next.com. This wasn't typical for a CEO in 1991. Email was still a novelty in most offices. Many executives didn't even have email addresses, and those who did might check them once a week. Most Silicon Valley workers chose to walk down the hall rather than risk their message sitting unread for days.

Steve was different. He lived in his inbox, firing off responses at 3:00 a.m., running his company from his keyboard. But the software was primitive. You couldn't search your messages, couldn't automatically sort them into folders. NeXT executives would spend hours manually dragging hundreds of emails into folders, one by one.

"Steve, how do you find that email again?" became a constant refrain in the hallways.

The solution came from Paul Hegarty, a talented NeXT software developer. His idea: keyword search for email. While the world was still figuring out whether email was even useful, NeXT was already solving problems that would emerge as universal headaches a decade later.

Steve's relationship with his own technology revealed itself in unexpected ways. When a new Canadian engineer named Steve Hayman noticed that nobody at NeXT had claimed the email alias steve@next.com—despite seven or eight Steves working there—he figured he could take it. Late one Friday night, two weeks into the job, he filled out the form to redirect steve@next.com to his own address, shayman@next.com.

The system approved it automatically. Then the avalanche began. Emails from reporters, CEOs, financiers—all thinking they were writing to Steve Jobs—flooded Steve Hayman's inbox. "Of course I didn't read any of it," he later wrote on his blog. But panic set in immediately. In a desperate attempt to undo his mistake before anyone noticed, Steve Hayman filled out the form again, this time redirecting steve@next.com to sjobs@next.com. Then he sent Steve a confessional email: "I did something dumb . . . This was a bad idea, I'm sorry."

But Steve didn't rip into him. "Great idea, thank you," he responded.

The next month, on June 14, Ross resigned from NeXT's board. His involvement had been shrinking for a while as his three-year-old company, Perot Systems—a technology services firm competing for lucrative corporate and government contracts—was taking off. The relationship between Ross and Steve had deteriorated, with Ross frustrated by NeXT's burn rate and lack of progress toward profitability.

Ross's departure dealt a blow to NeXT, particularly to its government business. When he formally left, his countless government connections walked out the door with him.

Eight months after leaving NeXT, Ross appeared on CNN's *Larry King Live* and declared his consideration of a run for the presidency. "If I can get on the ballot in all fifty states," he said, "I'll run."

The Texas billionaire who'd tried to teach Steve fiscal discipline took his message national. Armed with flip charts and infomercials, Ross called the national deficit the "crazy aunt nobody in the family wants to talk about." He bypassed both parties, positioning himself as a populist independent with a knack for speaking directly to voters.

"Absolutely I endorse him," Steve told a magazine. Steve didn't let their breakdown get in the way of his admiration for Ross. He pointed to Ross's "belief in the worth of the common individual."

In the 1992 presidential election, he captured 19 percent of the popular vote, the best third-party showing since Teddy Roosevelt.

For their married life, Steve and Laurene decided to leave the crumbling Jackling House behind and move to Old Palo Alto, nearer to schools and downtown. Their new place was more modest in size and featured wooden beams salvaged from the construction of the Golden Gate Bridge.

It was there that *Fortune*'s Brent Schlender had somehow convinced Steve and Bill Gates to sit for their first joint interview in a decade—Steve had insisted on holding home court advantage.

When Bill arrived fifteen minutes late, he stepped out of his black limo and knocked on the wrong door—the formal entrance instead of the kitchen door that everyone else used. The interior featured Steve's typical level of decor. The living room held two Eames chairs. Unhung Ansel Adams prints leaned against the walls. Steve's LPs were scattered across the floor.

Because Bill was late, photographer George Lange had exactly three minutes to set up for the portrait. As he hustled Steve and Bill through the house to the backyard, where he had originally planned to shoot the photo, he spotted an intriguing staircase.

"Let's bring our light in here," he called to his assistant.

Steve stood barefoot, waiting. "You might want to put on some shoes," George suggested. "It's for the cover of *Fortune*."

Steve went upstairs and returned shortly, clomping down the stairs in new golf shoes, laces untied. While George adjusted his lights, the two men stood on the stairs sniping at each other like teenagers.

"You will never beat me at anything," Bill said.

"You may tie me at something, but you'll never beat me," Steve shot back.

The perfect shot: two men standing on different steps, arguing about who stood taller.

As Brent steered the interview, Steve griped to his rival about Microsoft's domineering position. Windows 3.0, released just a year earlier, was already a massive success, on its way to selling four million copies and establishing Windows as the future of personal computing. Microsoft was becoming the gatekeeper of the PC industry. Hardware manufacturers needed to license Microsoft's operating systems to sell PCs, while software developers had to write for Microsoft's platforms to reach users.

Steve put it more colorfully. Hundreds of companies made PCs, hundreds wrote software, "but they all have to travel through this very small orifice called Microsoft to get to one another."

"It's a very large orifice!" Bill protested, laughing at Steve's word choice.

Steve did acknowledge that Windows was bringing what he saw as Apple's innovations, including the graphical user interface, to the masses. (Bill had long argued that both companies had taken these ideas from Xerox PARC, the Palo Alto research lab where scientists had invented the mouse-driven, windowed interface in the 1970s.)

But, Steve said, "In the meantime—and it's been seven years since the Macintosh was introduced—tens of millions of PC owners are needlessly using a computer that is far less good than it should be."

While Mac users had been pointing and clicking on visual icons since 1984, Microsoft had kept PC users in the Stone Age, forcing them to type commands into DOS, a primitive text-based system where doing anything—copying a file, opening a program, even seeing what was on your computer—required memorizing and typing arcane instructions on a black screen. Microsoft had the technology to liberate its users from this mess years earlier, Steve implied, but chose not to.

Steve told Brent about NeXT's automated factory and lamented the fact that IBM had buried his NeXTSTEP software like "a diamond got dropped in the mud and is now sitting on somebody's desk who thinks it's a clod of dirt."

And he explained how Charles Lindbergh had managed his world-changing, transatlantic flight. "Every time he came down on the side of increasing his chances of getting to Paris at the sacrifice of safety or comfort. That's why he made it." In other words: Revolutionary leaps required risk.

Bill saw things differently. "Smart people like Steve ought to try to build things from scratch," he conceded. But he argued that the real tests of digital performance—handwriting recognition, object-oriented systems, multimedia—would prove that evolution beat revolution.

As they talked, George looked for what he called "black keys," the revealing moments between planned poses. Once, his camera caught something unexpected: Steve and Bill actually laughing together. It was an outtake George wouldn't discover for years, a frame of shared humanity between two men reshaping the world.

At one point Bill turned to George with a question that had been eating at him: How much did his photography lights cost? George stared at the billionaire. "All my lights are worth about as much as the hubcap on your cheapest car," he said.

The question cast the two titans' mindsets in stark relief: As Steve dreamed of Charles Lindbergh and building perfect objects, Bill priced out someone else's lights.

16

MISSION CRITICAL

In the summer of 1991, Steve invited Andy Grove to a NeXT offsite retreat in Santa Cruz. Andy, the cofounder of Intel, had been a mentor ever since Steve had cold-called him for advice in the late 1970s.

Andy entered a meeting room with NeXT's senior leadership team gathered before him. He skipped pleasantries and posed a seemingly easy question: "What business are you in?"

The executives glanced at each other. Andy waited.

Hearing no response, he began polling each person in the room, one at a time. Some echoed Steve's pet phrase about building a "mainframe on a desk." Others insisted NeXT was competing with Apple in the premium personal computer market—they'd just released the lower-priced NeXTstation, after all. Still others cited NeXT's original vision of building a "scholar's workstation" for labs and universities.

"Andy asked profoundly simple questions," NeXT's marketing director, Ron Weissman, recalled. But revealing ones. After six years in business, NeXT's own leadership couldn't agree on what business they were actually in.

If they could, maybe they would have a better shot at reversing the company's fortunes.

In the third quarter of 1991, NeXT's already low sales plunged by half. The catastrophe unmasked an accounting trick that the team had been using to hide paltry sales figures from Steve. The trick was this: The team reported sales figures by determining the number of units given to distributors, not sales to final customers.

With the launch of the NeXTstation, NeXT required stores and distributors to take at least twenty-five machines each. Distributors didn't have to pay right away—they got the machines on credit. NeXT then immediately counted these as "sales," even though no money had changed hands and no actual customers had purchased anything. This practice, called "channel stuffing," made NeXT look successful on paper while machines piled up unsold in warehouses, as journalist Randall E. Stross reported.

When distributors failed to sell the machines, they couldn't pay NeXT either. Suddenly, NeXT's reported sales tumbled and the company was owed over $10 million from distributors holding all those machines.

The European operation, which was set up after NeXT sold the computer that built the World Wide Web, took the deception furthest. According to Randall E. Stross, VP Theo Wegbrans allegedly encouraged dealers who needed four machines to order fifty on credit they'd never pay. He reported these as real sales to headquarters. By the time Steve finally intervened after months of warnings, the truth emerged: Millions of dollars in "sales" were just unsold machines sitting in warehouses that NeXT would have to write off.

Steve summoned seven NeXT European country heads to London for what they assumed was a routine review. In the parking lot outside the meeting venue, the executives stood waiting, puffing cigarettes, as

Steve's assistant called them in one by one. Each executive emerged from the meeting with the universal gesture of the suddenly unemployed: hands thrown up in mock surrender, bitter grin. "Nice to know you guys," they told each other.

NeXT was yet again on the precipice of bankruptcy. It had burned through the $100 million cash injection from Canon two years earlier. Now that Steve had alienated Ross and IBM—which would have paid lucrative licensing fees for NeXTSTEP—the most straightforward paths to raising more money were shuttered.

That left Canon as the last major investor standing. So Steve got on a flight to Tokyo to beg Canon executive Hiroshi Tanaka for additional loans. Though Tanaka and his team were growing uncomfortable with Steve's mishandling of NeXT's finances and his continued failure to hire a COO as their previous agreement required, they found themselves in a catch-22. If they didn't extend another loan, NeXT might collapse, and their entire $100 million investment would go up in smoke.

Canon agreed to cut checks totaling $40 million for the rest of 1991. NeXT would need to completely retool its approach—and do so quickly. If the team failed this time around, their failure would be final.

NeXT's leadership team began taking a cold, hard look at the company's hardware business. The fact was that NeXT's computers simply weren't selling.

"[They were] too expensive," hardware chief Rich Page said. And third-party software options were still too limited. Even with "a great operating system, it didn't really have the right apps," he said.

Rich understood the ruthless reality of the technology adoption curve. After the early adopters bought machines, "they get exhausted. Sales slow down. There's no reason to buy the product," he said. As sales stalled, NeXT's Fremont factory struggled with an oversupply of inventory. The situation was so dire that Rich even found himself moonlighting as a salesman.

At the same time, Steve kept cycling through manufacturing leaders. He "would find one [VP of manufacturing], hire them, they'd be the VP for six, nine, ten months, whatever, he'd get frustrated, and he'd get rid of them," Rich remembered. Steve seemed to always blame them for his decision to build a machine for a market that didn't exist.

As NeXT's leaders studied the problem, a consensus began to emerge: They should abandon high-cost hardware in favor of selling high-margin software. But Steve wasn't on board with this plan. He clung to hardware like a lifeline. A software pivot would mean abandoning the beautiful objects Steve loved to make.

While the debate raged, NeXT's biggest customers made their preference clear.

A principal from O'Connor & Associates—a Chicago-based high-speed trading firm—showed up in HR chief Phil Wilson's office one day. He shut the door behind him.

The visitor had chosen his audience carefully. In his two years at NeXT, Phil hadn't gotten worn down by Steve's reality distortion field. The O'Connor representative knew he would offer a receptive ear for the company's feedback.

He proceeded to lay out O'Connor's worries about NeXT's long-term viability as a company. "Phil," he said, "you have to help me make Steve understand the value of NeXT computers to us is not in the hardware, it's in the software."

O'Connor made money by analyzing data and making fast trades in the market. NeXTSTEP allowed the firm to build proprietary trading software quickly, giving it an advantage over competitors.

The firm had developed a mutually dependent relationship with NeXT. O'Connor needed NeXT to survive so it could keep making NeXTSTEP. Without it, O'Connor would lose its edge.

Meanwhile NeXT desperately needed them as a customer. "O'Connor basically made payroll," Mike Slade, NeXT's new VP of marketing, recalled. Mike had just joined NeXT after seven years at Microsoft, where he'd launched Excel for the Mac. Mike had been lured away by Steve personally, becoming one of the few executives who could challenge him directly. "At the end of the quarter, [O'Connor would] come up and order the most souped-up, overpriced workstations they could find in the price list," Mike said. "Rip-off memory, rip-off server, rip-off RAM, big color monitor, just anything to help us make payroll."

Phil sat there absorbing the O'Connor representative's message.

Then he composed a long email to Steve to make the case. NeXT, he argued, should become a software-only company.

Steve didn't want to hear it. "You're an HR guy," he replied. "What do you know about this?" He followed up that charming note with a threat. If NeXT became a software company, he wrote, it would have to downsize dramatically and then "we won't need a guy like you."

Rather than take the feedback from his team and their customers seriously, Steve kept insisting that NeXT hardware was superior and worth the purchase. He still believed his hardware had a future and he didn't want to give up everything his team had sacrificed.

So he dreamed up a new rationale for keeping the hardware division. In late 1991, he recorded a new strategy video for employees. "A lot of light bulbs have come on over the last ninety days," he began. Steve revealed that he'd been visiting customers in the field, getting "firsthand information as to what they're doing with our products."

"We've had historically a very hard time figuring out exactly who our customer was," he said. He turned to a whiteboard where he sketched a diagram representing the computer market.

"Over the last year, we've oscillated back and forth between thinking that the PCs and Macs were our competitors . . . Or the workstations were our competitors," he said. NeXT had discovered that "every single customer we've talked to here has the need to write one custom application."

Yet instead of accepting the conclusion his staff and customers had been pushing—that NeXT should focus on selling development tools to meet that need—Steve came up with an entirely new market category to justify his obsession.

He called it the "professional workstation" market, supposedly distinct from both PCs and traditional workstations. This new segment, consisting of publishers, doctors, and lawyers, currently totaled just fifty thousand units. He pulled numbers out of thin air. "This marketplace in '91 is going to grow to about a hundred thousand units . . . And next year in '92, it's going to triple to about three hundred thousand units." Steve predicted NeXT could supply half of this imagined demand.

It felt like signature Steve. The team had seen him lose major customer deals, watch the entire team slump in dejection, only to return the next morning with electric enthusiasm—and no small amount of bluster. Steve had this ability to "confidently state things that he did not know to be true," software developer Leo Hourvitz observed.

NeXT's desperation bred new tactics for seeking attention. "We're an ant in an elephant war here," Mike said. The team watched as Sun and IBM battled each other to achieve the sector's highest sales while NeXT barely registered.

"Here's what you do when you have a bigger competitor with more money," Mike told Steve. "You pick a fight."

Mike and his colleagues had an idea for how to do this while demonstrating NeXT's true value. He proposed holding a videotaped competition between two software developers. One would be an expert on NeXTSTEP and the other with Sun workstations.

They were given the same task: Develop a troubleshooting app for a customer service call center as quickly as possible.

The NeXT developer used Interface Builder to drag and drop the foundations of his app from a preloaded palette of objects. After twenty hours of work over three days, he had completed his custom app without writing a single line of code.

Meanwhile, the Sun developer struggled with clunky development tools and turned in a prototype that lacked key features. He had written a full sixteen pages of code.

"If you're going to write an application on the NeXT, you're half done because we've already written half of it for you," Avie Tevanian explained in the video. "If you use your custom application to make money, which for example people on Wall Street do, the sooner you have it, the more money you're making."

The decision to poke at Sun created an illusion in the marketplace. "That put us on the map," marketing director Ron Weissman said. "We were like number twelve in the market, but the impression was that we were number two."

Inadvertently, the competition reinforced the fact that NeXT's true value wasn't in the beautiful hardware Steve loved. It was in the invisible code that could help traders corner markets and build fortunes.

By late 1991, the pressure to keep NeXT alive had begun transforming Steve.

"He was like a guy who's been waterboarded at Guantanamo," Mike recalled. "[He] couldn't sleep. . . . He was off his rocker every day." To keep the company afloat, Mike said that Steve was writing $10 million checks out of his own checkbook. He was starting to run out of personal cash too.

In 1991, Reed College invited Steve to speak to incoming freshmen. "Character is built not in good times," he told them, "but in bad times; not in a time of plenty, but in a time of adversity."

Three weeks later, on September 22, 1991, his son, Reed, was born.

As Steve's company flailed, he discovered something that mattered more. “Having Reed has been a different experience for me that I won’t even attempt to put into words,” Steve said in a magazine interview.

“It’s as if I never saw the color green before and all of a sudden when Reed was born, I could see the color green.”

Something was softening in him. As things went off the rails, Ron observed, “he’d get humble, he’d be very self-reflective.” Mike concurred. “When [Steve] was desperate, that was his absolute best,” he said.

The man who’d once ruled through sheer confidence even began admitting his mistakes for the first time. Occasionally, when things went wrong, Steve confessed to the team: “I blew it.”

Steve eventually acknowledged what everyone had been trying to tell him. “Corporate America discovered that they could use NeXT-STEP to build their in-house, mission-critical custom apps, five to ten times faster too,” Steve soon told an audience at his next product launch in San Francisco.

“And they came to us and said, ‘You don’t realize what you have. You have potentially the biggest breakthrough in the computer industry that we have seen in the last decade.’ ”

NeXT was teaching Steve something he’d never learned at Apple: how to transform failure into fuel.

17

SPOOKS AND DEADHEADS

In late 1991, Jim Diamond landed one of NeXT's biggest sales: thousands of workstations to the National Reconnaissance Office, an elite intelligence agency whose mere existence was a state secret until 1992.

After Ross's exit from NeXT, a few salespeople had managed to salvage government contracts, including this one. Though the scale of NeXT's government sales was nothing close to what Ross had envisioned, this deal would be huge for the flailing company. There was just one problem: The Los Angeles Air Force Base, which housed the agency office that had ordered the computers, didn't want to take delivery until the new year.

But NeXT couldn't wait until then. It needed to off-load its inventory, mark down revenues, and close its books. Between Christmas and New Year's Day, when the base was shut down, a dozen tractor trailers rolled up to the gates. Guards watched as trucks dumped thousands of black cubes at the base, which wasn't prepared to receive them. "A couple of tractor trailers ran over picnic tables," Jim recalled.

Jim got "in a little trouble," he recounted, but the relationship survived. The federal government kept buying NeXT computers, giving the company enough revenue to last another quarter. NeXT's survival now depended on the very agencies Steve had once snubbed.

But it created a conundrum. NeXT still needed third-party developers to build software for NeXTSTEP. However, the developer community wasn't exactly thrilled to be making tools for the CIA. They knew about the spies' relationship with NeXT because the three-letter agencies placed orders for their independent software, which only worked on NeXT machines. Steve needed someone with cultural cachet who could make NeXT seem cool again, someone who could convince hackers and idealists that the platform was still worth their time despite its new clientele.

John Perry Barlow—a Mormon cattle rancher, computer geek, and Grateful Dead lyricist—fit the bill perfectly. His friends called him "Barlow."

His platform would be *NeXTWORLD* magazine, which Steve had founded with publisher Pat McGovern. Pat, the billionaire founder of tech publishing empire International Data Group, had previously helped Steve launch *Macworld*, in a deal that included financial commitments and an agreement to provide computers for the staff.

NeXTWORLD took a similar shape. Dan Ruby, who edited the magazine, described it as split between two worlds, calling it "an in-house magazine, even though published out of house"—a captive publication that existed at Steve's pleasure. Steve hoped to use it to create a community of developers, enthusiasts, and influencers around the Cube.

Before writing for *NeXTWORLD*, Barlow had been a NeXT skeptic. But when Steve gifted him a NeXT machine so that he could write a column, the computer's elegant interface—"It has a kind of film noir quality," he wrote—hooked him. Soon he was writing like an addict: "Hi, I'm John, and I am a NeXThead."

His column quickly established him as a prophet of the NeXT gospel, despite the fact that he was still a new convert. "He didn't have all that much to say," Dan admitted to the Computer History Museum. "But he said it dramatically, with a [witty] turn of phrase."

Barlow and his fellow *NeXTWORLD* writers covered all things NeXT. But it wasn't just company-approved content. Barlow expressed concern about NeXT's pivot toward corporate customers—a concern Dan shared. "Like what's going on?" Dan recalled. "I thought Steve Jobs was all about anti-corporate."

This kind of gentle criticism was tolerable. It made the magazine seem authentic. But when *NeXTWORLD* crossed the line into actual news, NeXT executives erupted. Mike once fired off a furious email to Dan, upset that the magazine had revealed an unannounced product. "So you have to ask that familiar question, as the editor of *Pravda*, what is the goal?" In other words: Toe the official state line.

Since everyone knew about the funding, anything *NeXTWORLD* printed would become "official" NeXT news. "If your goal is to create a kick ass and independently funded magazine, the most critical thing you can do is help more machines get sold," he wrote to Dan.

While NeXT and *NeXTWORLD* fought over editorial control, they both overlooked the actual future. In August 1991, *NeXTWORLD* writer Daniel Kehoe spotted an announcement for a software app called "WWWNeXTStepEditor version 0.12." The app allowed users to edit the hypertext—the code—that made up the websites on the information system, spelled "WorldWideWeb." The name seemed to Daniel to be "a bit of a conceit since the only users at the time were high-energy physicists at a few research institutes."

Daniel wanted to cover the web for *NeXTWORLD*, but the editors weren't interested. They worried it had limited appeal.

Barlow also wrote for *MicroTimes*, a popular monthly tabloid that covered the Bay Area tech scene. He was scheduled to interview Steve for that publication and bought a nonrefundable airline ticket from Wyoming so they could meet. Two days before the interview, Steve cancelled the meeting. Then he abruptly changed his mind. Barlow was kept waiting in the lobby for forty minutes. Then Steve bounced in, telling Barlow he could only spare twenty minutes instead of the promised ninety.

"But not to worry," John wrote. "He could 'talk real fast.'"

They sat in a conference room together. Steve sat on the neighboring seat, one of his knees bobbing on his chair.

"You want to talk about our marketing strategy?" Steve asked. "Good. I want to talk about that too, since you're confused."

The dig landed precisely where Steve intended. Barlow had been publicly criticizing NeXT's marketing for months, circulating electronic rants about what he saw as "the apparent absence of any coherent approach to marketing and sales at NeXT." Steve had emailed him directly, telling him he was "all wet"—completely wrong—but had refused to elaborate.

"Believe it or not, when we did the Macintosh, we never anticipated desktop publishing," Steve began. "We weren't smart enough."

In other words, Apple's greatest success had been inadvertent. Now he claimed to have stumbled into a similar kind of discovery at NeXT. "The concept that all big companies have a ton of mission-critical custom apps they want to write . . . was something that never occurred to us," Steve said.

NeXT's pivot from universities hadn't been intentional. But by June, he explained, most customers were corporations. They were using NeXTSTEP to build their own mission-critical apps faster than before. "It was not a planned thing," he said.

Then Steve gave Barlow examples of NeXT's new clients. They revealed how far the company had strayed from its original vision. Steve told Barlow about an ad agency where an art director used the computer to write apps that scraped airline data. He claimed that the Royal Canadian Mounted Police in Toronto were using NeXT systems to manage the entire police department. "Multimedia out the wazoo," Steve enthused. He never specified what the multimedia was for, but surveillance seemed the likely answer.

The latter example particularly disturbed Barlow, who was a staunch advocate of digital freedoms. "I see a great deal of frustration and disaffection in the NeXT user community, which is about as rabidly devoted as anything I've seen outside a religious group, and they just don't feel like there's anything they can do," he told Steve. These, after all, were his people.

"Well, to make NeXT successful, we've got to make NeXT successful in corporate America," Steve said.

"You're probably quite right," Barlow replied. "But . . . eventually a company resembles its market more than its maker."

Steve paused, smiling thoughtfully.

"We'll see." Then, convincing himself: "So our path, for good or bad, is going to be more like IBM's." Steve proceeded to paint a portrait of NeXT's affinity for the corporate world, mentioning the O'Connor traders who "look like us" and "talk like us."

He rattled through his analysis of the market—computer dealers were dead, he told Barlow, and everything would be mail order soon.

Steve also forecast something radical. While the internet already connected universities and corporations through physical cables and dial-up modems, Steve envisioned computers with a built-in "radio net or something" that would make them wirelessly connected everywhere. Once that happened, he argued, being disconnected would feel "like having a telephone that's not plugged in."

When the conversation turned back to customers, Barlow said, "Actually, the Mounted Police don't bother me anything like as much as my recent discovery that the CIA is one of your biggest customers."

"I can't comment on that," Steve replied.

Despite promising only twenty minutes, Steve had stayed for nearly an hour. Barlow left the interview impressed with Steve—"Whatever his personal wrinkles, this guy really *is* a genius," Barlow wrote—but unsettled about his corporate pivot and his growing coziness with government surveillance organizations.

With the support of Apple cofounder Steve Wozniak, Barlow had started the Electronic Frontier Foundation, a growing chorus of developers, privacy advocates, and countercultural intellectuals who saw the internet as a borderless frontier to be protected against surveillance and corporate greed. Steve's vision of NeXT as a tool for corporate America and intelligence agencies ran counter to everything Barlow believed technology should be.

It looked to Barlow like something major had shifted. It appeared that the pirate, who had once flown the Jolly Roger over the Macintosh Division offices at Apple, was enlisting in the navy.

At the very least, he was selling the navy computers. Dozens of contracts from the early 1990s showed the U.S. Navy, Army, and Air Force purchasing NeXT hardware. As a Pentagon official told Steve: "The best software will win the war."

The NSA, too, had become a massive customer—a partnership that required compromises Steve wouldn't have imagined making during his Apple days.

As Steve grew closer to NeXT's government customers, he continued his efforts to win over developers. The best of them was someone Barlow called "a dirt hacker" from Albuquerque, New Mexico—in other words, a person who came from humble, nontradtional origins to become a skilled developer. His name was Andrew Stone.

Andrew built software at supernatural speeds, revising entire programs overnight and implementing features the same day they were suggested. His apps, sold under the name Stone Design, rivaled the quality of those sold by the biggest software companies. Where corporate software could feel bloated and bureaucratic, Andrew's work was "clean, extraordinarily self-documenting, and powerful," as Barlow put it. In programming terms, "self-documenting" meant that Andrew's software was so well written that other programmers could understand it without needing separate explanations—the mark of a master craftsman.

One day an envelope arrived at Andrew's home containing a purchase order for the database software he had designed for NeXT computers. The order was huge, a license costing more than $300,000. And it came from a small Texas town he hadn't heard of.

But he didn't think much of it. Andrew cashed the check and used part of the money to throw a rave with Barlow at the Palace of Fine Arts in San Francisco.

The invitation promised "Smart Drugs, Sense8VR [an early virtual reality installation from one of the pioneering VR companies], Ambient Lounge, Vegetarian Buffet, & Posliterate [Postliterate] Dancing to an [*sic*] Hypnotic, CyberTribal Beat." It asked for "people with an expanded sense of the possible."

As attendees gathered around at the Palace of Fine Arts—its rotunda and classical columns rising from a lagoon like the ruins of ancient Rome—the British occultist Genesis P-Orridge sang. Scantily clad tai chi dancers performed on elevated platforms while colored lights and fog played off their bodies. A man wearing a large hat carried around a bag stuffed with ecstasy pills and LSD for guests.

Andrew recalled a number of luminaries showing up: Bobby Weir of the Grateful Dead, the trailblazing singer Todd Rundgren, the founders of *Wired* magazine. "But we were all pretty high, so I didn't get a chance to greet everyone," he said. (The next day, the staff of *NeXTWORLD* had to give a business presentation to advertisers and showed up blitzed and hungover.)

Notably absent was Steve, who had been invited but didn't like partying. A clear split was emerging, Andrew noticed: "Steve in his Armani suits, trying to court all of the intelligence agencies and corporations, while the people holding the flag are, of course, Barlow and me, having the raves and realizing that it's about the community."

As they processed this growing distance, a Grateful Dead song haunted the growing community of NeXT developers. Titled "Estimated Prophet," with lyrics by Barlow, the song weaves together visions of Barlow's Mormon boyhood with a prophecy from the book of Ezekiel about an exiled priest who witnessed heaven's machinery spinning above the rivers of Babylon.

In the lyrics about a prophet wandering the shores of California, Andrew Stone heard the song of their exodus. "We didn't really know where we were," he said. "The spiritual part became a very dark place. Steve continued to seek markets that would not open for him"—after burning through universities, publishers, and anyone else who could fulfill Steve's original vision of democratizing powerful computing tools.

Steve's commitment to democratization had been negotiable. He'd been "flailing around" between strategies, Mike Slade recounted, chasing revenue rather than revolution. The developers believed in the mission perhaps more than Steve himself did. The pragmatic prophet left it to his disciples to carry the original faith.

Andrew called this place "bardo," the term Buddhists use for the space between death and rebirth, a twilight realm where souls wander. If NeXT collapsed, Steve's faithful developers would go out of business right along with him, their work lost to history.

But no one believed that the "Armani suit guy" was the real Steve. They felt the actual Steve was in hiding, lying in wait for something greater as he tried to reconcile the quotidian pressures of quarterly earnings with NeXT's higher calling—to build beautiful technology that would shape the course of history.

As they waited, the developers were falling prey to the same pressure to survive. They started selling their software to whomever would pay, even if those buyers represented everything the counterculture opposed.

After the rave, Andrew's phone rang. "Come on over and show us how to use this [software]," the voice on the other end said.

The caller identified themself as a representative of the National Security Agency, located in Fort Meade, Maryland, and revealed that the agency had just purchased a $300,000 license from Andrew using the false Texas address.

Andrew had just thrown a rave with NSA money.

Feeling conflicted, he boarded a plane to NSA headquarters. A self-described hippie, and a man who believed in "invocating the divine into what is normally just business," he wasn't on board with government surveillance. But money was money.

At Fort Meade, he discovered something unexpected. The NSA agents he met were Deadheads too. They knew the music, the culture, the references. They were, in their way, his people. To him, it made the whole thing more bearable.

One day, at NeXT, a software developer named Blaine Garst received an invitation to a mysterious meeting. "I didn't know what the meeting was about," he said.

Suddenly Blaine found himself in a room with NSA analysts, trying to explain fast elliptic curve encryption—a groundbreaking cryptography method that Richard Crandall had built into NeXT's email system.

"Do you know encryption?" Blaine asked the analysts. "Do you know how elliptic encryption works?" These were supposed to be the government's cryptography experts, ostensibly there to learn about NeXT's encryption technology.

They claimed they didn't get it. Or as Blaine later concluded: "They were playing dumb, or they were dumb, or they'd already made the decision."

In reality, the men from Fort Meade weren't there to learn. And they hadn't come to buy computers either. They were on a different mission: to kill NeXT's encryption capabilities before they could spread.

At the time, traditional cryptography software was classified as munitions. If you shipped it to other countries, you could face arms trafficking charges and three to five years in prison. In 1991, a cryptographer named Phil Zimmermann had created an encryption program called Pretty Good Privacy and given it to his friends. After the software spread worldwide, a grand jury heard evidence to indict him.

Richard's software for NeXT was as advanced as Phil's. He had made a breakthrough in the software's efficiency. Elliptic curve encryption could provide the same security as traditional encryption but with much smaller keys, making it fast enough for everyday consumer use. If traditional encryption was like using a massive padlock that took forever to open and close, Richard's system offered a sleek combination lock—just as secure, but small and quick enough to use that your computer could lock and unlock email messages without skipping a beat.

Steve announced the feature at a NeXT product launch event at San Francisco's Moscone Center. "If you want to encrypt a file when you send it," Steve demonstrated to the audience "it's as easy as flipping this little lock right here." Click. Done. The system would automatically encrypt the email for each recipient. No computer science degree required.

But Steve's new friends at the NSA weren't keen on the feature. The officers did not want to be locked out of emails sent internationally.

Back in the conference room, Blaine tried to salvage something from Richard's invention. Elliptic curve technology could do two separate things, he explained: encrypt messages—locking out everyone including the NSA—or it could just provide digital signatures, proving the sender's identity without hiding its contents.

Blaine volunteered that NeXT could ship the second option, providing users with an authentication feature but avoiding the encryption option that scared the government. Since the government only regulated encryption, not authentication, this solution might also let NeXT ship the technology overseas without breaking the munitions law.

But the NSA wanted to quash the authentication feature too. And it wasn't open to discussion. NeXT executives might've pushed back but they didn't want to anger the NSA, a major customer that could pull its contracts.

Shortly after the visit, Richard left the company. He could see the writing on the wall for his pioneering encryption technology. "He went on sabbatical, went back up to Portland," Blaine remembered. "And he handed me the elliptical encryption code as he left."

NeXT's encryption features were dead. "They talked Steve out of [it]," Blaine said simply. The NSA remained a major customer.

Steve, the one-time rebel, had learned to play ball with the keepers of secrecy.

It wasn't just NeXT. In 1992, the NSA engineered a calculated compromise with the industry at large. The agency had negotiated with the Software Publishers Association (SPA), the trade group representing major software companies like NeXT and Microsoft, to create a two-tiered system.

Under the agreement, American companies could export encryption software, but only with 40-bit keys—weak enough that any serious adversary could break them. The government, meanwhile, protected its own secrets with 56-bit encryption—more than 65,000 times stronger. The upshot was that SPA members like NeXT could ship encryption globally, but only if it was weak enough for the NSA to crack.

From the NSA's perspective, this made sense. The agency needed to prevent strong encryption from reaching hostile nations or transnational criminal organizations. But the deal forced American software companies to play security theater, pretending that they were offering serious security, while everyone knew it was breakable.

Avie ran the numbers and found that if NeXT chained together a few hundred workstations, the team could crack the "secure" messages in a single day. The very machines NeXT sold could easily shred the encryption technology the government allowed them to use for export.

The Bay Area NeXT Group, an informal club of NeXT enthusiasts that assembled regularly at Stanford's Terman Engineering Center, was growing alarmed by government intrusions into the digital world.

In one April 1992 session, the group invited tech journalist Jim Warren to lay out the new threats, which extended far beyond the NSA. California's new driver's licenses embedded magnetic strips that retailers could swipe, harvesting names and addresses with every purchase. Toll roads were installing automatic vehicle identification to log every passing car. Caller ID, an invention that revealed who was calling, turned every phone call into a data point that could be sold or subpoenaed. Landlords pooled tenant histories into shared blacklists. Credit bureaus compiled permanent dossiers on consumers.

The digital surveillance state was being assembled. The group feared that their NeXT machines, with their powerful databases and networking capabilities, were the exact systems that could enable this infrastructure.

It didn't help that when Steve talked about NeXT's government contracts in public, he referred to them obliquely. As the company developed real-time collaborative software for intelligence agencies—an early precursor to Google Docs allowing multiple users to simultaneously edit the same document—he used deliberately anodyne examples to demonstrate it for the public: "Ralph has the template on his Sun. Vicky has the headline on her NeXT. Kevin has the text file on his PC."

The reality was more dramatic. Replace "Ralph" with a CIA analyst in Langley, Virginia, "Vicky" with a field officer in Moscow, and "Kevin" with a station chief in Berlin. Steve was selling spy tech as office collaboration. “It just works,” he said, dragging and dropping files across machines like magic.

An additional NeXT app called LiveWire, made by Adamation, would also allow intelligence officers to look at simulated battlefield maps, watching tanks, aircraft, and missiles move in real time. The CIA wrote a $70,000 check for a license.

In March 1992, Steve wandered the floor of the NeXTWORLD Expo, named after the magazine that hosted the event with NeXT. The Expo was NeXT’s annual trade show—the company’s chance to announce new products and rally the developer community. At the expo, Steve was “openly available to anyone who sought his ordinarily hard-gained company,” Barlow noted in the second part of his interview with Steve in *MicroTimes*. He was “amiable and engaged.”

When Steve took the stage, his two-and-a-half-hour presentation contained flashes of his old showmanship but, as Barlow wrote, “a lot more steak than sizzle.” The newly announced products were “pretty prosaic stuff”—enterprise software for financial trading, healthcare, and corporate clients.

The scene would have been unrecognizable to Ross or Dan’l Lewin, the executives who had begged Steve to embrace exactly this kind of pragmatic focus three years earlier. Steve was finally doing everything they had pleaded with him to do: Listen to customers. Talk about sustainable market segments instead of revolutionary dreams.

He had finally become the CEO they had hoped for then.

But the transformation had come too late. Steve’s pivot might have saved NeXT if he’d done it in 1988 or 1989, back when he was blowing up the IBM deal and chasing perfect control over his hardware and software rather than sustainable profit. As it stood, the markets had matured and competitors Sun and IBM had caught up. The company that might have succeeded with pragmatic focus five years earlier was now just another enterprise software vendor arriving late to a crowded party.

And the change wasn't complete. He had finally mastered both sides of the game—hardware and software. The problem was that only one side mattered anymore, and he couldn't bring himself to let the other one die.

18

ROCK BOTTOM

Steve had been chasing Peter van Cuylenburg, a British technology executive, for eighteen months. At first, Steve wanted him to run sales and marketing at NeXT, but Peter wasn't interested.

Steve wasn't going to give up. He'd learned that the best people were worth the wait. "When you meet somebody that good . . . you know you're going to be settling for second best if you compromise," he told students at MIT. "I've always found it best not to compromise and just keep chipping away."

Peter was a proven turnaround artist. He had run Texas Instruments' European office, then revived failing telecommunications firm Mercury Communications, building it from a $400 million to a $2 billion company in two years.

In March 1992, Steve finally got his man, hiring him as NeXT's chief operating officer. This allowed Steve to follow through on his promise to Canon three years after the fact: that he would hire an operations executive to bring order to his highly personalized company.

Employees came to know their new colleague by the initials PvC.

In an unusual arrangement, Steve and PvC shared a newly created Office of the President at NeXT, formally splitting day-to-day management duties between them, a degree of power sharing rarely seen in Silicon Valley companies. Steve gave PvC operational authority equal to his own, including a board seat.

Some saw echoes of the John Sculley incident.

PvC believed in business process as the remedy for all ills. NeXT executives recounted that he devoted himself to keeping Steve in check, armed with spreadsheets and McKinsey-style slide decks. He took up the mantle of enforcing discipline at the company and slashing the number of vice presidents.

Behind the scenes, the team found him two-faced and obsequious.

PvC arrived at NeXT in a BMW 850i, which was the hot executive car of the early 1990s, Mike recounted. Within weeks, he'd traded it for a Porsche—just like Steve's car.

"I liked that 850," Mike said to him one day. "What happened?"

"Porsche, man," PvC replied. "You know, Steve."

To Steve's face, PvC acted the part of a perfect president, aligned in all things. Behind his back, PvC derided him as a madman, Mike said.

Mike didn't appreciate the shtick. "This guy Peter van Cuylenburg is a slimeball," he told Steve. "He trashes you behind your back. He's a bad guy, and we all hate him."

Steve's face went cold. "No, he's a good guy," he said. "You're wrong."

Around the same time, Steve made another big hire. Feeling certain that Rich, his VP of engineering, would quit soon because he was getting burned out, he hired Jon Rubinstein as backup. Jon, an HP veteran, had just watched his graphics supercomputer start-up Ardent fail spectacularly despite its brilliant technology.

Jon was awake to the game Steve was playing. On paper, Jon would report to Rich, who was still running engineering. But everyone understood the real arrangement. As Jon recalled, "Steve was about to undermine Rich."

When Jon met with Rich, they didn't pretend otherwise. Both men knew Steve's pattern: bring in a successor, undermine the incumbent, wait for them to quit. The two struck a pragmatic deal in which Jon agreed to keep Rich informed of whatever Steve was planning behind the scenes.

Though nominally reporting to Rich, Jon led the team developing NeXT's new flagship computer, the NeXT RISC Workstation (NRW, for short). It was positioned to save the company's hardware future. Mike called it "an absolute masterpiece" that NeXT hoped would run at "50 or 100 megahertz—like lightning." In 1992, when most high-end workstations topped out at 40 megahertz and even premium personal computers struggled to reach 66 megahertz, those speeds represented a huge leap forward.

The NRW would employ a clever strategy. As Mike put it, NeXT would be "a fast follower to Apple on chip decisions." Like a cyclist drafting behind the leader, NeXT would let Apple do the heavy lifting—selecting cutting-edge chips—and then the leaner NeXT would sprint past at the last moment, beating Apple to market with an NRW using the latest chip.

Motorola's newest chip—the 88110—offered NeXT its best shot yet. Designed to let two processors share the same workload, it promised exactly the kind of power NeXT's multitasking software was built to harness. By the end of 1992, the company planned to "literally leapfrog over everyone" in performance, Mike recalled.

Then Motorola executives called with news.

They were joining forces with IBM and Apple to create PowerPC—a new family of processors that would all speak the same language, letting software run across IBM servers, Apple computers, and Motorola systems. Instead of three companies making three different processors, they'd pool their resources to beat Intel. It was great for the industry, but death for NeXT's hardware strategy.

The 88110 chip NeXT had bet everything on? Dead before it could ship. Motorola would fulfill existing orders, then cut NeXT off altogether. Mike summed up Motorola's message: "Fuck you and this new chip." Motorola had supplied every processor NeXT had ever used starting with the Cube. Now NeXT was left with a computer it had spent months building on top of a chip that it couldn't use.

The full horror of the situation hit Mike as he listened to the Motorola call. This maneuver was about more than chips; it was about power. IBM, Motorola, and Apple controlled the processors, the operating systems, and the manufacturing. But NeXT? The company was a mouse in a field of giants. "We had no leverage," Mike said. "We were completely at their mercy. And they had no mercy."

The moment crystallized eight years of strategic mistakes. Steve had been offered every path to scale: IBM's partnership that could have put NeXT on millions of desktops, Ross Perot's connections throughout the federal government, distribution deals that could have moved them beyond boutique sales. Each time, Steve had walked away, betting that his superior technology would create its own demand, that if he built something perfect enough, the world would beat down a path to his door.

Instead, his competitors' ecosystems grew massive while NeXT stood still. Apple's user base now reached the millions, deepening its supplier relationships. IBM's enterprise dominance had solidified. Microsoft captured the PC revolution and had spent eight years building an unshakeable foundation of developers, users, and hardware partners.

These companies could dictate terms to chipmakers like Motorola because they commanded ecosystems that had grown exponentially during the years Steve spent perfecting his platform. If NeXT had been bigger, it would have been setting industry standards instead of being crushed by them. But everyone could see NeXT was failing, and no one wanted to tie their future to a sinking ship.

"This is the single most important thing that ever happened to NeXT," Mike said.

Steve promised that he would never again let himself be dependent on other companies' road maps. He kept his word, spending $278 million to buy chipmaker P.A. Semi in 2008 after he returned to lead Apple. The purchase would allow Apple to design its own processors for the iPhone and iPad—and eventually create Apple silicon chips to power Macs. The lesson of NeXT's dependence on Motorola and other suppliers had stuck.

"The NeXT NRW thing was a great product," Jon told the Computer History Museum. "It would have been a very successful product, but we never got a chance to come to market."

The team knew it was time to make a radical change—one that Steve had resisted with all his might. It was time to port NeXTSTEP to run on Intel 486 chips.

This wasn't a mere pivot. The 486 and successive Intel chips would power most of the world's PCs, potentially giving NeXT access to millions of machines versus the few thousand workstations that NeXT had ever sold. It would give everyone buying PCs from IBM, HP, Compaq, and the other manufacturers the option of running NeXTSTEP.

It would finally turn NeXT into a software company, competing directly with Microsoft and Windows.

Andy Grove himself had helped bring about the decision. Many months earlier, he stood before NeXT's leaders and told them that porting to Intel was do-or-die. "Steve's a dear friend of mine," he said, "and I'm just gonna tell you guys, you're not gonna make it if you don't run on Intel chips."

Andy's logic was based on simple market math. Without Intel's massive installed base, NeXT wouldn't be able to attract the software developers the company so desperately needed. Developers made software for platforms with many users, and users bought computers that had the best software. More users meant more software sales, which meant more developers creating apps, which meant more reasons to buy Intel-based PCs, feeding Intel's dominance.

Software developer William Parkhurst begged Steve to heed Andy's warning. But Steve had staked everything on beautiful black cubes with custom chips—not beige boxes running on commodity processors. Porting NeXTSTEP to Intel would involve the dirtiest word he knew: compromise. And it would be tantamount to admitting the failure of his grand hardware vision.

William knew the problem by heart now. NeXT had burned through its tiny pool of maverick customers who could ignore corporate procurement rules. Many companies loved NeXTSTEP but refused to bet their business on NeXT's proprietary machines. Their purchasing departments demanded the ability to buy computers from multiple vendors—Dell, Compaq, IBM. As long as NeXTSTEP was chained to NeXT hardware, the software would remain a beautiful prisoner.

The 486 project would break those chains. And after a year of lobbying, Steve finally gave in to William. They would call the project NeXTSTEP 486. But, he added, "I can't finance it. You have to go arrange your own financing."

So William flew to Intel and pitched Andy. Andy listened, calculated, and cut a check. He did so not because of his belief in NeXT or his loyalty to Steve. He needed what amounted to a bargaining chip against Microsoft.

By the early 1990s, Microsoft was becoming dangerously powerful.

It was so dominant in software that it could dictate terms to its hardware partners. Intel made the chips, but Microsoft controlled what ran on them. If Microsoft ever decided to favor a different chip architecture, or worse, develop its own processors, Intel could find itself cut out of the most lucrative computing market.

As William understood it, Andy wanted "a foil against Microsoft"—something else to wave around in negotiations. Having NeXT as an alternative operating system meant Andy could walk into those Redmond meetings with a little more swagger. It was a humbling position for NeXT. Steve was reduced to being Intel's insurance policy.

It was going to take a lot of work to port NeXTSTEP. When NeXT controlled its own hardware, every component was chosen to work perfectly with the operating system. Now William's team had to make its elegant software work with whatever graphics card Dell shipped that month, whatever disk drive Compaq chose for cost reasons. That meant writing thousands of lines of translation code—or drivers—for each component.

When NeXT's hardware team heard about the Intel deal, they were shattered. It meant abandoning the iconic machines they had poured their hearts into.

"What the fuck, William," one engineer exploded. "We built this beautiful hardware for you."

By later in 1992, Steve claimed it had been the plan all along, "the strategic model that we've always had: We're a software company that happens to make great hardware," he told *NeXTWORLD*. Steve claimed it was evidence of an ascendant NeXT. Onstage at COMDEX 1992, the computer industry's largest trade show, he called his company "the only serious challenge to Microsoft."

In reality, the switch to Intel meant bending the knee to Bill Gates, who'd long argued that closed systems would always lose to open ones.

Now Steve was listening to his customers and accepting their help. "And boy, we need it, so that's good," he told an audience at MIT.

In June 1992, Avie was home at his apartment when he got a call from Steve. He was nearly in tears, Avie recounted to the Computer History Museum.

"You're not going to believe this," Steve said. "Bud is leaving."

"Really? Where's he going?" Avie asked.

"You're not going to believe this," Steve said again. "He's going to Sun."

For Bud, the new job simply made sense. He had looked carefully at the increasingly competitive PC market. "I felt like NeXT was not going to be able to compete," he said.

New manufacturers like Compaq and Dell were selling cheaper options and had plunged the industry into a price war. In a lower-margin environment, Bud didn't like NeXT's prospects. He wanted to build software that would scale, that people would actually use. As Sun's VP for software, he would be able to build apps "and get them on an awful lot of desktops," he said.

On a Sunday night, Bud had called Steve to deliver the news. "He tried to talk me out of it," Bud said. "But I was firm."

When he went into NeXT that Monday morning, Steve had deprogrammed his key card.

Bud's decision to defect to a competitor deeply hurt Steve, and it came at the worst possible time for NeXT. Without Bud to lead NeXT's software division, Steve had no choice but to delay the NeXTSTEP 486 release by almost a year—all while Microsoft Windows ate up vast market share.

Bud was indispensable, having built the software division from the ground up.

Steve angrily undercut Bud in public, just as he had tried to do with Dan'l. He told the Associated Press that senior executives had declared a "no confidence" vote in Bud a few months earlier. Bud later said he didn't remember a "vote." Steve "dissed me in the press," Bud recalled.

Six months later, Steve's anger had cooled. As Bud would put it, they were "back on reasonable terms." Bud was now at Sun, and Sun had something Steve needed: powerful workstations that could run NeXTSTEP.

In Silicon Valley, rifts have an expiration date when there are deals to be made.

Steve's desperation was growing. For months, the financial reality had been closing in on him, but he had refused to face the truth that he was running out of money. He was bleeding money on two fronts—pouring his personal fortune into both NeXT and Pixar. When Steve recruited an Intel executive named Marcel Gani as the NeXT CFO earlier that year, Steve had called him at 2:00 a.m. and told him that he wouldn't reveal his accounting books because he wanted to hire "risk-takers." Steve insisted that everything was fine because NeXT had the backing of Intel. Marcel had believed him.

Then Marcel dove into the books and discovered the devastating truth. NeXT was effectively bankrupt. Steve had been living in a financial fantasy. Marcel soon quit.

In December 1992, Steve picked up the phone and called Canon for what Jon called a "cram-down." The Japanese company had already poured over $140 million into NeXT and remained convinced they could succeed in the computer business.

"If you don't deposit another check for $20 million by Monday," Steve told them, "I'm going to shut the doors." Canon had the weekend to decide.

It wasn't a bluff. Steve meant it literally. He would close NeXT's doors if Canon didn't wire the money. The company had reached the point where survival was measured in days, not weeks.

The two companies came to hastily negotiated terms. In exchange for $20 million, Canon would purchase NeXT's hardware division—the factory, the designs, the engineering processes. Canon believed it could build and sell the computers. "Are you sure?" Jon had asked them. "Yes, we're sure," said an executive.

Jon called himself "the bagman," working to load NeXT's debt onto the hardware division Canon was buying. "My goal was to take as much of the Canon debt as possible and roll it into the hardware division, so the software division could keep going and not have the large debt on the books," Jon recalled. Canon agreed.

In exchange, NeXT would keep the cash—enough runway to survive—and hold on to its software operation. After a weekend of chaos in Tokyo, $20 million appeared in NeXT's account on Monday morning.

Steve was despondent about breaking up the company. "Everyone here can leave except me," he said at a meeting of the remaining NeXT executives. And many did leave, assuming that NeXT would go bankrupt once the hardware business collapsed.

On January 9, 1993, Rich handed in his resignation letter. "It gets a little tiring to get yelled at so much," Rich recounted. That left George Crow and Steve as NeXT's last two remaining cofounders. Over the following few months, Mike and Todd followed Rich out the door.

The chaos at NeXT had become so apparent that even Canon executives were confused about who was actually in charge. Canon called Jon with an extraordinary question: Who should they trust—PvC or Steve?

PvC plotted his exit almost a year after joining. But according to Jon, he didn't go quietly. In a move that eerily echoed John Sculley's coup eight years prior, PvC allegedly tried to sell Steve's company out from under him.

PvC called Scott McNealy, the Sun CEO, with a proposition: Buy NeXT, fire Steve, and install him as the new leader. A clean decapitation.

Jon was in the room with Steve when he saw the betrayal unravel firsthand. "McNealy called Steve," he recalled. "[Scott] goes, 'Hey Steve, they just tried to sell me your company. What do you think?'"

Mike could never forget the aftermath: "Steve just lost his shit. He was *betrayed*."

Sun didn't want any part of a deal. In fact, Scott barely considered NeXT worth his attention. He'd only called Steve as a courtesy, perhaps for the kick of ratting out a conspirator.

PvC has disputed this version of events. In his telling, Scott approached him about a potential partnership. "I brokered a meeting with him and Steve at Steve's home in Palo Alto," PvC wrote. "The three of us met there and discussed alternatives, but Scott and Steve did not agree on possible approaches. There was not, at any time, a discussion about me replacing Steve as CEO."

By March 1993, PvC had left the company too.

Those who worked closest to Steve noticed something changing, though the process looked anything but graceful. The pattern that had defined him for years was finally breaking apart, the wild emotional swings that colleagues had learned to brace for. *Up, down, up, down,* they recounted.

But now the crashes seemed to hurt more, and the highs couldn't lift him as high. Each betrayal left him rawer than the last.

Dan'l Lewin, who had mended fences with Steve after their falling out, pointed to a passage in Ernest Hemingway's novel *The Sun Also Rises* that captured what everyone was witnessing:

"How did you go bankrupt?" asked one character, Bill Gorton.

"Two ways," explained another, Mike Campbell. "Gradually, then suddenly."

Steve's transformation was following the same excruciating arc. The powerful energy that used to sustain him for days would collapse into periods of hollow exhaustion.

Friends watched him struggle with something he'd never had to face before: the possibility that intensity alone might not be enough. The financial terror brought him closer to losing everything he'd built. The personal betrayals cut deeper because he'd allowed himself to trust people who then walked away.

Steve was being forced to find something he'd never needed before: a center that could hold when passion failed, when vision wasn't enough, when everything around him collapsed. Learning to live without the extremes that had defined him was perhaps the most painful education of his life.

The press smelled blood.

"They always knew it before it broke," said Allison Thomas, who ran the public relations firm that represented NeXT, Allison Thomas Associates. "They spread [the news of NeXT's hardware collapse] like wildfire."

The press was primed for a negative story. They no longer trusted Steve and were fed up with his outlandish claims. Soon, journalists were calling about rumors of imminent firings.

In *Fortune*, Alan Deutschman wrote, "Sometimes it's hard to tell whether Steve Jobs is a snake-oil salesman or a bona fide visionary, a promoter who got lucky or the epitome of the intrepid entrepreneur . . . Jobs' dream of building another great computer manufacturer like Apple . . . is dead, dead, dead."

Then, in February 1993, Allison's team drafted a confidential press release announcing the final end of the hardware business. "NeXT to Become Software Company" read the release's headline.

Before the official announcement, someone in Allison's office accidentally left a copy of the confidential press release on their fax machine. Someone discovered the document and leaked it to the press. "It was a catastrophe and really unfortunate," Allison said.

That Tuesday, February 9, 1993, NeXT employees opened *The Wall Street Journal* and tuned to the local radio station, only to hear the devastating news that they were being fired. "Black Tuesday" is how the ignominious day became known.

A day later, Steve gathered the hardware employees in a presentation room and confirmed the reports. NeXT would be laying off 280 of its 530 employees, he told them, almost the entire hardware division. It would close the unprofitable Fremont factory and sell whatever remained of the hardware division to Canon. "We all cried together," said Nina Serpiello, an art and production manager. "It was like having a funeral."

In the wake of the sale, George, the head of analog engineering, threw in the towel too. "I just didn't think Canon knew how to sell computers," he later explained. His departure didn't surprise anyone. His rare analog expertise, which engineers called a "black art" because it wasn't a common specialty, guaranteed work anywhere. This confidence had defined his relationship with Steve from the start, where unlike others, George had felt comfortable going toe-to-toe with him.

George's departure left Steve the sole cofounder remaining. The band of conspirators was no more.

NeXT's hardware division had built computers so gorgeous that they ended up as sculptures of industrial art. The magnesium cube is still studied at design schools today. NeXT machines are part of the collections of the Smithsonian's National Museum of American History, the Computer History Museum in Mountain View, California, and the Science Museum in London. In 2024, Christie's, the prestigious fine art house, auctioned a Cube for more than $20,000. Computers from NeXT's beige-box competitors ended up in landfills.

NeXT's hardware failure came down to timing. The company's features were too early to market—shipping optical discs before storage was cheap and reliable, employing object-oriented programming before developers embraced it, creating megapixel displays when everyone else made do with small, blurry screens.

Meanwhile the company's hardware strategy itself was too late. The computer industry had fundamentally shifted while NeXT was stuck endlessly perfecting its Cube. By the early 1990s, corporate America wanted commodity hardware they could buy from multiple suppliers, not elegant sculptures from a single vendor. The age of proprietary computer architectures was ending, killed by Microsoft's software dominance and the rise of interchangeable PC clones. NeXT was trying to win a hardware war that was already over.

"We made a really great computer," Steve later told *Fresh Air.* "But the world had changed enough to where the door to establish a new hardware company really had closed even before we started the company. We just didn't know that at the time."

Steve had been trying to recreate past glories at Apple when the rest of the world had moved on. He took that lesson to heart: When the world changes, you have to change with it.

Almost a month after the hardware division closed, Steve's adoptive father, Paul Reinhold Jobs, died at seventy years old, on March 5, 1993.

Steve invited his old friend Dan'l to the burial, which took place at Alta Mesa Memorial Park. A few mourners circled the grave: Steve and Laurene and their infant son, Reed; Marilyn, Paul's second wife, and her daughter and son-in-law; Dan'l and his wife, Susan; and the cemetery workers preparing to lower the casket.

Susan looked after Reed, who, at eighteen months, had just learned to walk. He toddled among the headstones.

Dan'l knew Paul from NeXT company picnics. He was a salt-of-the-earth machinist, the kind of guy who got along with everyone. Dan'l remembered one gathering where he'd walked over, put his arm around Paul, and said quietly, "Hey Paul, if friends can't tell you, who can? Your zipper's down."

Now Paul would be buried beside Clara, who had died almost seven years earlier.

Steve spoke briefly about his father. He felt lucky to have been his son—in the family's Los Altos garage, Steve had watched Paul carefully sand the backs of cabinets and fence posts, learning the lesson that the parts of a product you can't see should be as beautiful as the parts you can. Paul had taught Steve how to work with his hands, to respect craftsmanship, to never cut corners even when no one would look.

Steve, the man who commanded audiences of thousands, stood before a handful of mourners, saying goodbye to the mechanic who'd raised him.

19

BURNED

The death of the hardware division ricocheted across the NeXT community. On Black Tuesday, as news of NeXT's hardware shutdown had already leaked to the press, the company's warehouse shipped a final batch of computers to dealers across the country.

Eric Bentley, who ran a small Oklahoma firm called Computronics Consultants, had spent the previous year courting NeXT to become an authorized dealer. He'd paid for special NeXT training and invested another $100,000 preparing for what looked like his company's big break. Just four months before NeXT shuttered its hardware division, he'd landed a $275,000 contract with the Tulsa Police Department for NeXT computers—massive money for a small consultancy. NeXT had even endorsed his performance bond, vouching that he'd deliver.

At precisely the same time Eric had been investing in selling NeXT computers, NeXT executives had begun planning to wind down the company's hardware business, which one leader referred to as an "Apocalypse Now scenario" in a November 1992 email.

The collapse left Eric stuck. The Tulsa Police Department, discovering they'd bought into a dead platform, abandoned the deal. Eric was left with computers no one wanted. The final insult came in the mail in the form of a $156,000 invoice from NeXT for the discontinued hardware.

Eric sued for fraud—NeXT had known since at least November that the hardware was going to be discontinued yet kept shipping equipment until the day before the announcement.

NeXT countersued for the six figures that Eric owed for the final shipment. Despite the fact that the industry standard was to provide sixty to ninety days' notice before discontinuing products, NeXT's dealer contract didn't require any.

The federal court sided with NeXT and Eric was ordered to pay for the computers that had ruined his business.

Other clients and distributors dragged NeXT into court as well, accusing Steve of deception, fraud, and breach of contract. NeXT's channel-stuffing scheme had left everyone confused about who actually owned what. Distributors had taken machines on credit; now they demanded NeXT take back the unsold inventory.

Steve was unmoved. His position: Once distributors accepted shipment and signed the credit terms, the machines were theirs. The fact that NeXT had pressured them to take fifty machines when they needed four? The fact that European sales heads had allegedly inflated orders to hit targets? Not his problem.

Accessory manufacturer Software Logistics Corporation had bet the factory on Steve. It had retooled its entire operation with expensive custom molds and specialized assembly lines to make NeXT's sleek black keyboards and mice. When NeXT killed its hardware division, it walked away from $1.1 million in peripherals that Software Logistics had already built.

When Software Logistics demanded payment, NeXT offered reassurance. "We have $20 million in the bank," an executive told the company. The same week, *The Wall Street Journal* reported that NeXT was nearly broke. After not receiving payment, Software Logistics sued NeXT in May 1993. The judge ordered NeXT to pay up.

Meanwhile, Steve's developer community—the one he had fought so hard to cultivate—began eating itself alive. By 1993, half the indie software companies building for NeXT had gone out of business, according to historian Hansen Hsu. The market simply wasn't growing as fast as they had hoped.

Inside the company, some disgruntled employees even turned to looting. The day the hardware division shuttered, someone went to the Fremont factory, opened up the metal office supply cabinet where DRAM chips were stored, and took them all, probably to hawk the valuable chips on the open market. The alleged thief was never caught.

Other employees simply walked off with Cubes.

Office phone lines lit up with angry customers. Universities that had just spent hundreds of thousands of dollars on computer labs found themselves with what marketing director Ron Weissman called "dead-ended boat anchors"—machines that still worked but had no future. His academic computing colleagues called him personally: "What the hell did you guys just do?" they asked.

NeXT scrambled to contract third-party support providers to keep the abandoned machines running for three to four years, which would give universities enough time to depreciate their investments and plan replacements. But customers knew this was really just life support. The Cubes would get repairs and maintenance, but no upgrades.

On May 25, Steve took the stage at San Francisco's Moscone Center in his somber gray suit to unveil his next round of plans for NeXTSTEP. Filling the audience: the customers he'd just abandoned.

He declared that "the transition is officially over . . . we are now, as of today, a software company!" Later, he unveiled a company name change, rebranding from NeXT Computer to NeXT Software.

He demonstrated NeXTSTEP running on Compaq and Dell machines that cost $795—a fraction of the price of the discontinued Cubes. Then he did the unthinkable. He demonstrated Bill Gates's Microsoft Excel running inside NeXTSTEP emulation software.

Then he showed how you could build a custom app on a Compaq computer, dragging and dropping the same object technology these customers had spent an exorbitant amount to access on their Cubes and NeXTstations. Many felt resentful and upset.

Then the finale. "I thought this might inspire you as you prepare for your upcoming battle against Microsoft," he said, cuing up the climax scene from *Star Wars: A New Hope*. In it, Luke Skywalker (representing NeXT) fires two proton torpedoes from his X-wing to destroy the Death Star (Microsoft).

As it exploded on screen, audience members checked their watches.

John Perry Barlow hosted Steve's celebrity roast at the NeXT convention dinner. Some wondered if the roast would be in good humor—Barlow was about to publish a devastating column for *NeXTWORLD* calling Steve "a genuinely tragic figure" with epic levels of hubris. He'd skewer Steve's management style, saying he created dysfunctional families filled with people too dependent on his approval to tell him when he was wrong.

"Roasts are usually meted out to people who are doing well, but the somewhat hollow quality of this roast might actually have been the nadir of Steve's career," Barlow later wrote. "My roast of him consisted mainly of gallows humor about the state of the company."

Steve wasn't at his own roast, contrary to custom. The next day, Steve's wife, Laurene, confronted Barlow on the conference floor. "Steve is not going to be happy to hear you said that," she said.

"I don't care whether he's happy or not," Barlow replied.

Despite his words, Barlow later admitted that he did care what Steve thought. But Steve never confronted him about the roast.

Apple executives picked up the first issue of the tech newsletter *The Future Image Report*, which explored the lessons from NeXT's hardware collapse. The publisher, Alex Gerard, judged NeXT to be "all over the place."

Though the jettisoned hardware was top-notch, it hadn't connected with customers. Even the company's nascent software pivot looked doomed to failure—Alex's research determined that it was coming too late. "Not falling prey to a commodity market will require exactly what NeXT took too long to acquire: Clear knowledge of customers, and a single-minded focus on satisfying their needs," the report said.

Apple, meanwhile, had drifted into a fog of its own. The company had squandered its dominant position, going from $1 billion to $8 billion in revenue and spending its newfound cash developing glamorous innovations with no practical use. Meanwhile its product line had become a mess of divergent offerings. In 1993 alone, the company released more than seventy products.

Apple poured hundreds of millions into its Advanced Technology Group, founded under John Sculley, where luminaries like Alan Kay—the man who had first inspired Steve at Xerox PARC—dreamed up futuristic devices. Engineers worked eighteen-hour days on John's pet project, the Newton personal digital assistant, which was stuck in development for five years. In December 1992, a Newton programmer named Ko Isono, exhausted from trying to fix the faulty touchscreen, killed himself.

John promised the device would transform how people worked—recognizing your handwriting, adapting to your writing style, and helping you organize your notes and ideas as easily as with a pencil and paper. The reality fell far short, and the Newton flopped.

So did the company's new $3,400 PowerBook. Apple launched an advertising blitz called "The Hard Way / The Easy Way," trying to convince buyers that the competing computer notebooks were ergonomic nightmares with unreadable screens while the PowerBook offered the elegant solution. But customers weren't buying it.

Instead of managing Apple's problems, John jetted off to Washington, DC, telling his colleagues he was seeking a political appointment. He would even step out of board meetings to take calls, telling directors the White House was on the line.

As John focused on his future, Apple's present crumbled. In June 1993, the board called John into a meeting and forced him to resign. A few days later, the company announced a $188 million quarterly loss and 2,500 layoffs, amounting to 15 percent of the workforce.

John spent the next fifteen years coping with his failure. "I wish I had reached back to Steve and told him, 'I want to help you come back to Apple,'" he told *CNN Money*.

Steve's verdict on John was less generous. "What can I say?" he told interviewer Robert X. Cringely. "I hired the wrong guy."

He had watched from exile as John turned Apple into everything he despised: a bloated bureaucracy that confused activity with achievement, releasing more than seventy products while neglecting to consider what would make any one of them truly great.

"John Sculley got a very serious disease," Steve continued. "It's the disease of thinking that a really great idea is 90 percent of the work."

The staff of *NeXTWORLD* magazine decided to mark the occasion of NeXT's hardware death with a Cube funeral pyre. Senior Technology

Editor Simson Garfinkel had been toying with the idea of burning the Cube and photographing it for two years, when he'd first asked NeXT for an empty chassis to burn.

On a Tuesday morning in spring 1993, Simson picked up Sally Chew, *NeXTWORLD*'s managing editor, at the train station. Together they drove to Lawrence Livermore National Laboratory, a weapons facility outside San Francisco. Somehow, Simson had convinced the Department of Energy to let him use its weapons lab to destroy the Cube after submitting safety data on its black matte paint.

Arriving at the laboratory, they were guided through the enormous complex to the burn cell at Site 300: a twenty-by-thirty-foot brick-and-steel box with sophisticated ventilation and two large metal doors. The place smelled like a campsite the morning after a bonfire. Next to it were sheds that scientists used to simulate the inside of a nuclear reactor.

A government pyrotechnician with a long reddish beard suited up with fireproof pants, coat, and helmet, squeezed into a respirator, and climbed into the burn cell with a gas torch. The photographers and magazine staff watched from outside through the open metal doors. The pyrotechnician directed the torch at the black magnesium cube, waiting for it to ignite. But it remained pristine.

Steve had stymied them by choosing an exotic magnesium alloy for the Cube with a higher ignition point than the torches could reach.

"This is so NeXT," Simson told Sally.

The pyrotechnician, eyes gleaming, wheeled out a more powerful torch and put on his protective mask. This one—hot enough to cut through steel—only made the metal start to droop like melting wax.

Finally, they wheeled in a natural gas burner fed by a three-inch pipe and placed the Cube on top like an altar sacrifice. Before lighting it, Simson scattered magnesium shavings inside the Cube to make it burn more brilliantly. Finally—*finally*—the metal began to glow. The pooling magnesium burst into white flames.

That's when Simson decided to use the backup Cube he'd brought in case something went wrong. He grabbed it from his car and the pyrotechnician placed it on top of the burning wreckage. The fire leapt even higher, white and blinding. They had finally managed to destroy the indestructible machine.

The technician grabbed a hose and doused the fire with quick spurts of water, which instantly turned to steam. Thick clouds of white smoke covered everyone in fine white powder from the burned magnesium. It looked like fallout from a nuclear blast.

Simson laughed hysterically. He believed they had recapitulated NeXT's entire experience as a hardware manufacturer in four hours: grand ambitions, technical perfection, and ultimate consumption in a pit of flames. The resulting story, titled "Pyromania!," ran in *NeXTWORLD*'s June/July 1993 issue.

By then, *NeXTWORLD*'s relationship with Steve was turning to ash as well. *NeXTWORLD*'s publisher, the International Data Group, had been bleeding money on the magazine since its founding in 1991, and Steve wasn't willing to step in to save it.

When president Gordon Haight called Steve in November 1993 about overdue payments, Steve allegedly threatened to put *NeXTWORLD* out of business and start his own magazine.

Then Steve kicked the magazine out of its own annual expo at the Moscone Center and changed the event's name from the NeXTWORLD Expo to NeXTSTEP Expo. The magazine had been collecting a fifth of the expo's profits—its one reliable revenue stream. The International Data Group responded by suing Steve for racketeering under the Racketeer Influenced and Corrupt Organizations Act, known as RICO, the statute prosecutors use to take down mob bosses.

To win its case, International Data Group had to prove that Steve ran an ongoing criminal enterprise. Their evidence? Press releases and emails about a computer conference. The lawyers argued that Steve had perpetrated an elaborate bait and switch: Companies had paid good money for booths at NeXTWORLD Expo. Steve pocketed their checks, renamed the event NeXTSTEP Expo, kicked out the magazine, then told the confused exhibitors their contracts still stood—for an entirely different show that no longer included the magazine. The International Data Group submitted as evidence every email and press release about the event.

But neither party could produce the one document that mattered: a signed contract for the profit-sharing arrangement. International Data Group claimed that NeXT mysteriously couldn't locate its copy. NeXT simply denied the agreement ever existed.

The publisher's case imploded. In April 1994, *NeXTWORLD* ran its final issue.

To mark this moment, Simson sent an invitation: "You are PERSONALLY invited to a WAKE for NeXTWORLD Magazine, to mourn the passing of our esteemed journal into the annals of computer history." Attire: Black. Refreshments: sushi, hard cider, and "of course, KOOL-AIDE [*sic*]." Charitable donations should go to "Steve Jobs' Home For Little Runaways."

On the evening of April 9, 1994, the evangelists gathered to mourn, raising their Kool-Aid glasses to the prophet who'd abandoned them.

PART THREE

20

EATING CROW

The operating system wars were beginning—Sun on one side, Microsoft on the other. Everyone waited for the first shot to be fired.

Sun expected Microsoft, through Windows NT—its operating system for corporate enterprises—to lay siege to its server business. Bill Gates had also promised a new operating system code-named Cairo, which promised to be an object-oriented paradise where developers would build tomorrow's software using Microsoft tools, for Microsoft systems.

Sun couldn't be caught unarmed. It needed its own object weapons to stand a chance. To get them, it briefly considered acquiring NeXT. But it ultimately chose the cheaper option: licensing NeXT's software.

In the $10 million deal that emerged, Sun would work together with NeXT to develop a new program called OpenStep. OpenStep would bottle some of NeXT's magic, making NeXT's revolutionary development tools available to programmers working on different computers. Now developers could write software once and have it run on Sun workstations, IBM machines, or NeXT hardware—instead of being confined to NeXT platforms only.

At the press conference to announce the deal, Ed Zander, the president of Sun's software subsidiary SunSoft, stood at the podium scanning the room for Steve and Sun CEO Scott McNealy.

"If I could find these two guys, I can get going," he said to the assembled press. "Maybe they're calling the deal off, I don't know. Or they're into a fight back there."

Nervous laughter rippled through the room. Everyone knew about Steve and Scott's long-running rivalry. "Sun said they'd rather stick needles in their eyes than help us do this. That's a quote," Steve had once said about his early attempts to partner with Sun.

When the pair finally emerged, Ed announced: "Ladies and gentlemen, let me welcome the Yasser and Yitzhak of Silicon Valley"—two and a half months earlier, Yasser Arafat and Yitzhak Rabin had signed the Oslo Accords on the White House lawn. The crowd laughed nervously.

Steve spoke first. "We believe this industry needs an alternative to Microsoft," he said, projecting a vision of unity.

Scott, too, never hid his contempt for Microsoft. He had recently called the company "the evil empire in the Pacific Northwest" in a video for developers. Now, on the podium, he joked that if Sun failed it might just "become the Safeway for Microsoft diskettes."

Microsoft wasn't Scott's only target. He couldn't resist taking subtle potshots at NeXT's failed hardware, despite their new partnership. "We're doing [NeXTSTEP on SPARC workstations] pure and simple because SPARC is the best price performance platform out there in the world, and we think that's the best way to accelerate the NeXTSTEP environment." SPARC was Sun's hardware platform. By touting it, Scott was also implicitly reminding everyone of NeXT's hardware failure.

Then, catching himself: "Hope that wasn't disagreeing too much. Is that okay? We're kind of on our honeymoon right now."

The audience laughed. Even standing together as partners, Scott had to let everyone know: Steve Jobs needed Sun. Sun didn't need Steve Jobs.

But Steve still occupied his own universe. A few months later, at the NeXT East Coast Developer Conference, Steve stood before his dwindling ranks of developers and declared: "As many of you know, we announced a relationship with Sun recently where they are fundamentally betting their company on NeXTSTEP."

He played down the fact that Sun was also pursuing half a dozen other strategies—other Unix standards and Windows compatibility, as well as its own competing technologies. Far from betting the company on Steve's software, Sun was spreading its bets across the table.

NeXT's Redwood City offices were quieter now. The hardware engineers had gone. The remaining team had a quiet determination, recognizing that NeXT's survival as an enterprise software company would hinge on spreadsheets, not inspiration.

Heading up the charge: Dominique Trempont, NeXT's new CFO and the guy people called when the spreadsheets were bleeding. He had spent more than thirteen years at Raychem, the $2 billion materials science giant, turning $15 million losses into $75 million profits for its electronics group in a year and a half. Now Steve needed him.

His recruitment had started on a quiet Sunday morning. Dominique was repainting his living room, and his wife picked up the phone.

"This is Steve Jobs," the caller announced.

"Yes, and I'm the Queen of England," she replied.

Dominique had first read about Steve years earlier in *Fortune* magazine while he was an MBA student at INSEAD, France's elite business school. Something about Apple's culture had spoken to the Belgian-born executive, pulling him from France to Silicon Valley in the 1980s, though he'd never worked for Apple itself.

When the two finally met, their one-hour meeting stretched to seven. They walked Palo Alto's streets as Steve evangelized NeXT's technology—the multimedia experience, the drag-and-drop interface that made Microsoft look prehistoric. They talked about software architecture. Dominique discussed his photography hobby, Steve brought up his obsession with design.

Steve also told Dominique about NeXT's disconnect. The company had built tomorrow's technology for customers who didn't know they needed it yet—at a price they couldn't afford. "Basically, at the time, NeXT was what you see on the Mac today," Dominique reflected, "with the multimedia experience, drag and drop."

At hour seven, Steve made his move. "I want to make you an offer," he said.

"I'm not ready for that," Dominique replied. "I need to do my homework . . . Six weeks. I want to meet your customers, your engineers, your businesspeople. And I want to talk to people who've worked with you."

Dominique knew about NeXT's troubles—the negative press, its poor financial health—and wanted to evaluate the company's potential for himself. After six weeks of due diligence, he reached a conclusion. "With the right openness, this company could really take off like a rocket," he said.

Steve needed Dominique so badly that when Dominique became hospitalized with kidney stones, Steve and NeXT's VP of sales and marketing, Warren Weiss, showed up at his bedside with an employment contract. Laurene also dropped off a "basket of goodies and a book, *The English Patient*," Dominique recounted. "I later joked that it took a good dose of morphine for me to sign on."

As CFO, Dominique imposed discipline. "[Dominique] was a great steadying force for Steve," Warren said. He developed a top ten process that Steve immediately embraced. Unlike the reactive Deep Shit List, which catalogued unfolding crises, the Top Ten was proactive—"the art of making the impossible possible," as Dominique called it. Each item had an owner, a deadline, and an ambitious goal that, if achieved, would move the company forward.

Every Monday morning, the executive team gathered to review progress. "If we were falling behind in one of the top ten, we would basically all focus on that and say, how do we fix it? How do we transfer resources to it?" Dominique said. The Top Tens cascaded through the company—engineering had one, sales had one, even the Japan office had its own list.

Dominique understood that focus meant saying no. When one team proposed an internet venture incubator, Dominique nixed it. The company would have to wait until it had more money in the bank. Every decision came down to one question: Could NeXT afford it?

Dominique also worked to restructure NeXT's $400 million mountain of debt. One creditor proved to be a challenge. Canon had stopped communicating with Steve entirely. Without Canon's agreement to restructure, NeXT was facing bankruptcy. So Warren spent six months convincing Canon's executives that restructuring was the only option—without it, NeXT would collapse, and they'd recover nothing.

Canon, which had once dreamed of selling the black cubes in Asia, wanted an end to the nightmare and sold all of its holdings in NeXT as soon as it could.

Steve had injected about $50 million into NeXT and $54 million into Pixar. Combined, Dominique estimated Steve was burning through $50 to $60 million a year keeping both companies alive. Exactly how much he had left was unclear. Ed Catmull later estimated that Pixar represented about half of Steve's net worth, while Warren guessed Steve was down to his last $150 million.

Against this backdrop, NeXT's extravagant headquarters were looking like a more serious liability than ever. The floating staircase still commanded the atrium. The custom-designed spaces still gleamed. The overpriced phones still rang.

Venture capitalist Bill Janeway of Warburg Pincus walked in one day. Warren had brought him to the offices to explore a potential recapitalization. Bill looked at the floating staircase. He walked away and the deal never happened.

In the midst of the financial carnage, Steve summoned Warren. His agenda: merge NeXT with Pixar.

Warren couldn't believe what he was hearing. "That's like two Titanics going down together," Warren told him. His answer: No.

Steve turned to another adviser during this challenging period: his friend Larry Ellison, the founder of Oracle. Back when Steve had just left Apple, the two were neighbors in Woodside.

Their friendship began with an argument over Steve's pet peacock, which had been a gift from an ex-girlfriend. "The peacock wandered over and woke me up," Larry later recounted at the All Things Digital conference. When he complained to Steve, Steve commiserated with him—he didn't like the peacock either, he said. The disagreeable pair hit it off right away. Neither Steve nor Larry ever disclosed what became of the peacock, though it's likely that Steve sold it or gave it away.

Larry operated like Steve did. They were both human magnets turned to maximum strength, either pulling people into their orbit or flinging them away. There was no neutral ground with either man. "I say Steve's my best friend, and Steve says I'm his best friend," Larry told his biographer Mike Wilson. "And he says, 'Well you're my only friend, so you must be my best friend' . . . I could use the same joke."

While Steve burned through his fortune keeping two companies alive, Larry's wealth grew. Oracle made the unglamorous software that ran corporate back rooms, the databases and digital plumbing no one saw but every company needed. Larry was proof positive that boring could make for a better business proposition than beautiful.

In May 1993, Steve recruited Larry to join NeXT's board. Larry brought his extensive enterprise software experience to bear, noting that "70 percent of the IT projects fail in the world," Dominique recounted. Larry advised the NeXT team to start a professional services group "to ensure that [the] success rate is 100 percent on your projects."

So NeXT did exactly that, establishing an internal group to consult on company projects. It was a valuable addition. "It gave us insights into what our competitors were doing," Dominique said. The group also came up with ideas for new products.

Larry emphasized that consistent execution was everything in enterprise software. That meant fixing problems as they arose. Where Dominique had his top ten process, engineering director Karl "Charly" Kleissner, who had recently joined NeXT after leaving a start-up called DataMind and the massive computer maker Digital Equipment Corporation, became the keeper of NeXT's bug database. It had ballooned to tens of thousands of problems, categorized as "boulders" (gargantuan bugs), "rocks" (medium fixes), and "pebbles" (small bugs).

In NeXT's early years, bug tracking had been ad hoc, with no systematic documentation. Charly's comprehensive approach finally let the team triage what could realistically ship with each release—which "boulders" were essential and which "pebbles" could wait. The result was software that, despite the company's turmoil, consistently delivered. "What went out into the world of developers was very solid," Charly recalled.

Charly managed all of it with a spreadsheet. It symbolized a departure from before—a company-wide transformation. NeXT's future was no longer going to be shaped by revolutionary tools but with cells and Monday morning triage.

Even so, the engineers still worked off of their discontinued NeXT computers. "The beautiful hardware was everywhere," Charly remembered. "It held up until we left."

Even if boring could pay the bills, it couldn't hold Steve's interest. As the company pivoted to enterprise software, Steve's attention wandered. Dominique saw Steve nearly fall asleep in meetings with CIOs.

So he began stepping away from NeXT. “He let us [manage] the company,” Dominique said. It was a major shift for the infamous micromanager. And as it turned out, Monday morning meetings ran more smoothly without him there.

Steve began spending more time at Pixar, trading NeXT’s elegant designer headquarters for the ratty sofas of Pixar’s bare-boned offices. Two different worlds, both burning Steve’s money.

By early 1994, things were beginning to turn around for NeXT. That year, the company achieved its first profit of $1 million on revenues of $49.6 million, thanks to the Sun licensing agreement and financial austerity. After nine years of losses, NeXT was finally stepping into the black.

The company was unrecognizable from Steve’s original vision. No more black cubes, no beautiful factories. In their place: bug tracking and the unsexy plumbing that made corporate systems work.

The young man who had wanted to put a dent in the universe was beginning to think smaller, measuring progress in pebbles rather than boulders. And while his fortune evaporated, his wisdom condensed. He now understood that genius without discipline ends in expensive failure.

At NeXT’s East Coast Developer Conference, Steve’s newfound humility peeked through. “I wanted to close by saying something to all of you who’ve been with the NeXT community through ’93, which is: Thank you,” he said. “We put you guys through a difficult year.”

“Everybody else thought it was our epitaph,” Steve said.

21

FOUNDATION

NeXT fell into an intense, quiet focus. Steve often materialized in office doorways after dark. "Hey, what are you working on?" he'd ask engineers. No ulterior motive. He genuinely wanted to know.

One-on-one, Steve transformed, leaving behind the role of humiliator in chief that he played in larger team meetings. This Steve was calm and curious.

He couldn't code, but he could grasp the essence of any technical problem instantly. An engineer might explain to Steve why something couldn't work—whether because of memory constraints, processing limits, or fundamental physics—and Steve would probe gently. "Yeah, but what if . . . ?" he'd ask. He had a gift for connecting disparate ideas and suggesting combinations that violated conventional wisdom. He refused to accept the thousand reasons why something wouldn't work.

As much as the problem-solving interested him, Steve struggled to put his greatest strength to work: selling the software innovations.

Technology needed drama to capture imagination. How could he dramatize a class in object-oriented programming? How could he make sorting algorithms sexy?

Back in Cupertino, Apple had finally decided to embrace objects.

The company had been falling behind in the software wars, and it was losing out on outside developers as a result. The number of applications developed for Windows was doubling every year while applications for Mac were growing at one fifth that rate.

All the most exciting new software was appearing on PCs first, if it came to the Mac at all. Even pro-Apple industry analysts were now telling corporate clients to replace their Macs with machines that ran Windows.

Apple had commissioned a confidential report to figure out how to right the ship. After years of dismissing NeXT's approach, the report finally conceded what Steve had been saying all along: "Objects are Apple's future," it declared. "This is a war for survival."

Apple understood that whichever company controlled object technology would control how software communicated, essentially becoming the owner of the world's digital railroad tracks. If Microsoft won the war, Apple would be beholden to its northern rival for the foreseeable future. Or worse, it might collapse altogether.

"Apple today is like a young adult, still living in a small hometown, who has a fabulous career opportunity in a distant city," the report concluded. "It's scary to leave home, but there's no opportunity here, and if we wait too long the job will be gone."

In May 1994, current and former Apple employees raised their glasses to better days. They had gathered at the Fairmont Hotel in San Jose to mark ten years since the launch of the Macintosh. Steve was conspicuously missing, and the reunion program didn't even mention him.

"The sad part was they had a picture frame on one of the tables with a list of all the early employees who had passed away," Rich Page recalled. "The list was much longer than I expected."

As the old guard passed on, so did their approach to building computers. Apple's confidential report spelled out why, describing the Mac's predicament: "Computer platforms don't age gracefully. . . . Sales of a successful platform actually tend to keep on growing right up until they collapse and when the collapse comes, it can be shockingly fast."

Steve couldn't stop watching Apple die.

He had a window into the problems in Cupertino through Tom Suiter, whose design agency CKS Partners handled both NeXT and Apple accounts—a conflict Steve allowed.

"How's it going over there?" Steve would ask Tom. When Tom showed him the latest release of Apple's Newton MessagePad, Steve played with it briefly before handing it back. "This thing is so lame," he said.

While Apple fumbled with Newton's handwriting recognition, Steve was playing with a different new technology. He'd rigged up voice activation on his cell phone. Warren Weiss later called it "a version of Siri," fifteen years before the real thing was released.

Steve would call Warren and laugh as he experimented with this primitive voice technology. But there was no large company to build it with, no platform to launch it from. Just Steve and his engineers tinkering in their office.

As 1994 went on, a violent first-person shooter game called *Doom*, released at the end of the previous year, exploded around the world. Players wandered through a military facility on one of the moons orbiting

Mars, blasting demons in gruesome detail, with unprecedented speed and realism. It was so good that it even sparked congressional hearings on video game violence.

The NeXT team watched in awe as the game conquered millions of computers and reshaped the industry. They learned that John Carmack, the game's twenty-three-year-old creator, had built the entire thing on NeXT machines.

"The first major personal purchase I made wasn't a car, but rather a NeXT computer," John later wrote in a Facebook post.

For a young programmer frustrated by the constant crashes and primitive development tools of DOS and Windows, the Cube was a revelation. It didn't crash, and its development tools were years ahead of everything else on the market. While other developers fought with their machines, John could focus on what mattered: building the best game he could.

Before the game blew up, John had requested to include a "Developed on NeXT computers" line in *Doom*'s opening credits. NeXT said no. Steve didn't think very highly of games. To him, they were toys. NeXT built computers for serious work.

When *Doom* became a success, NeXT scrambled to reverse course. But by then, John wrote on Facebook, "that ship had sailed."

NeXT had attracted exactly the kind of revolutionary developer Steve claimed to want, only to push him away because his work didn't come dressed in a suit.

In October 1994, NeXT and Sun released their promised collaboration, OpenStep. It flopped—and most people chalked up the failure to Sun. For Sun, "OpenStep was just another offering on their platforms," Bud Tribble said. Sun didn't make it central to its software strategy and NeXT paid the price.

OpenStep's fizzle taught NeXT another harsh lesson about partnerships. It could build great infrastructure and watch it gather dust when partners treated it as an afterthought.

Meanwhile, HP and Digital Equipment Corporation were porting NeXTSTEP to their machines, buying NeXT a little more time. The licensing revenue helped stabilize the company. Combined with the $75 million from the Sun deal, NeXT had clawed its way from $400 million in debt to almost breaking even, Dominique recounted.

NeXT engineers were becoming masters at porting NeXTSTEP to other companies' hardware. "That was our specialty!" said Avie Tevanian, who had now risen to become NeXT's VP of software. "Give us the funding, or commit to go, and six months later, we'd have it running."

NeXT survived the year 1994 by building practical solutions to mundane problems. These projects were called Foundation, Enterprise Objects, OpenStep—the boring software that made interesting things possible. It was all very un-Steve.

The software porting team, led by Avie, kept plugging away on new enterprise solutions. And they grew very close in the process. Every Friday night, they would let off steam with a game of poker.

The team developed other bonding rituals as well: When anyone left NeXT for another job, they would take them outside and give them a ceremonial toss into the creek running past NeXT's office.

In February 1995, Laurene threw a surprise fortieth birthday bash for Steve at Larry's home in Pacific Heights. A modernist behemoth of glass, steel, and concrete, it looked down on San Francisco and the Bay beyond, spread out like a circuit board.

Larry had become a billionaire two years earlier. He wanted to help Steve find a similar path. But a life of riches didn't motivate Steve. "He wasn't trying to be famous," Larry would later say at All Things Digital.

"He wasn't trying to be powerful. He was obsessed with the creative process and building something that was beautiful."

As Steve celebrated his birthday, the tech journalists who once covered him enthusiastically now ignored him completely. In their eyes, he had fallen from the pantheon of tech visionaries. *Newsweek* editors had recently dropped him from a feature on the fifty most important people in tech. Number one on the list: Bill Gates. Everyone in the industry was eagerly anticipating his launch of Windows 95.

While the tech world fixated on Bill, Steve was discovering satisfaction in quieter pursuits. At home in Palo Alto, away from the industry spotlight, he was learning to find meaning in everyday family decisions.

The Jobs family had been making do with a subpar washer and dryer, and it was time to shop for replacements. So Steve and Laurene began discussing the pros and cons of various laundry appliances around the dinner table.

They agreed that American washing machines were fast but rough. Steve observed that European machines took twice as long but treated clothes like precious objects. "We ended up talking a lot about design, but also about the values of our family," Steve told *Wired*.

He sounded like a different Steve than before. "The problem is I'm older now, I'm forty years old, and this stuff [technology] doesn't change the world," he said. "Having children really changes your view on these things. We're born, we live for a brief instant, and we die. It's been happening for a long time."

His reflective mode continued in an interview with the Silicon Valley Historical Association. "All the work that I have done in my life will be obsolete by the time I am fifty," he said. He later told them: "You're building up a mountain, and you get to contribute your little layer of sedimentary rock to make the mountain that much higher. But no one on the surface, unless they have X-ray vision, will see your sediment."

Steve's deliberations over laundry machines continued for about two weeks. At forty, the man who had once vowed to put a dent in the universe was finding profound satisfaction in sharing time—and sharing his love of technology and design—with his family.

They ended up buying a Miele.

22

BEGINNER'S MIND

By 1995, the World Wide Web was growing fast. Twelve million people were online and about 18 percent of American adults had a computer with an internet modem. The web had moved beyond a few hundred university sites and was building critical mass with the public.

But it was still a nightmare to use. Websites took minutes to load via the typical modem—unless the connection crashed. Then you'd be forced to start all over again. Once the page finally loaded, you'd see an unaesthetic clash of colors, text, and grainy images.

The web was still in its creation phase, Steve told *Wired*. Nobody knew what it would become. At NeXT, Steve had been largely ignoring it. "Steve ignored the web because it was not his idea," software engineer Nico Popp recalled.

At NeXT, Steve had created a culture where engineers were free to pursue side projects—a freedom that would prove crucial. He wanted his team to follow their curiosity.

One problem: Every day, NeXT's engineering team dealt with the same paper chase—bug reports arriving by fax and email from developers, fixes going back the same way. Everyone knew there had to be a better solution.

One morning, Steve appeared in Dominique's doorway without knocking, as was his way, and asked Dominique to come with him. Steve had been doing his usual rounds through the engineering building when a team of three software engineers sent Steve a proposal for a creative project: Why not use the emerging World Wide Web to enable the back-and-forth exchange of bug information automatically?

Steve and Dominique walked to the engineering building, where the team, consisting of Nico and two others, explained how they had whipped up a new communication tool. As he sent bug reports back and forth, the website could update itself with the new information. When they saw it working, both men were blown away.

What stunned Steve and Dominique wasn't just that the engineers had built a website—it was how ridiculously easy it had been for them to do it. They spent the weekend building another demo for Steve, a car-dealer website where customers could select models, colors, and options, then calculate lease payments—all generated from database information, proving that web pages didn't need to be static documents.

Steve liked to describe technology as archaeological layers in a mountain—each innovation built upon countless hidden foundations. NeXT's architecture embodied this philosophy: a rock-solid Unix foundation, sophisticated graphics rendering, object-oriented frameworks, and development tools, each layer built on the ones below. For years, these seemed to outsiders like expensive abstractions.

Now, suddenly, all those layers were paying dividends no one had foreseen. The website was assembled like Lego blocks from components that had been waiting years for this exact moment.

Where competitors needed armies of programmers writing everything from the ground up, NeXT's architecture let a small team snap together their prebuilt, battle-tested pieces, while writing very little code.

Each component did one thing perfectly and connected seamlessly to everything else.

This was the vindication of every software decision NeXT had made. Every dollar Steve had spent on "unnecessary" abstraction layers. Every heated engineering debate about proper object design. Every month spent building frameworks that seemed to have no immediate application.

"Of course!" Avie exclaimed when he saw the engineer's demo. "This is the way it should be."

The demonstration triggered a cascade in Steve's mind that led to an epiphany. In the web, Steve had found NeXT's killer application.

After years of wandering, here, finally, was a viable market on the horizon. "This is typical Steve Jobs in action," Dominique said. "When we hit that sweet spot, it was like, *this* is why we exist."

The team felt that the web was *their* technology. Tim Berners-Lee had invented it on a NeXT machine. And they believed it could become the perfect home for the projects they'd been refining in obscurity: objects, dynamic content, and distributed intelligence.

Steve prepared a presentation that outlined his three predicted stages of the web's evolution. It started with the one-way publication of information (the current stage). Second, it would facilitate the two-way exchange of information through a server. This is what Nico had just demonstrated. Third, the web would enable electronic commerce—processing transactions, managing inventory, and supporting complex business applications.

Steve demonstrated the third stage by showing how someone might be able to book a flight on the web—selecting departure cities, destinations, and dates through the interface. Steve planned to unveil this vision at his opening speech at the WebMania conference in San Francisco in January 1996.

The response was immediate. Engineers throughout NeXT stopped what they were doing to see the demo. Groundbreaking software was born: WebObjects. It breathed life into the dead pages of the World Wide Web.

Steve saw WebObjects as truly transformative. He envisioned a future where online stores could offer thousands of products without the massive expense of printing and mailing catalogs. Instead of sending thick booklets to every household—the way Sears and JCPenney did—retailers would be able to show each customer exactly what they wanted to see, when they wanted to see it.

When a user entered information, Steve envisioned a server processing the request and sending back a custom page. Shopping for a red Honda Civic with leather seats? The server could create that exact page—with current inventory, local pricing, and available options—just for you, in that moment.

As he imagined the web future, an excitement Steve had lost during years of enterprise sales suddenly flooded back to him. "If you look at things I've done in my life, they have an element of democratizing," Steve told *Wired*. "The Web is an incredible democratizer."

He rhapsodized about how his tools would allow any lone online developer to build things that once took entire corporate teams to create.

So that he could visualize WebObjects in his presentations, Steve had his engineers build a captivating dynamic image, NeXT Director of Operations Greg Brandeau said. The demo showed several software objects on screen: a customer, a product, a shipping address, and so forth.

When Steve changed one object during the demonstration—when he updated an address or modified customer information—"you saw the system automatically change everything else," Greg explained. The engineers had built "a display of all of the objects talking to each other." When one changed, the system would automatically update all the other objects. Steve had found a way to make object-oriented programming beautiful and comprehensible.

In 1995, this idea was a revelation. At the time, each and every web page was hand coded, resulting in an identical experience for every visitor. That made building the online future impossible. "Every time [an online store] had a price change, you'd have to touch ten thousand web pages to rebuild," Steve said at a product demonstration at the Sharper Image store on San Francisco's Sutter Street. "That's untenable."

And it's what WebObjects would fix.

He gathered the company together in the auditorium. "We have this new technology called WebObjects," he announced. "The internet is going to be the most important technology transformation of the next fifteen to twenty years. We're going to burn the boats. The future of this company is WebObjects."

Steve was making a gamble that would have seemed unthinkable just months earlier. After years of pouring resources into NeXTSTEP, he was now betting the company's future on WebObjects instead, an act that Dominique called "a bit of sacrilege."

Meanwhile, Microsoft had canceled Cairo, causing Sun to lose interest in OpenStep. Despite OpenStep's limited market success, the Sun partnership had still provided a third of NeXT's revenue through licensing fees. Instead, Sun was chasing another programming language called Java. That left the WebObjects market wide open for NeXT.

With a major revenue stream disappearing and fewer enterprise customers for the company's traditional software, NeXT also needed a new growth market. WebObjects offered a way to ride the exploding web rather than depend on fickle corporate partnerships.

To approach the problem, Steve employed what Buddhists call "beginner's mind"—a concept he had discovered after dropping out of Reed in 1972 in a book called *Zen Mind, Beginner's Mind*. In it Shunryu Suzuki writes, "In the beginner's mind there are many possibilities, but in the expert's there are few."

The myriad opportunities that WebObjects enabled let Steve view enterprise applications with fresh eyes. Instead of dull corporate tools, he envisioned dynamic, consumer-facing websites that happened to be powered by enterprise data. In his telling, humdrum airline booking software became a way for customers to plan trips from their home computers. An inventory database didn't just enable corporate bureaucracy, it became the engine that would power personalized shopping experiences.

By 1996, Steve compared the inevitability of the web's growth to that of the telephone. When you have just two phones, "it's not very interesting," he told *Wired*, "it's probably not until you get to around ten thousand telephones that it really gets interesting." The web had achieved critical mass, he explained, and things were about to get exciting.

He also emphasized his open approach to the web. "There's a tremendous open possibility to the whole thing," he said. "And it hasn't been confined, or defined, in too many ways. That's wonderful."

On August 9, 1995, Netscape debuted on Wall Street. Netscape made the web's dominant browser, and its IPO grew into the biggest tech-finance story of the year. *The New York Times* declared it Wall Street's "darling."

It was trading at a monumental $2.9 billion market cap. That was more than eighty times Netscape's annual revenue and made it worth almost as much as better-established tech companies like Adobe Systems ($3.3 billion) and Lotus Development Corporation ($3.5 billion).

At the time of its IPO, Netscape had only been in existence for seventeen months. More puzzlingly: The company had never posted a profit. Its outrageous success signaled the birth of a new financial phenomenon: the market assigning valuations based on web companies' exponential potential, not current profits.

The age of Silicon Valley was ascendant.

Two years before, Netscape's founder Marc Andreessen had come to Steve with a demo of an earlier browser called Mosaic. Dominique remembered Steve telling him: "Anybody can write thirty thousand lines of code," explaining why he had dismissed Marc out of hand.

Now all Steve could do was watch Marc rake in billions while he burned through his savings to keep the company afloat.

But maybe, in this new world where potential mattered more than profits, he could engineer another path forward. Pixar's first feature film, *Toy Story*, would be released in November. If it succeeded, he hoped that perhaps Pixar could ride the new IPO wave, buying him enough time to figure out NeXT's future.

The web boom was changing Steve's calculations about everything. Nine years earlier, he had resisted any talk with his investors of going public, determined never to lose control the way he had at Apple. But he wasn't the same person anymore. He had learned to trust others.

Five days after Netscape's blockbuster IPO, Steve emerged on the stage at the Object World Conference in San Francisco to promote WebObjects. He followed Larry Ellison's playbook. "We are absolutely moving into the consultant selling mode," Steve announced. "Following in the footsteps of probably Oracle would be the best example."

Instead of simply selling WebObjects software licenses, NeXT would deploy teams of consultants to work on-site with clients for months at a time, implementing and customizing WebObjects for each company's specific needs. This approach would generate much higher revenue per customer and deeper client relationships.

Steve had struck a chord. "Everybody was lining up," Dominique said. "We had meetings every fifteen minutes with big customers."

A week and a half later, Microsoft's Redmond campus became the center of the tech universe. Microsoft was launching Windows 95. The release turned into a watershed for the industry, with customers lining up outside electronics stores for the midnight release.

Within the first four days, Windows 95 sold one million copies, breaking every record for software sales. The Start button quickly became an icon, showing up on billboards, in TV commercials set to the Rolling Stones' "Start Me Up," and on the front page of every newspaper.

"Windows 95 is so easy to use, even a talk show host can figure it out," Bill told Jay Leno, who stood onstage with him at the launch.

At thirty-nine, Bill became the wealthiest man in America with a net worth of $14.8 billion. It appeared to be a straight triumph for Bill's philosophy of flexible computing—suggesting that consumers clearly didn't care about design or an elevated user experience and that companies should focus instead on capturing market share.

By now, Steve had fully bought into Bill's belief about open systems. WebObjects ran on HP servers, Sun machines, even Windows NT. (Windows 95 didn't run WebObjects because it was built for home users checking email and playing solitaire, not Fortune 500 companies.)

Despite this, Steve continued to lob potshots at Microsoft. "They have absolutely no taste," he told Robert X. Cringely in 1995. "I don't mean that in a small way, I mean that in a big way. In the sense that they don't think of original ideas, and they don't bring much culture into their product."

But while Steve criticized Microsoft's aesthetics, Bill had already won the war that mattered, and Windows 95's success highlighted just how precarious NeXT's position remained, even with WebObjects gaining traction.

On a hike together through the Santa Cruz mountains, Steve and Larry Ellison hatched a plot for regaining dominance. They had watched Apple's steadily declining stock price, its chaotic product lines, and its plunging market share.

As the company's influence and price ebbed, it became the perfect takeover target. Steve and Larry settled on rough details: Larry would marshal a team of investors to buy Apple and install himself as its CEO. Steve would return as his lieutenant—head of products, maybe, or chief technology officer. Oracle would become the parent company to Apple, which would then take the Mac operating system and merge it with NeXT's technology.

Larry even brought his Oracle executives to Apple headquarters, walking with them along the roads and parking lots of Infinite Loop and declaring, "Someday this will all be mine." He consulted junk-bond trader Michael Milken, who had just spent ten years in prison for securities fraud, about financing a deal. The prospect of playing corporate raider with his best friend's former company thrilled Larry.

But Steve felt conflicted about the plan: Taking Apple by force would require him to return to a company he wasn't even sure he wanted to lead again. And he certainly couldn't stomach forcing his way in through a hostile takeover.

"If I do this I need to do this standing on the moral high ground," Steve told Larry.

Steve turned back to NeXT.

Serious customers continued to line up for WebObjects. Disney, Shell, Chrysler—members of the Fortune 500. Within a month, WebObjects had racked up more than $2.5 million in sales.

One customer was Michael Dell. The soft-spoken founder had built Dell Computer Corporation from his dorm room at the University of Texas at Austin in 1984. His biggest innovation was cutting out the middleman and selling PCs directly to customers via mail-order catalogs. By the early 1990s, Dell had grown into a roaring success. Then came its first annual loss and a cash squeeze that nearly killed the company.

Michael saw the web as his salvation. He wanted to build a website that would allow customers to configure their PCs online—choose processors, memory, features—then check out with a credit card. A complete vision for e-commerce before e-commerce existed.

When he asked IBM to build the website, the company quoted Michael a two-year timeline. Then he tried NeXT. As Michael explained the concept to Dominique and Sina Tamaddon, VP of professional services, Sina took notes, disappeared, and returned during the same meeting with a working demo, built using objects. "We can get that ready for you in one week," Sina said.

Michael signed up almost immediately. "Nobody had ever [built a website like that]," Dominique recalled. It was ambitious and novel.

Though WebObjects had become NeXT's focus, Steve couldn't help but pitch Michael additional products. Steve went over to Michael's house to pitch NeXTSTEP as a replacement for Windows on Dell computers, Michael later recalled. But he politely declined.

Within a year, Dell's WebObjects-powered online sales exploded, growing to $3 million a day and quickly becoming the core of the company's distribution strategy. Dell represented the next generation of tech manufacturers, leaving behind the giants like IBM and Sun that Steve had spent the last decade courting.

The web was a clean slate that would place the aging behemoths and nimble challengers back at the same starting line, together.

23

HERO'S JOURNEY

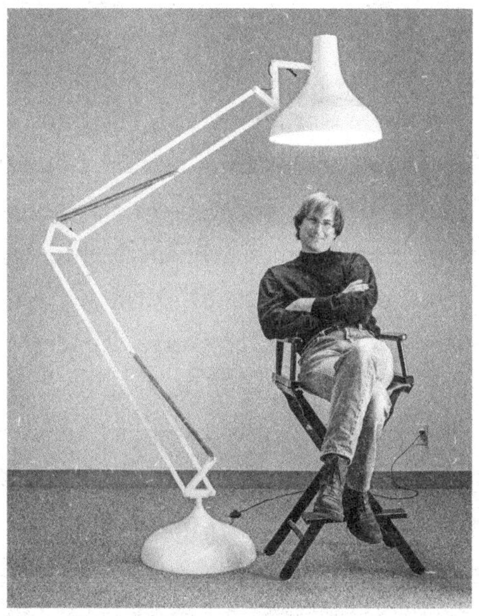

In spring 1995, Steve sought refuge with designers, artists, and marketers. He took his friend Paul Vais, the former NeXT executive director of marketing, on a drive in his Mercedes sedan.

Steve popped a cassette tape into the dashboard and pressed play. A jazz ensemble burst from the stereo, playing a lilting melody. Then came the voice of the pop singer Randy Newman: "You've got a friend in me / You've got a friend in me."

"What do you think of this?" Steve asked him, explaining how it was going to become the theme song for *Toy Story*.

"I don't get it," Paul said.

Then the true meaning dawned on Paul. There was a deeper vision that informed all of Steve's work, whether at Pixar, NeXT, or Apple.

He cared about imparting a story, not merely building technology. "No amount of technology can turn a bad story into a good story," Steve later reflected.

"That's what Steve was really thinking about," Paul said. "[NeXT] had the best technology, and it wasn't going to win the day if it didn't have great storytelling. That fusion of art and science . . . was one of his most powerful insights."

Toy Story was a monument to this insight. It had taken the Pixar team four years of nonstop work to execute. Woody alone required 723 control points—the invisible digital joints that animators pulled like a puppet's strings. Pull one point, his eyebrow raises. Adjust another, his mouth forms a smile. Each animated tree in the film had 10,000 leaves. The film's 81 minutes contained 114,000 frames and 34 terabytes of files from the company's graphics software, RenderMan. No one had attempted computer animation at this scale before.

"It is not only an exercise in artistic creativity and in computer science technology," Steve said. "It is also an exercise in managing scale and complexity that we have not seen in the likes of computer graphics very often."

Steve's colleagues pointed out the irony behind the accomplishment. At NeXT, he had obsessed over every detail and every decision, and the company struggled as a result. He'd assumed a very different role at Pixar. After shuttering the hardware division in 1990, he'd pinned the company's survival on John Lasseter, the animator behind *Tron*'s groundbreaking computer graphics.

John and Pixar President Ed Catmull had effectively managed Steve away from the creative process, asking him to stay out of meetings with the company's brain trust of creative decision-makers. That left John and his team to craft characters and storylines, while Steve focused on the business side. In part, that meant writing big checks. "Steve knew that making movies was not his forte," Dominique explained.

Steve, Ed, and John had secured a major three-film deal with Disney in July 1991. While Steve handled the financial negotiations, he deferred to John, the executive producer, on creative matters—an arrangement that had been crucial to convincing the Pixar team to accept Steve's leadership when he bought the company from Lucasfilm. John wouldn't have allowed things to happen any other way. Steve had learned that respecting this boundary was essential to keeping Pixar's creative talent.

But Steve remained Pixar's nominal CEO. "I remember it was kind of weird for him to be CEO of two companies. He was getting crap for that," said Paul.

Behind the scenes, the two companies had begun to blur at the edges. When Steve showed up at the NeXT boardroom, he sometimes brought Pixar and Disney creatives in tow to workshop *Toy Story* storyboards. It made for a strange juxtaposition: pictures of animated toys hanging in the conference room of an aspiring enterprise software company.

In August 1995, Steve took the stage at SIGGRAPH, the annual gathering for computer graphics professionals. He was there to talk about the technology behind *Toy Story*. As he spoke, audience members saw a different Steve from the serious software leader they had come to know. As he talked, he appeared lit from within, boyish in his excitement about making film history.

"We are at the centenary of this incredible invention," he told the audience. A hundred years after the Lumière brothers' first motion picture, decades after Walt Disney gambled on color with *Snow White*, he said that Pixar was picking up the baton and delivering the next evolution in cinema. *Toy Story* would be the first completely computer-generated feature-length motion picture, he told the audience.

Pixar let Steve dream about making a dent in the universe again.

As he regained his spirit, Steve's colleagues witnessed him maturing in other ways.

In March 1996, Chris Palermo—the company's number two lawyer—faced every parent's worst nightmare.

Chris had joined NeXT nine months earlier as associate general counsel. Chris had previously worked for Jack Brown, of the firm Brown & Bain, who had aggressively represented Apple in its lawsuit against NeXT. During his interview, Steve looked at his resume and asked, "So, why did you work for that dick brain Jack?"

Chris, without skipping a beat, said, "Well, I had the good judgment to leave, didn't I?"

From that moment, they'd been in sync.

Now tragedy struck Chris's family. A drunk driver in New Orleans hit his two small daughters and their babysitter. When Dominique learned what had happened, he immediately called Steve.

According to Dominique, Steve listened without saying a word. Then he promised to call back in ten minutes.

When he did, he had a plan ready. "I have a whole team at Stanford ready to take care of them," Steve said. "I'm sending an airplane to pick them up and bring the whole family back. One thing: You don't talk to anyone about this."

It was an extraordinary gesture. Chris had only been at the company nine months and reported three levels down from Steve. He was, in his own words, "kind of a rank-and-file employee."

Though Chris couldn't accept the medevac—the children needed immediate, urgent care that made a cross-country flight impossible—the offer revealed a newfound spirit of generosity. Dominique was moved by the act and by Steve's desire to keep it quiet. "It's almost like he didn't want that in his image," he said.

Both children lived—Chris's older daughter was saved by a six-hour surgery at Tulane University. Two weeks later, when she had stabilized, she was finally able to fly back to California. "I don't think [Steve] gets sufficient credit for those basic acts of humanity," Chris said.

In upstate New York, a relative of NeXT salesman Jim Diamond's sister-in-law was dying of an aggressive form of breast cancer. The twenty-seven-year-old woman had weeks—maybe days—left to live, and her final wish was to watch *Toy Story* with her two-year-old daughter.

Initially Steve demurred. The film wasn't out yet, and he worried about something leaking and preempting its release. But a few days later, Steve changed his mind and dispatched a team to New York. A luxury car pulled up to the woman's home and out stepped a couple of Pixar employees carrying videotapes and *Toy Story* merchandise.

The young mother was confined to a hospital bed in her living room. The Pixar employees set up the Woody and Buzz toys and transformed the room into a private premiere. The little girl crawled into bed with her mother and the toys as they watched the movie together.

When the film ended, the employees packed up the videotapes and disappeared into the car, the film's secrets safe. The daughter fell asleep that night clutching Woody. And five days later, the mother died.

"Steve had that type of compassion," Jim said.

Ed later recalled that this wasn't unusual behavior for Steve. When Pixar employees fell seriously ill, Steve would visit them in the hospital and arrange access to top specialists.

On Thanksgiving Eve 1995, Disney and Pixar released *Toy Story* to critical and commercial acclaim. The film soon entered the canon of American pop culture, a recognition that Steve—who saw himself as a cultural creator, not just an innovator—cherished. The American Film Institute would later rank it number ninety-nine on its list of the greatest American films of all time.

Six days after *Toy Story*'s theatrical release, with the film on track to gross $373 million worldwide, Pixar was ready to go public. The IPO had been planned for three months, but its timing was deliberately tied to the film's release. Pixar needed *Toy Story* to prove that computer animation could succeed commercially before investors would back the company. The film's strong opening weekend had given Pixar's underwriters the confidence to move forward with the public offering.

Steve and the Pixar team gathered at the offices of their investment bank, Robertson Stephens. And at 9:30 a.m., they watched as the opening bell signaled the start of trading for Pixar's 6.9 million shares on the NASDAQ.

The shares were priced at $22, the same price Apple had set for its IPO years earlier. According to Ed, the parallel was pure coincidence. Steve hadn't remembered. After endless struggle at both NeXT and Pixar, the IPO finally brought vindication.

Within an hour, Pixar's shares rocketed to $49 and closed the day at $39 a share.

Steve excused himself and picked up the phone in one of the bank's side offices, according to journalists Brent Schlender and Rick Tetzeli in their book *Becoming Steve Jobs.*

"Hello, Larry?" Steve asked, according to the book. It was Larry Ellison.

"I made it," Steve said. With Pixar's stock price closing at $39 per share, Steve's stake in the company was now worth approximately $1.2 billion. He had just become a billionaire.

The magnitude of this reversal was staggering to Ed. Back in 1986, Steve paid only $5 million for Pixar, which looked like a bargain, from George Lucas. But over the nine years that followed, as Pixar struggled to make a profit, Steve kept writing checks to fund it. Just before the IPO, he was down $54 million total—what Ed called "a substantial portion of his net worth."

Each check he'd written during those lean years had been an act of faith in his team. Now, in a single day, that faith had been vindicated beyond his wildest projections.

Colleagues who were in the room heard something almost relieved in his tone. The man who had always professed not to care about money calling to announce his entry into the three-comma club. They believed

Steve was using the money to keep score—proof that he'd finally won, despite all the failures.

But more than that, the IPO finally gave Steve leverage. He had learned to trust his team at Pixar, and as a result, he could maneuver going forward from a position of strength.

Ed had watched Steve undergo what he called "a fairly major transformation" in the four years leading up to this moment. The period began with personal milestones in 1991: Steve's marriage to Laurene, Reed's birth.

Steve was also learning hard lessons about timing. His vision often outpaced reality. At NeXT, he decided not to include a floppy disk drive in the Cube; he was technically correct that floppies would eventually disappear, but the decision was commercially disastrous for its time. Almost everyone with a computer stored their data on floppy disks. "You can't get ahead of the curve too much," Ed observed. Steve "didn't understand that." The computer industry was littered with companies that had been right too early.

But with Pixar's IPO, Steve had finally learned the lesson of timing. Computer animation was ready for mainstream audiences and *Toy Story* had proved the market existed. This time, Steve hadn't jumped too far ahead of the curve. He'd ridden it exactly when it crested.

Throughout their partnership, Ed had developed a unique approach to working with Steve that avoided the explosive confrontations others experienced. "I never had sort of one of these loud yelling arguments with Steve ever," Ed said. The secret was understanding how Steve's mind worked: "Steve did not want to be guided in his thinking. He wanted to know what the facts are on which to base something."

Ed once had a disagreement with Steve that stretched across three months. "He was just wrong," Ed said. "The fact that he has a powerful personality and he could talk and think faster than I could didn't make him right." Rather than escalate, Ed would present his case then wait. Eventually, Steve would say, "Oh, you're right, and that's the end of the discussion."

The transformation was real and lasting. "The people who were with Steve by the end of '95 pretty much stayed with him for the rest of his life," Ed observed. By November 1995, Steve had become the kind of leader people wanted to follow long-term.

And he was humbled. "If you don't treat [talented workers] right, they can go get another job in ten minutes, right?" he later recounted to an interviewer. "So a strange thing happens, which is the sort of the hierarchy of power inverts, and the CEO is actually at the bottom. So I sort of feel like I work for most of these people, because they're the ones that are doing all the brilliant work, you know."

Looking back, Ed saw Steve's arc as "more like the hero's journey. He came back, he learned from the experiences and mistakes he made." The man who had emerged by November 1995 was different. He was still demanding, still visionary, but tempered by failure and success in equal measure.

After the IPO, Steve joined Larry Ellison in Hawaii. The conversation turned again to the possibility of taking over Apple. While Steve had previously resisted the idea on principle—not wanting to force his way back—now at least the money was there. Larry's wealth was valued at $4.7 billion. Steve had his Pixar windfall. For the first time, their combined resources could make an Apple acquisition realistic, if Steve could overcome his reluctance.

Steve hired NeXT's former CFO Susan Barnes to advise on the takeover plan. "He and Larry had come up with this idea of, could we go in and take Apple private?" Susan explained. "Could we do a hostile [takeover]?" She researched other proxy fights, examined board structures, and mapped out the mechanics of shareholder warfare.

"Steve had lined up a lot of money to do it," Susan recalled. He was watching Apple deteriorate and felt compelled to intervene before the company collapsed, she said.

The old Steve Jobs—the one who had stormed out of Apple in 1985—might have seized the moment to launch an assault and force his way back in. But a decade of struggle had changed him. He arrived at the same conclusion he did last time Larry talked about a takeover. "I decided I'm not a hostile-takeover kind of guy," he told *The New York Times*. "If they had asked me to come back, it might have been different."

The corporate raider who'd once taken Xerox PARC's graphical interface, who'd built his career on audacious moves, discovered a line he wouldn't cross. Taking Apple by force would prove he'd never really belonged there. He'd rather wait forever.

So he decided to stay at NeXT and sell more WebObjects. He wanted redemption, but he wanted it on his own terms.

More than almost anyone else he knew, one man embodied the values Steve cherished most—big thinking, creative rebellion, a distaste for corporate complacency. That man was Paul Rand.

By March 1996, a decade had passed since the two had worked together on NeXT's logo. Steve and Paul had barely stayed in touch. Steve heard that Paul was about to publish his next book, *From Lascaux to Brooklyn*, a treatise on the history of art and graphic design, so he thought it might be a good opportunity to rekindle the friendship.

Steve drafted an email with the subject line "Howdy."

> Paul,
>
> A friend of mine just gave me your email address, and I couldn't wait to drop you this line. I hope this finds you and Mirian [*sic*] well and in good spirits. I imagine you both at home, looking out the window into your cold, barren Connecticut meadow.
>
> Things are well with me. My family continues to grow, with the birth of our daughter Erin in August. She is a delight, and the entire miracle

> of it all still stops me in my tracks now and then. Reed is four and a half, and he is a wonderfully curious boy. Lisa is finishing her last year in high school and is off to Harvard next year. I guess Lisa's impending departure from the nest makes me realize that Reed and Erin will leave soon as well. Life is fleeting . . .
>
> Paul, your NeXT logo continues to serve us well. The company has not yet achieved the success of your logo for it, but we are still trying. Some new products look very promising, so maybe this time next year we will grow into our logo after all.
>
> Its [*sic*] been a long while since we have spoken, but you are both in my thoughts often.
>
> Steve Jobs

Paul was elated to hear from his old friend Steve. He wrote back:

> We're both in good form. We now have two grandchildren. One is tackling the computer, and the other is tackling anything that gets in his way.

Paul then offered to send Steve a copy of his book, which Steve accepted then replied:

> I guess one decides to give away all of one's secrets and special perspectives at some point, before they are lost forever. Since I am sure that you are going to live to at least 150 years old, you may have begun too early . . . giving your competition a leg up.

Eight months later, in November 1996, Paul died of colon cancer. It had initially been misdiagnosed as an ulcer.

At eighty-one years old, the legendary designer was gone.

24

PIZZAS AND ROADSHOWS

In August 1996, it was finally NeXT's turn to plan for an IPO. Goldman Sachs and Merrill Lynch assembled the deal at their San Francisco offices, with Robertson Stephens—the bank that had just taken Pixar public—as co-underwriter. They planned to release five million shares with the NASDAQ ticker symbol NXXT, priced at $15 to $17 per share.

Steve stayed out of the room for most of the preparation work. Eleven years of struggle had taken its toll. For all his enthusiasm for selling WebObjects, he was tired of pushing the boulder uphill. He'd become, according to Dominique, someone who "just wanted to go run Pixar." He hoped the IPO would allow him to retreat to a more hands-off role at NeXT.

Steve's exhaustion with NeXT ran deeper than most people realized. From his perch at Pixar, Ed had been watching the contrast between the two companies with growing unease. Pixar was soaring after its November 1995 IPO, while NeXT continued to struggle for broader relevance, despite the success of WebObjects. Then Ed read a NeXT press release that troubled him deeply.

Steve was quoted talking enthusiastically about how exciting and successful NeXT was with financial companies buying their software for analysis. "When I read that, I thought, 'Oh, crap, this is not what Steve is all about,'" Ed recalled. "That's not the exciting thing he wanted to do with his life."

Sensing what was coming—that Steve might abandon NeXT to focus entirely on Pixar—Ed asked Steve to dinner at a restaurant they frequented in Palo Alto. He didn't explain the purpose until they arrived.

Steve asked what the meeting was about.

"Well, I read this press release," Ed said, then paraphrased Steve's comments about selling to financial companies. "Steve, this isn't you."

Steve's response was immediate and revealing. The financial clients were pleasant enough to work with, but that wasn't the point "I know I hate this, and these are nice people. This isn't what I want to do."

The admission confirmed Ed's fears. Steve was selling software to customers who didn't excite him.

Still, the IPO had to be sold. It fell to others to craft the story about why investors should buy shares in the company and why the press should cover it. NeXT was still deep in debt, after all, with Steve personally guaranteeing $17 million in loans to cover operating expenses. But the bankers saw a huge opportunity: NeXT had brought WebObjects to market before anyone else developed similar technology. More big companies were expressing interest and Merrill Lynch had just signed an enterprise-wide license.

NeXT's bankers decided to harness the buzz and pitch NeXT as the enterprise backbone of the web revolution. They hoped to borrow some of the same web magic that had made Netscape soar—emphasizing NeXT's future promise over its present circumstances.

The lawyers required NeXT to disclose all the company's downsides in gory detail. NeXT would need to be clear with investors that, despite its promise, WebObjects was untested. It had only launched seven months prior. And NeXT's SEC filings said that "only a limited number" of customers had actually deployed the product that Steve wanted to bet the company on.

Then there was the matter of the CEO. "Mr. Jobs spends approximately half of his time at NeXT and is not committed to spend a certain amount of time at NeXT nor is he able to devote his full time and resources to NeXT," said the filing. It later clarified: "It is likely that NeXT will seek to hire a new Chief Executive Officer over the next 12 months or so."

The team would have to overcome a lot in order to pull off a successful IPO. The NeXT brand—and Steve's personal image—still looked unattractive. Many still considered NeXT to be little more than Steve's hardware misadventure. The team would need to make Steve a hot commodity once again.

The challenge of rehabilitating NeXT's reputation fell to Nicole DeMeo, the company's director of worldwide communications. Before coming in-house, Nicole had spent three years at public relations firm Porter Novelli advising NeXT as a client. She had watched NeXT struggle to win positive press despite genuine technical breakthroughs. Since joining the company, she had been running messaging workshops with the executive team, trying to find a story that would stick.

And she'd have to do something else, too: make infrastructure sexy. The bankers needed something tangible for the January road show, when NeXT executives and their bankers would have to travel from New York to Boston to Chicago pitching investors. They needed something physical for reporters to photograph, something investors could visualize and remember.

Then, through their network of start-up contacts in Seattle, Nicole's PR team came up with a piping-hot answer: pizza. A company called

CyberSlice was using WebObjects to build the world's first nationwide pizza delivery website.

By telling a story about pizza—a concept everybody gets—NeXT wouldn't be forced to talk about boring enterprise middleware or back-end infrastructure. Instead, they could tell the story of pizza, ordered online and delivered to your door.

When she told Steve, he loved the idea. "[Steve] saw this as a way to bring some attention, bring some energy," said Tim Glass, one of CyberSlice's cofounders. "It's hard to say 'pizza' with a frown on your face."

Tim and his cofounder, Bryan Cupps, were inspired to build CyberSlice after seeing the 1995 Sandra Bullock thriller, *The Net*. The film is about an eccentric and reclusive computer hacker named Angela Bennett who works out of a home office, advising company leaders on their information technology systems. But when she stumbles on government secrets, her identity gets stolen, and she's forced to go on the run from assassins and the police.

Though critics considered the film tacky and far-fetched, it predicted technological change with uncanny accuracy. It depicted remote work, identity theft, a digital fireplace, online flight booking, and—in an iconic opening scene—online pizza delivery. None of these innovations were broadly available at the time.

Tim remembers watching the opening scene in which Angela Bennett loads a website called Pizza.net, chooses a large pizza, then selects anchovy, garlic, and extra cheese as her toppings. All for fourteen dollars. "Your pizza will arrive in 45 minutes. Gratuity not included. Thank you for your order, Angela Bennett!" reads her computer screen.

"Did this exist anywhere?" Tim and Bryan wondered. Surely someone had thought of it already. Two years earlier, in August 1994, Pizza Hut ran a limited experiment of an online delivery service called PizzaNet in Santa Clara. But it required a Pizza Hut employee to call your home to verify the order, defeating the whole purpose of online ordering. Other than that, Tim and Bryan couldn't find any examples.

"What if we really did that?" Bryan asked Tim. They came up with an idea that would be far more ambitious than Pizza Hut's experiment: giving local, independent pizzerias in cities across the country the ability to sell pizza online.

In September 1996, they started CyberSlice and moved into an office overlooking Elliott Bay in Seattle. Bryan, an engineer, became CyberSlice's chief technology officer. Tim, a charming and gifted salesman, took the role of president. He would be in charge of building the sales team.

Even before starting in earnest, the cofounders ran into problems with their business model. The entire concept of web delivery sounded alien—even a little scary—to mom-and-pop pizza joints and their customers.

"They heard about this thing called the internet, but they had no idea what it was," Tim said. "So how could you get all these restaurants connected? How could you get their modems connected? It was just too complex."

They weren't the only ones with reservations. When Tim and Bryan pitched CyberSlice to venture capitalists, some were eager to invest. Others, not so much. "I'm gonna tell you about an invention," one VC shot back after hearing their pitch, "it's called the telephone!"

Critics didn't realize that online deliveries could solve a critical problem in the pizza industry. Local pizza shops were struggling to achieve citywide reach. Outside of the yellow pages, marketing happened by word of mouth, paper menus, and refrigerator magnets. In practice, that limited businesses' reach to a few-mile radius and restricted customers' options to what was in their neighborhoods.

CyberSlice planned to unlock the vast potential of the internet to allow users to access restaurants around their city and let businesses finally achieve a wider reach. Everything would come together on the CyberSlice website, which is where NeXT's WebObjects came in.

Google Maps did not exist and the geographic data sold at the time cost millions of dollars. So Bryan had to start from scratch to build the geographical database of pizza restaurants. Bryan divided the United States into a grid, with each square less than an eighth of a square mile. Then he gave each square a unique ID. The system would identify which grid the customer was located in, then display each restaurant delivering to that grid.

Because of the project's ambition, it carried an enormous risk of failure. In the ninety days between CyberSlice's founding in September and its planned December demo, Bryan and Tim had to build a company from scratch using new technology.

"One of the problems was, how are we going to get 12,000 or 13,000 pizzerias connected to this thing?" Tim explained. So the team again turned to WebObjects. With the help of NeXT consultants, they turned each restaurant menu into a collection of objects that could be assembled quickly. "This is the ticket," Bryan said, "because it allows us to glue everything together."

The second step: building a massive database of restaurants and their locations. The team would have to manually map out each pizzeria's delivery boundaries. Tim and Bryan hired Steve Green, a veteran owner of pizza stores, to facilitate it. Under his direction, CyberSlice employees mailed a cover letter to every pizzeria in a few target cities, starting with Los Angeles, Washington, DC, and Chicago. Restaurants were asked to shade in their delivery areas on a paper map, enclose a menu, and mail it back. Then the employees inserted the data by hand. "We had this whole factory of people keying in all the shades and squares," Tim remembered.

With the delivery database constructed, the cofounders had to solve yet another challenge: how to make the CyberSlice delivery system actually work. How could they guarantee that any pizzeria, including those without an internet connection, would be able to receive and deliver an order?

Ironically enough, the team turned to the telephone. They created a digital system that would call restaurants, translate online orders into a computer-generated voice, and prompt the restaurant to confirm the order by pressing numeric phone keys.

Because pizza ingredients were no match for the day's text-to-voice software—"The word *pepperoni* might come out pay-per-own-ee," Bryan said—the team hired a voice actor to record all of the words in every pizza menu.

As the launch date approached, CyberSlice became consumed in a frenetic scramble to get the website working. NeXT executives raised the stakes, telling Tim and Bryan that they wanted to host the event at their headquarters in Redwood City. Steve himself wanted to introduce the product in a demonstration of the power of WebObjects.

Steve would be the first person to order pizza on the system. This demo had to work, for the sake of both companies—it would be a centerpiece of NeXT's IPO story. NeXT provided CyberSlice with substantial technical support, sending engineers to work at CyberSlice's Seattle offices, helping with Objective-C coding, and recommending specialized consultants for the project.

On launch day, the team loaded CyberSlice onto a giant screen in the NeXT auditorium. Steve planned to place a web order for a tomato and basil pizza with no cheese—the vegan choice—from Amici's East Coast Pizzeria, which was a ten-minute drive away.

In order to allay the technologists' ritual concern about demos failing in front of everyone, NeXT's communications department preordered pizzas to keep backstage as backup. No one at NeXT or CyberSlice informed Amici's of the CyberSlice order ahead of time. If it had been coordinated, journalists at the event would call the pizzeria and ask if they knew about it and the whole presentation would be an embarrassment.

About an hour before stage time, Bryan felt a tap on his shoulder. He turned around.

"Hi, I'm Steve Jobs."

Bryan had heard horror stories of Steve ripping into people at a moment's notice. He felt nervous. Was something amiss for launch day?

"Killer app. Love it," Steve said.

"He thought it was cool," Bryan said. "He was very down to earth with me."

An hour later, Steve, Tim, and Bryan all took the stage for the product launch. Steve pulled up the CyberSlice website, which included an animated graphic of a spinning pizza, and searched for Amici's delivery menu. Then he selected his order for a vegan pie, while Bryan and Tim ordered meat and cheese pizzas.

"This is the future," Steve announced to the crowd.

Steve handed the stage to Bryan and Tim, who talked about the incredible uses for WebObjects. "*Newsweek*, *Time*, and all these different people were in the audience," Bryan said.

All of a sudden, an unsuspecting Amici's deliveryman walked in with about twenty pizzas for the audience. As surprised as he was to see the press, the press was surprised to see a real delivery driver appearing from the wings. They had assumed the demonstration was staged.

Usually, Steve disappeared after his presentations. But with CyberSlice, he stayed for the entire event, hanging around and mingling with the crowd, contributing to a joyful mood.

Here was Steve, planning his exit from NeXT, suddenly engaged because someone had used his technology to deliver pizza. He still couldn't resist a good demo.

"In the future, we're going to order everything online," he told the crowd.

With road-show planning still underway and the CyberSlice demo done, NeXT finally had momentum. And Goldman Sachs had its story—NeXT, the engine of e-commerce itself—complete with a cheesy hook.

25

OPERATION REBOOT

In August 1996, Apple CEO Gil Amelio sat alone in his office staring at a checklist. Elsewhere in the building, engineers were still arriving for work, still debugging code, still pretending that Copland—Apple's next-generation operating system named for composer Aaron Copland—had a future.

Five hundred engineers had been working on the project for two years now, at a cost of $500 million, and Apple had next to nothing to show for it. Copland was bleeding the company of time, talent, and cash.

For his checklist, Gil wrote out three possible courses of action:

1. Start from scratch with a new operating system.
2. License an operating system from another company.
3. Purchase an existing operating system outright.

Each option amounted to an admission of failure, an acknowledgment that the company behind the personal computing revolution could no longer build its own operating system. But without a modern OS, Apple users were left stuck in the dark ages, facing the spinning beach ball of death every time an application froze. One bad piece of software could force users to reach for the computer's power button.

Gil, the chairman of Apple's board, had been tapped a few months earlier to take over an Apple in crisis. He had come from the chipmaker National Semiconductor, which he had turned around after four years of heavy losses. Gil was a PhD physicist who insisted on being called "Doctor." He was portly and conservative, always dressed in a suit and tie.

As he took office, signs of Apple's imminent death abounded. The company's internal newsletter ran an article from human resources titled "Surviving a Layoff." Be open to change, it advised. Find something important about what you're doing. Believe you can make a difference.

Another newsletter article was titled "Why Does Apple Get Bad Press?" It read like a cry for help:

> Want a series of challenges? Try smoothly announcing lower-than-expected earnings, a series of top-level executive departures, aggravating product shortages, a product recall and [a] number of adjustments in key corporate initiatives. As a backdrop, your competition is flooding the media with the biggest, most expensive and over-hyped product intro in world history.

That product was Windows 95. Behind closed doors, Apple employees mocked Microsoft's interface, its instability, and what they saw as its shameless copying of the Mac. But the bravado rang hollow. Apple had no hits of its own to speak of—it produced a mess of middling products with bewildering names like Cyberdog, AppleScript, HyperCard, FireWire, OpenDoc, QuickTime VR, PowerPC. The old Apple had made two things—the Apple II and the Macintosh—and had made them well.

The product recall mentioned in the newsletter? That was the Power-

Book 5300, a $6,500 laptop that had started catching fire. Literally. *The New York Times*' John Markoff savaged Apple: "For months, Apple Computer Inc. had been contending that once consumers looked at Microsoft's new Windows 95 software, the comparison would help Apple's own business catch fire. Now, in a sense, its prophecy has come true, and . . . Apple's newest portable machines have burst into flames."

The fires, caused by defective lithium-ion batteries, were ruining Apple's reputation. The company had hoped to position the new laptops as symbols of high-tech glamour, even securing a $15 million product placement deal to feature them in *Mission: Impossible*, starring Tom Cruise.

Instead, Apple had to recall several thousand laptops, issuing replacements at a hundred-dollar discount and with hard drives that held only two thirds of the storage originally promised. Customers felt ripped off.

"When I walked in the door, I was facing five crises," Gil told *Fortune*:

> We were dangerously low on cash; the quality of our products was poor; the development of our next-generation operating system was behind schedule and in disarray; Apple's famously contrarian corporate culture was almost impossible to manage; and our product line and development efforts were fragmented to the point that the company was completely unfocused.

He discovered a total of three hundred active research and development projects. After slashing the number to fifty, he still thought it was too many. The engineering culture had devolved into anarchy. Gil kept hearing variations of the phrase "Steve Jobs can get away with whatever he wants, so I'm going to do whatever I want."

One routine financial review meeting pushed Gil over the edge. Apple's CFO casually glossed over a $50 million quarterly loss to currency exchange, as if hemorrhaging money were just another line item. When Gil pressed him on it, the CFO shrugged. "That's pretty much what we do every quarter," he said.

At the center of this chaos sat Copland, the operating system that was supposed to save the company. The project had started with noble ambitions—to compete with Windows 95 by offering memory protection, preemptive multitasking, and object-oriented programming. Preemptive multitasking allowed multiple applications to run smoothly at the same time, so one demanding program couldn't hog the computer and make everything else sluggish. It was a basic feature that Windows 95 already had but Mac OS still lacked.

By 1996, Copland had metastasized into something monstrous. Competing software teams had turned the project into a battlefield, with each faction demanding their pet features be included. The feature list exploded. And deadlines kept slipping away. When a beta release in November 1995 failed to reassure developers, Apple pushed Copland's release date all the way to January 1997.

At the Worldwide Developers Conference in May 1996, Gil had announced that instead of shipping Copland as one revolutionary OS, Apple would release it piecemeal—a feature here, an update there—in a last-ditch effort to save face and buy time.

But developers weren't easily fooled. And neither was the press. It confirmed what they saw as Gil's unfitness for the job—coming from National Semiconductor and stocking Apple's executive ranks with semiconductor experts who had never run a computer company. Gil and his team knew how to manufacture chips, not create magic for consumers.

He also faced criticism for slow decision-making. One Apple executive told journalist Brent Schlender, "It's as if Gil was a microprocessor running at 25 megahertz when the rest of the industry, and many people at Apple, have clock speeds of 200 megahertz. He takes six weeks to make a decision that should take only one."

At a cocktail party that spring, Gil had described Apple as "a boat. There's a hole in the boat, and it's taking on water. But there's also a treasure on board. And the problem is, everyone on board is rowing in different directions . . . My job is to get everyone rowing in the same direction so we can save the treasure."

A fellow CEO turned to his companion after Gil walked away. "But what about the hole?" he asked.

Gil brought in Ellen Hancock to serve as Apple's chief technology officer and enforcer. At the age of fifty-four, she had already served as the highest-ranking woman at IBM and National Semiconductor.

She credited her success to a type A personality and twelve-hour workdays. Where Apple engineers slouched in jeans and sandals, Ellen showed up in conservative suits and short-cropped gray hair, with rosary beads clicking in her purse. She could drink any engineer under the table and then show up the next morning without flinching. She earned the nickname "the Iron Grandmother."

She had broken through Silicon Valley's glass ceiling by, as a colleague put it, demanding "to be included in that all-male-bastion world, and they obliged because of her hard work and intelligence." She had earned a master's in mathematics from Fordham University and spent decades managing complex technical projects at IBM, including overseeing the development of mainframe computers and semiconductors. However, the Apple faithful still dismissed her as a corporate suit who lacked the creative vision they valued.

Gil's mandate for Ellen fell under a cost-cutting project he called Operation Reboot. Her assignment: figure out if Copland could be saved. After sitting through presentations from the Copland team—watching engineers struggle to explain their own code, seeing features that contradicted each other, and discovering that despite its overlong feature list, the

OS didn't embrace the innovations of the internet—she delivered her assessment to Gil: It was a basket case.

Meanwhile, Steve watched Apple's continued implosion with disgust. "I try not to talk about Apple too much, but what I will say is that the day I left Apple, we had a ten-year lead over Microsoft," he told *Fresh Air.* "The problem at Apple was that they stopped innovating. It wasn't that Microsoft was so brilliant or clever in copying the Mac. It's that the Mac was a sitting duck for ten years."

Gil ruled out option one on his checklist—starting from scratch. Apple had just proved it couldn't build a modern OS with unlimited time and money. It made no sense to try the same thing and expect different results. The next best options—shopping for someone else's operating system—would require admitting that Apple couldn't deliver by itself.

But that was the truth.

Gil had promised Wall Street that he would announce a new operating system strategy by January 1997. So he made a decision: He would scrap Copland and give Ellen less than five months to find, evaluate, and secure Apple's future operating system, according to journalist Jim Carlton.

She started making calls. Using Sun's Solaris, the operating system that powered high-end workstations and servers, looked like a possibility. Embracing Windows NT, while technically an option, would be corporate seppuku. But one other name kept coming up: Jean-Louis Gassée's BeOS.

Six years after leaving Apple, Jean-Louis still wore the crown of Silicon Valley royalty. He had been working in secrecy on his start-up Be, building what Apple now desperately needed: a modern, multimedia-savvy operating system. If anyone understood Apple's DNA and could deliver its future, it was Jean-Louis.

Jean-Louis arrived at Apple's Cupertino campus. Suave, confident, and still beloved by many Apple engineers, he presented Ellen and her team with what he called "seven ways to use Be's technology."

The demonstration impressed them. BeOS was stable and built for the internet age. It could run multiple applications without crashing. It handled multimedia with elegance. The Apple executives watched as Jean-Louis navigated through the interface, showing off features that made their Mac OS look prehistoric.

Ellen pushed forward with the deal, insisting that Apple needed to buy Be outright, not just license the technology. In October, Gil and Jean-Louis met at the Kauai Marriott Resort and Beach Club in Hawaii for negotiations. Usually, they would have met in the San Francisco Bay area, but Gil was on Kauai to speak at a conference. They had three months until Apple's deadline.

As waves crashed on the beach, Jean-Louis laid out his terms for returning to Apple. He would bring his entire fifty-person team from Be. He would report to Ellen but oversee all future operating system development, essentially becoming Apple's software czar. Jean-Louis offered to work for a dollar a year, a gesture of magnanimity. But his investors wanted 15 percent of Apple and a seat on the board.

Gil was stunned. Fifteen percent of Apple? The company might have been struggling, but it was still worth billions of dollars. At most, Gil valued Be at $50 million. Jean-Louis's start-up had impressive technology, but it would still take years of expensive development before Apple could ship it as a Mac operating system.

The negotiations continued through early November, with Apple making a cash offer that Jean-Louis said was well below $100 million. But he remained convinced that he held all the cards. Gil heard from a colleague that Jean-Louis said, "I've got them by the balls, and I'm going to squeeze until it hurts."

His logic: Apple had given itself mere months to make a decision. The clock was ticking, with two months until the deadline. According to someone close to the negotiations, Jean-Louis allegedly said, "A man in the desert doesn't bargain on the price of water."

Jean-Louis felt so confident in his position that he leaked news of the negotiations to the press. The stories appeared everywhere—*BusinessWeek*, the *San Jose Mercury News*, *The Wall Street Journal*. Now everyone knew that Be was in talks to save Apple and that Jean-Louis was likely coming home. The coverage put pressure on Apple's stock price and made Gil look desperate.

Apple executives were furious. From their perspective, the leak revealed Jean-Louis as someone who couldn't be trusted, someone willing to use public pressure to get his way. By mid-November, Jean-Louis's negotiating tactics were wearing thin. Gil quietly told Ellen to look at alternatives, including desperate ones like Windows NT and Solaris (though Sun's board had already rejected a merger), or reviving Apple's failed joint venture with IBM, a doomed project called Taligent that had tried to build a new operating system from scratch. Anything but cave to Jean-Louis's demands.

On November 15, Ellen told the Copland engineers to salvage what they could from their doomed OS. Maybe they could release a less ambitious version and buy some time. It was a hedge against the Be deal falling apart.

Two days later, at the COMDEX show in Las Vegas—the computer industry's massive annual trade gathering—Gil and Jean-Louis met for their final negotiation. The setting teed Jean-Louis up: thousands of industry insiders, press everywhere, the perfect audience to herald his return to Apple.

Apple's offer: $125 million cash.

Jean-Louis's response: No less than $200 million.

"Outrageous," Gil called it.

The talks collapsed. Jean-Louis left COMDEX still believing that, with the January deadline mere weeks away, Apple would come crawling back. He couldn't have known that soon after Ellen arrived back in Cupertino, she would receive a voicemail that would change everything.

This caller didn't promise to squeeze Apple's balls. He offered to solve the company's problems.

“Why don’t we just frickin’ call Apple?” Garrett Rice, a product manager at NeXT, asked a group of fellow managers. They were assembled in a common space at the Redwood City offices. Though he asked the question in jest, he was genuinely angry.

An English major who’d fallen in love with the original Mac, he then became obsessed with NeXT. He had even volunteered to work for free just to be near it. Now he saw in the newspapers that Apple was prepared to spend tens of millions of dollars on Jean-Louis’s operating system, which the NeXT team saw as a pale imitation of NeXT’s technology.

If Apple was looking at Be, why not just buy the real thing? Garrett believed NeXT stood on “a dragon’s hoard of technology” that everyone seemed to be overlooking.

Garrett left the group of managers, walked back to his office, and took a risk. He picked up his designer phone and called the head of software at Apple. He left what he described as “one of my more inspired sales pitches” on the man’s voicemail, explaining why Apple should be looking at NeXT instead of Be.

The executive called back: “I’m leaving the company,” he said. “Here’s Ellen Hancock’s number.”

So Garrett called Ellen and left the same pitch on her answering machine. He didn’t focus on Steve, instead talking about NeXT’s technology. He argued that if Apple wanted to be thorough it should at least look at NeXT.

“I hadn’t even thought about that,” Ellen later told journalist Jim Carlton.

“Ellen did something that was unusual for a person in her position,” Steve recounted to *The New York Times*. “She returned his phone call.”

Garrett rushed to his boss Mitch Mandich, who ran sales at NeXT. He laid out what had just happened—the call, Ellen’s interest, the door he might have just cracked open. Mitch looked shocked but smiled “like, holy shit, this could be a really great opportunity,” Garrett recalled.

Mitch went and got Steve and Avie. "Ellen Hancock wants to meet," Garrett told them.

In any other universe, Garrett's call might have gotten him fired. But in this timeline, it worked out. And thanks to him, Steve was about to enter Apple's airspace once again.

It was good timing. NeXT's IPO had skeptics inside the company. One profitable year in eleven wasn't a story investors wanted to hear. And Steve continued to drift away. He planned to hand off oversight of the company's day-to-day operations to the Office of the President, consisting of Avie, Mitch, and Dominique.

During IPO planning, the team began to get acquisition interest from suitors like Novell, Oracle (which came around twice), and Microsoft. Despite the antagonism between Steve and Bill, Microsoft's interest made business sense. For a year, NeXT had been adapting its software tools to run on Windows NT. This gave Microsoft's corporate customers access to NeXT's tools while still using Microsoft's operating system.

NeXT's object-oriented software did things Microsoft couldn't match, like speeding up app development for corporations. "If you put our stuff on top of it," Dominique said, "it legitimized Microsoft NT, which was very important for Microsoft."

While Microsoft owned the market, NeXT had a corner on elegance. "The user experience on Microsoft was not good," Dominique said. "It was getting a bit embarrassing." Acquiring NeXT could help Bill solve the problem.

But the talks fell apart. Microsoft executives feared what would happen if NeXT's engineers came inside. These weren't just programmers, after all—they were Steve's handpicked assassins, people who'd spent years building technology that made Microsoft's best efforts look clunky.

IBM also looked at buying NeXT, but Steve called the matchup a "total lack of chemistry." IBM executive Jim Cannavino—"Cousin Jim," as NeXT executives remembered him from their collaboration a decade earlier—remembered it differently. According to him, Steve called IBM offering to sell NeXTSTEP.

Regardless, the company wasn't interested in making a deal. "Steve, get another script here," Cousin Jim said. "We write operating systems as a lunchtime hobby."

But now Apple was calling. And for Steve, Apple was different from any other potential purchaser. As Larry Ellison later explained to journalist Brent Schlender:

> It's as if Apple is an old fiancée from college that Steve met again at a 20-year class reunion. Steve is happily married now with children, and has a great life. When he meets his old girlfriend again, she's an alcoholic and is running around with a bad crowd and has made a mess of her life. Even so, in his mind's eye, he still sees the beautiful woman he once thought was the love of his life. So what's he supposed to do?

The metaphor captured Steve's paralysis. A year earlier, he had entertained a hostile takeover of Apple with Larry. But when it came time to pull the trigger, Steve balked. Since then, he'd told his NeXT executives, including Dominique and Jon, that he had no interest in returning to Apple.

He had spent eleven years proving he didn't need Apple—building NeXT and Pixar. At Pixar, his ongoing work had given him entrée into Hollywood. He could be something beyond a computer executive. He could be a film mogul.

Yet Steve couldn't let go of his care for Apple. Every failed product was personal. It was proof that the board had been wrong to fire him but also evidence that his creation was perishing without him.

Dominique got a call from Ellen on November 27. "I'm looking at acquiring Be, and it's a very green operating system," Ellen told him. "Would you be okay if I sent our senior engineers this afternoon to kick the tires?"

Apple's engineers and managers were stopped cold by what they found at NeXT. NeXTSTEP boasted technical elegance that Mac OS could only dream of. The development environment cut programming time dramatically. The sophisticated architecture had been running stably for years while Copland couldn't even compile.

But what really caught Apple's attention was something so basic as to be almost embarrassing: memory protection. Windows NT had it. Unix had it. Even BeOS had it. But Mac System 7, the operating system running on millions of Macs around the world, didn't. When one program crashed on a Mac, everything crashed. Your unsaved work, gone. Your other applications, frozen. Your only option: restart your computer and pray.

Apple's engineers reported back, "Ellen, it looks better than we thought." In a conference room, Ellen gave numerical scores to each of Apple's five OS options using a rubric that scored ease of use, internet accessibility, memory protection, multitasking, and the speed with which the new system could hit the market. NeXTSTEP came out highest, and Be came out second.

This despite the fact that, from NeXT's perspective, NeXTSTEP was yesterday's news. Steve had already pivoted the company to WebObjects and web development tools.

The growing competition between NeXT and Be for Apple's acquisition was becoming Silicon Valley's worst-kept secret. Around this time,

Dan'l Lewin, by then CEO of intellectual property start-up Aurigin Systems, was having dinner at Il Fornaio in Palo Alto with a former Apple executive. They sat in a booth right behind the maître d' stand, with Dan'l facing the front door.

Just over a low divider decorated with plants, in another booth with his back to the door, sat Jean-Louis, dining with another former Apple executive, John Couch.

Steve walked in. He immediately spotted Dan'l and gave him a wave of acknowledgment before veering away. As Steve walked around the divider toward the other tables, he saw John and said hello. Then he noticed who was sitting across from him.

"Jean-Louis!" Steve said, his voice dripping with sarcasm. "I hear you're going to save Apple."

A few days later, just after Thanksgiving, Steve called Gil directly to give him a simple message: BeOS was the wrong choice for Apple.

Steve told friends he wasn't even trying to sell NeXT when he made the call. He just wanted to warn Apple away from Be. He thought Jean-Louis's software was all wrong for the company. But Gil, intrigued by Steve's certainty, invited him to come make his case in person.

On December 2, with NeXT's IPO struggling to materialize and Apple approaching its self-imposed deadline, Steve walked into Gil's conference room on the eighth floor of Apple's headquarters. He pitched Apple's leadership on an entirely new strategy, built around NeXT. Yes, he said, NeXT had the software to shore up the Macintosh. But there was a greater opportunity too: NeXT could enable Mac software to work on standard PCs, opening up new markets that Apple had never been able to touch.

Steve was at his charismatic best. But Gil understood the magnitude of what he was considering. Steve had been forced out of Apple for good reasons. He was impossible to manage, mercurial, destructive to corporate order. Bringing him back would be inviting chaos.

Two days later, Ellen informed Apple's board that NeXT was in play. They gave the green light for what Gil called a "shootout." The two archenemies would face off in Cupertino, each pitching his respective company: Steve Jobs, the exiled cofounder, versus Jean-Louis Gassée, the prince who'd replaced him.

26

SHOOT-OUT

On Tuesday afternoon, December 10, 1996, Apple executives filed into the Garden Court Hotel in Palo Alto. They were eager to see a showdown.

Apple had selected the venue—a posh, Spanish-style hotel—for its privacy. The technology press had been following this story for ten days, after the conversations first leaked in *The Wall Street Journal*, and would be looking closely for any action happening at Apple's campus.

Steve stepped into the hotel's conference room to present first.

As he began to detail NeXTSTEP's innovative features, Gil noticed something different about Steve. He wasn't the same person as the self-absorbed entrepreneur Gil had once known. In his place stood a "pragmatic, specific, precise" executive, Gil wrote in his memoir, *On the Firing Line*. In command of the facts, praising his system's virtues without pushing too hard.

It helped that, despite NeXT's many troubles, Steve wasn't desperate to make a deal with Apple. NeXT had positioned itself as a strategic partner, not a company seeking rescue. Steve still left open the possibility of the IPO.

Even as he extolled NeXTSTEP's virtues, he was transparent about the company's financial situation. He opened NeXT's books to reveal losses of $50 million from 1993 to mid-1996.

Steve clearly recognized NeXT's limitations. And it seemed he was beginning to recognize his own too. When the time came for a technical demo, he turned the floor over to Avie instead of doing it himself.

As Avie pulled out a laptop to start the demo, the Apple executives leaned in. Then Avie began to open applications. At a time when most personal computers struggled to play a single video file smoothly, Avie showed that NeXTSTEP could handle them and more. "We had productivity apps, we had games, we had QuickTime movies—four of them on the screen, 3D models, all going at the same time," Avie told the Computer History Museum.

The Apple team knew they were witnessing the future.

Then senior Apple engineer Wayne Meretsky began asking Steve and Avie pointed questions about any shortcomings of using NeXT software for Apple. The room's energy shifted, and for a brief moment, the presentation threatened to become adversarial.

But Steve didn't dismiss Wayne's concerns or deflect as he might have in the past. He acknowledged them, suggesting that they were the kind of solvable engineering problems that accompany all technological advancements. "Steve was, as one would expect, smooth," Wayne later recounted to former Apple executive Jay Elliot. "Everyone in the room understood how valuable software that could control so much processing power could be for Apple."

After a little more than an hour, team NeXT left the room. They had made a strong impression. "Between them, Avie and Steve were a very compelling duo," Gil concluded. It would be a tough act to follow.

When Jean-Louis entered the conference room, it looked like he was pursuing a different approach. He hadn't brought anyone else from his team. He wasn't carrying a laptop. In fact, he had no prepared presentation whatsoever.

Because the two teams had been kept separate, Jean-Louis had no idea what Steve had just done. He wasn't prepared for the fight. "Jean-Louis . . . did not understand that this was a shootout, or else still thought he had the decision locked up," Gil wrote in *On the Firing Line*, "even though stories had been appearing in the papers for ten days about my conversations with Steve."

Jean-Louis's presentation lasted mere minutes. According to Gil, he essentially said, "Your technical people have met with my technical people, so you know the strengths of our solution." He didn't deliver a pitch and didn't invite a technical discussion as his opponents had.

The Apple executives watched Jean-Louis's nonperformance with resentment. They had carved time out of their schedules to watch a substantive technical presentation. Where Steve and Avie had demonstrated their product's superiority through working code, Jean-Louis offered only entitled assumptions. Where NeXT had treated Apple's team as serious evaluators, Be treated them as inconvenient hurdles getting in the way of an inevitable conclusion.

"Everything pointed toward Steve Jobs and NeXT," Gil concluded, "but Jean-Louis had made it a no-contest." The Apple engineer in the room, Wayne, agreed.

When the presentations ended, Steve and Avie walked out into chilly Palo Alto, past the coast live oaks lining the streets, for one of his "signature Steve Jobs walks around Palo Alto," as Avie called them. The pair encountered one of the Apple team members on the street.

"You guys won easily, no problem," he told them. "You have nothing to worry about."

Three days later, Steve invited Gil to his Palo Alto home. He boiled water for tea, gave him a tour of the house, then led him to the kitchen table. With steaming mugs between them, the negotiation for NeXT began.

Steve opened, offering the company at $12 a share, which would have made the total acquisition price $500 million. It was a high opening offer and Gil knew it. But not an entirely unfair one. Apple would be buying more than just code—it would be integrating an existing operating system, assuming $50 million in additional annual revenue from NeXT's software business, harnessing the promise of WebObjects, and acquiring a team of seasoned engineers. Most importantly, it would be getting Steve himself.

Apple would be taking on serious debt obligations too. NeXT owed $28.2 million to Canon, $11 million to J. P. Morgan, and $8 million to Merrill Lynch—nearly $50 million in debt that Steve had personally guaranteed $17 million of.

Dominique had embarked on aggressive cost cutting for the previous three years, when NeXT's debts stood at $400 million. But even at almost a tenth of the original debt load, the number was still substantial for a company that had posted only one year's worth of meager profits.

"[Twelve dollars] isn't possible," Gil told him, according to *On the Firing Line*. "I can't see that kind of money. It's more than I want to spend. I don't think I can meet it."

"What's the number you're looking at?" Steve asked.

"I think I have a shot at convincing the board to take ten dollars. I don't think I can get a penny more than that."

The negotiation turned out to be speedy and terse. Steve didn't care about squeezing every penny from the deal. He wanted to get NeXT off his plate so that he could focus on Pixar.

The negotiation was different from any Gil had experienced. The traditional scenery, a corporate boardroom, and the typical players, corporate lawyers, were replaced with two men haggling in the kitchen.

Dominique, who had prepared the financials but wasn't in the kitchen that day, later called it "the fastest acquisition I've seen in the world."

By his estimate, the whole pricing discussion took five minutes. It was remarkably brief for a deal of this magnitude.

The two CEOs shook hands. The price: $10 a share. Apple began planning a grand celebration to mark the homecoming of its founding father. Apple executives envisioned flying Steve in by helicopter while employees gathered on the campus lawn holding candles—a sea of lights welcoming back their exiled founder, Dominique recounted.

Steve had mixed feelings about his return to Apple—according to his negotiation with Gil, Steve would be merely an adviser, not an executive, and he would remain CEO of Pixar. He hadn't decided how long he'd stay or what role he would ultimately want to play.

A helicopter arrival with thousands of people holding candles would create expectations he wasn't ready to meet. This wasn't a homecoming; it was a trial run.

Steve nixed the ceremony.

Even as he worked to seal the NeXT deal, Gil's allies gave him stark warnings about what Steve's return might mean for his own leadership.

"I remember sitting in a meeting and saying to Gil, 'If you buy NeXT, Steve will end up running the company,'" a former senior Apple executive told John Heilemann of *The New Yorker*. "But Gil didn't understand how much firepower Steve had. Either that or he felt he could harness it. And you can't. Steve doesn't know how to do anything but lead."

An Apple alumnus who had known Steve since the early eighties put it more colorfully. He called Ellen directly and, according to Heilemann, said: "Ellen, Steve is going to fuck Gil so hard his eardrums will pop."

Ellen herself told Gil that she suspected Steve would succumb to "founderitis"—the inability of company founders to work under anyone else's authority.

But the warnings didn't dissuade Gil. He felt certain that Steve's return would boost morale among Apple's despondent employees and revive the company's spirit of innovation. He also believed in his own prowess as CEO—he felt he could hold his own against Steve.

NeXT executives thought Gil failed to grasp what Steve's twelve years in the wilderness had given him. Steve came away not only with better skills for building technology but better strategies for getting exactly what he wanted.

In retrospect, Gil said his decision to bring back Steve was the correct choice, even if it turned into an act of self-sacrifice. Be's software impressed him, but NeXT's technology was stronger and more mature. Bringing Steve back could cost him personally, but Gil knew it gave Apple its only real chance at survival.

"I was driven not by what was right for Gil Amelio but by what was right for Apple," Gil told Heilemann.

In preparation for Steve's return, Apple's legal department began drafting a standard employment agreement: Steven P. Jobs, incoming senior adviser. This is what Steve had agreed to with Gil.

But now Steve had other ideas. "That [employment agreement] was not going to happen," NeXT lawyer Chris Palermo said. As detailed negotiations proceeded, Steve dismantled every constraint on his role. He was no longer willing to be anyone's employee, instead insisting on remaining an independent consultant. He wanted to keep his options open.

Final negotiations stretched past midnight on December 16, missing that day's deadline for announcing the deal. While the price was settled, Steve refused to commit to any defined leadership position at Apple. He wanted to remain CEO of Pixar, wanted the freedom to come and go, and wanted to assess Apple's dysfunction before deciding how deeply he would get involved.

Gil needed Steve as part of the package—NeXT without Steve would be like buying the Starship *Enterprise* without Captain Kirk. Steve knew this and used it as leverage.

The negotiations revealed Steve's deep ambivalence. He demanded a consultant's fee but no executive title. He wanted influence without obligation, presence without commitment. As talks continued through December 19, Chris, along with Nancy Heinen, NeXT's general counsel, worked through draft after draft, trying to define a role that was hard to pin down: How do you contract with someone who hasn't decided if he really wants to be there?

The solution that emerged after midnight gave Steve everything he wanted: He would be free to assess Apple's situation and define his role later. No obligations, no constraints. Gil got NeXT's technology and the promise of Steve's involvement—somehow, somewhere. Apple paid north of $400 million for NeXT and gave a blank check to Steve to write his own future at Apple. One man was betting the company. The other was keeping his options open.

Chris left the office at 1:00 a.m. on December 20, exhausted.

At 8:00 a.m. on December 20, 1996, Gil sent a letter announcing the deal.

The $427 million acquisition announcement was straightforward enough—Apple would buy NeXT, with Steve receiving $120 million in cash and 1.5 million shares of Apple worth roughly $37 million. Steve had initially demanded all cash, as had his fellow NeXT investors Canon and Ross Perot. Gil pushed back. He needed Steve invested in Apple's turnaround. Steve took the stock.

On paper, the arrangement looked almost quaint. Apple's banished cofounder would return as a senior adviser with no operational authority, reporting to the CEO.

"In this new era, the 'Not Invented Here' syndrome has been banished far beyond the horizons of our vision," Gil wrote in a letter to

Apple employees. "We will be open to new technologies, and where they're developed doesn't matter. In this new era, we will not be an island in the industry; but rather build a bridge to the center of an open standards world based on industry alliances."

To the engineers who'd been working eighty-hour weeks trying to salvage Copland and fix Apple's OS problems, this was not reassuring. It sounded like a public admission that their work had failed, delivered by their own CEO. He'd just announced that the company had given up on them in favor of NeXT. Engineers read his letter as their professional obituaries.

In the afternoon of December 20, Gil and Steve signed the contract that made the deal official. Then, at a 6:00 p.m. press conference, Gil said, "We picked plan A instead of Plan Be."

"I'm not just buying software, I'm buying Steve," he said.

The media's coverage of the deal was ecstatic. Satellite trucks and hundreds of members of the global press gathered outside Apple's headquarters as the acquisition dominated tech headlines worldwide.

The New York Times framed it as Apple's desperate attempt to reverse the perception that it "was washed up" by acquiring NeXT's operating system. The paper quoted Sun CTO Eric Schmidt, who said NeXTSTEP was "somewhere between five and seven years ahead of everyone else." CNET called it a "stunning move," with analysts noting that while Gil and Ellen were "extremely competent," they lacked charisma—exactly what Steve would bring back to the mix.

Jean-Louis, meanwhile, conceded defeat. "Congratulations for all aspects of an extremely well-crafted deal," he wrote to Gil after hearing about the acquisition. "Clearly we were not in the same technical and financial league."

Steve, meanwhile, still wasn't excited about returning to Apple. At 9:24 that night, he wrote to all his Pixar employees that the acquisition was actually a great opportunity to cultivate more work with them because Pixar was his true love. As quoted in *Make Something Wonderful*:

> This [the Apple acquisition of NeXT] is great for Pixar—it will free me up from running two companies, so I can devote even more of my energies to Pixar. There may even be some possibilities for Pixar and Apple to work together in the future (if creatively driven!).
>
> And, this is really great for me. I have been working with a group of wonderful colleagues at NeXT for over a decade, and having our work finally become mainstream will be very gratifying (a feeling everyone at Pixar already knows). I will be advising Apple on their product strategy, and I will get to spend even more of my time at Pixar:).
>
> I am very happy and excited.
>
> Steve

By February 1997, nearly everyone had left NeXT's Redwood City offices; according to Gil, 350 "exceptional NeXT employees" were joining Apple. One by one, they filed out, past the grand floating staircase, past the dock where engineering teams used to ceremoniously throw departing colleagues into the creek. The expensive offices overlooking the marina, with their $10,000 sofas and Ansel Adams prints, became a ghostly monument to NeXT's run. The floating staircase—which would later inspire similar designs in Apple retail stores—turned into a metaphor for the company itself: beautiful, gravity-defying, but unsupported.

NeXT was no more. And at forty-three years old, Steve had returned to the former home that had thrown him out. He walked back in the door not as the prodigal son but as hired help.

In the time he'd been gone, he'd experienced a deep shift. He had lost the desperation of a couple years earlier. He could now take a larger view, staring down challenges with confidence and calm. He had learned how to step back, delegate, and let go. He understood how to choose his battles instead of fighting every single one. That's how dozens of NeXT executives remembered him during this time.

And now, for the second time, he had relinquished control of a company he founded. He was free to take up the mantle of an independent consultant—for the symbolic sum of a dollar a year—with proximity to power and the freedom to maneuver.

The position was enough for Steve. He had Pixar to focus on and had no intention of running Apple again. Steve told his former NeXT colleagues that his consulting role would give him the maximum flexibility to engage as much or as little as he wanted—allowing him to test the waters at Apple while maintaining his primary focus on Pixar and retain the freedom to walk away if things didn't work out.

But soon he would actually start working at the company he had cofounded, carrying twelve years of hard-won wisdom about technology and leadership. What no one could predict: how he would react when he saw how Apple had transformed in his absence or how quickly emotional attachment could override his best-laid plans.

27

ONE FOOT IN

At the Macworld conference in January 1997, Apple hoped to reassure developers, journalists, and employees that a new and better Apple was on the horizon.

Gil kicked the presentation off by explaining how NeXT software was going to enable a much-needed retooling of Mac OS. Then he rambled for more than two hours, reading from a detailed outline rather than a prepared speech. He explained that Apple had established sixty criteria for evaluating operating systems. He clicked through arcane diagrams on the screen, lectured about preserving investments and retrospective compatibility, and announced many, many new things.

He explained that the Mac's forthcoming operating system would be designed to run two different systems at once—one he'd code-named "Blue Box" to run old Mac programs, another called "Yellow Box" to run new, modern software. Then he rambled about why Apple needed Java, the web programming language. "We need Java in here. So let's, let's put in some Java, and let's make sure the machine meets the minimum requirements, preserves your investment, provides stability, performance, and predictability of the modern OS."

Each announcement seemed to spawn three more. The cascade of product names and timelines suggested Apple was trying to solve every problem at once rather than focusing on the one that mattered most: staying alive.

As Gil droned on, people in the room could feel the audience lose interest. "It was amazing to watch," Avie would later recall to the Computer History Museum, "and I say that in a not good way."

Two hours later, Gil made a belated aviation analogy to attempt to illustrate what he'd been saying. "If you can imagine the Macintosh being analogous to a small Cessna, a small airplane," he said, arguing that the Mac had started small, but Apple had kept adding things—passengers, cargo, weight. "Then you realize that the engines really weren't strong enough. So you switch from the 68k prop engine to the PowerPC jet engine."

"That's no way to design an airplane," he said. In other words, time for a reset.

After his ramble, Gil finally handed things off. Along with the tech from the acquisition, he said, "we also got this guy named Steve Jobs."

As Steve took the stage, the energy in the room shifted. The audience gave him a standing ovation. But those closest to him knew this moment represented something more complex than a triumphant return. According to former NeXT head of hardware engineering Jon Rubinstein, who would follow Steve to Apple, Steve had been reluctant to come back to Apple at all. Laurene had opposed his return, concerned about how the stress from dealing with Apple's dysfunction would impact her husband. "She was worried about him, and rightfully so," Jon said.

"Thank you. Thank you very much. Let's chat for a few minutes about what we are trying to do here," Steve said onstage, as if the previous two hours hadn't just happened. Then he made things insanely simple.

"This is our mission," he began, speaking without notes. "What we want to try to do is to provide relevant, compelling solutions that customers can only get from Apple." He paused as the audience applauded. "If we can't figure out how to do that, then I think there's a lot of other options for people to buy their computers from."

Where Gil had spun up a tortured airplane metaphor, Steve's slide showed a clean outline of a building, with each floor representing a successive level of software development. He explained that DOS, the most basic operating system, put developers on the ground floor by offering virtually nothing in the way of prewritten code. The Mac's toolbox brought developers up to the fifth floor. But, with Windows 95, Microsoft had caught up. "That's not good for us," Steve said.

Thanks to NeXTSTEP, Steve said that Apple could take the lead once again, lifting developers up to the twentieth floor. He demonstrated NeXTSTEP's capabilities by running five QuickTime movies simultaneously. Then he built a working application in real time using NeXTSTEP's Interface Builder, dragging components together like blocks and connecting them without writing any code. This way of building software without writing code was central to NeXTSTEP's appeal but still alien to most Mac developers.

The audience was glued. Steve had learned to harness his charisma—instead of overtly selling the product, he simply showed them why his software was special.

Gil took the reins back and ended the event with a surprise: a staged reunion between Apple's two founders. Even this he bungled. Steve Wozniak, also an incoming adviser to the CEO, emerged from the wings instead of the back of the theater, where Gil expected him.

"You're supposed to be in the back!" Gil said to him over the applause.

Then Gil gave the two Steves commemorative Macs with special serial numbers: Steve Wozniak got number one, like his original employee badge. Steve Jobs got zero because even in 1976, Steve had refused to take badge number two.

The next day, Apple's press office found a dismaying report in the *San Francisco Examiner.* It lambasted Gil for his speech that "meandered from point to point in the fashion of Bob Dole, and droned on for 150 minutes in the best tradition of Fidel Castro." Worse still, the article said that, for all its endless information, the presentation lacked the one thing the expo attendees wanted to see most: "a plan to survive."

In his book, Gil pinned the poor performance on his speechwriter, blaming him for being insufficiently prepared and missing deadlines. But colleagues said Gil had taken a vacation before his keynote to his home in Lake Tahoe and failed to rehearse the speech.

In the fallout, Steve notched his first victory against Gil, whom he derided as a "bozo" in private. The CEO had bored everyone to tears while Steve, who held no operational authority as a senior adviser, had commanded the room. As Jon observed: "Gil was a very nice man, but completely clueless. He had no business in that role. He was just a fish out of water, and Steve was really pissed at the whole thing"—Apple's chaos.

Within weeks of Steve's return, the company's leadership structure began bending toward him.

Gil had tried to delineate their respective roles. "I said, 'Steve, I'll never be as charismatic as you, and you'll never be as good an operating guy as me.' He agreed," Gil told John Heilemann of *The New Yorker.* He imagined Steve offering input here and there.

But Steve quickly planted a stake in the ground. The first major personnel decision following the merger was where to put Avie, NeXT's software chief. As the architect of NeXTSTEP, he would be the obvious choice to lead the renovation of Mac OS. After all, he'd already led the porting of NeXTSTEP to Intel.

Gil wanted Avie to report to Ellen, but Steve objected. Ellen was well-liked by Gil's inner circle, but she hadn't written software for a few decades. In Steve's eyes, that made her unqualified to manage Avie, his star. At a staff meeting with Avie, Ellen had made a clumsy comment about a technical detail. It was a minor incident that Steve trumped up as reason to remove her. Steve called her a "bozo" behind her back—and it leaked to the press.

Gil, in thrall to Steve, complied with Steve's wishes. He agreed that Avie was, in fact, more technically qualified for the role. And because the operating system would be so central to the company's success, technical competence mattered a great deal. Steve told an audience at Stanford that "the management team he [Gil] was inheriting from NeXT was actually quite a bit better than the one he had at Apple. And so I was trying to make sure these people didn't get totally crushed."

Avie would report instead to the even-tempered Gil, bypassing the CTO, Ellen. It made a nice change, Avie said, from things at NeXT. With Steve, he had always had to brace for the worst.

As "Apple's new 'Mr. Fixit,'" as *The Wall Street Journal* called him, Avie took over a team of engineers who had an industry-wide reputation for being pampered. He exhorted them to forget elegant technical details and just get products out the door.

Steve pushed for another NeXT alumnus to join Apple's leadership as well: Jon Rubinstein. Jon had run hardware engineering at NeXT before departing to found a start-up that he later sold to Motorola. Gil agreed that he was top talent and made him head of hardware at Apple.

Just like that, Steve had installed his people to head up Apple's core technology divisions—even though, as Jon later recalled, Steve "wasn't around that much the first six months." The fact that Steve could orchestrate such strategic personnel changes while barely present revealed

Apple's desperation, not a master plan to take the company over. It was so close to collapse that its CEO was eagerly handing over key divisions to proven talent, regardless of their loyalties.

But some Apple executives speculated that Steve was orchestrating an overthrow, methodically placing his loyalists in key positions. Gil himself wondered about Steve's true motives.

"Maybe Steve really was just setting me up, putting his own people in place, ready for a palace coup," he later wrote. "If so, the decisions I made were bad for me. But they were beneficial for Apple, and I would likely have made them even had I known for certain that Steve was being guided by ulterior motives."

Gil's calculation was simpler than palace intrigue. Apple needed the best talent it could get, and with the company months from bankruptcy, there was no time for anything but competence.

On February 3, 1997, Avie and Jon attended their first executive staff meeting at Apple. They had arrived the same day—Avie from NeXT as part of the acquisition, Jon as the new head of hardware engineering tasked with saving a dying company. Within minutes of listening to what was going on around the conference table, Jon caught Avie's eye.

"Oh my God, what did we get ourselves into?" Jon thought, looking at his fellow engineer. "This is a disaster."

Nobody was running the place. Apple managers oversaw their own fiefdoms with no coordination. The ideas people proposed struck Jon as "nuts." The result was madness: Each division was building its own basic computer start-up software and independently developing identical computer chips. "The company was in shambles, absolute shambles," Jon would later recount to the Computer History Museum.

When NeXT engineers joined, some were told they'd have until the end of the year to revive Apple. But a new financial reality compressed the timeline. Apple—worth $4 billion in the early 1990s but now valued at just $1.5 billion—had lost $816 million the previous year. Perhaps one quarter of cash remained. If they failed to turn around the disaster in the next three months, the company could go under.

They'd have to overcome a lot. Gil's pet project, the Twentieth Anniversary Mac—a technical marvel created in honor of Apple's twentieth anniversary—had taken so long to build that its parts were already obsolete. When half of the displays manufactured by LG failed, Jon demanded legal action against the South Korean giant. But Apple's lawyers were sheepish. "We haven't finished our agreement yet," they said. In other words, Apple had shipped products without contracts in place.

In a Sacramento warehouse, $1 billion of printer inventory gathered dust, "like that warehouse scene in *Raiders of the Lost Ark*," Jon said. When asked why, executives shrugged. "Who knows? It was mismanagement, right?" he told the Computer History Museum.

To buy the company precious days of runway, Apple's CFO Fred Anderson played three-dimensional chess with creditors and suppliers.

At the executive team meeting, Jon and Avie made the decision to make deep spending cuts to buy time. "The marching orders were 'let's whack the company in half,'" Jon recalled.

They laid off seven hundred engineers and slashed entire divisions. Jon had to eliminate the entire Singapore office—more than seven hundred people—because their products were "unreliable" and had "enormous" failure rates in the field. He shut down a big group in France that was working on address book software. The server division: gone. The low-end computer division: gone.

In his youth, Steve might have rushed in to fire people personally and use the power vacuum to implement his vision for Apple. But this more mature Steve had learned when to step back and trust his people. Steve didn't advise him to make decisions, Jon recounted. He was simply not involved.

Steve's distrust of Apple management ran so deep that he didn't even rely on the company's IT support for his personal computers.

When Steve needed technical help at home—setting up his Mac, troubleshooting software—he called Pixar instead of Apple. For months, Ed Catmull recalled, "the systems person at Pixar was the one who was providing the Apple support in his home . . . because he actually didn't have the people he trusted at Apple at the time."

On February 4, 1997, Gil announced the layoffs. Rumors spread throughout the company and the press that Steve was plotting to take back Apple. Steve kept denying it. "People keep trying to suck me in," Steve told *BusinessWeek*. "They want me to be some kind of Superman. But I have no desire to run Apple Computer. I deny it at every turn, but nobody believes me." NeXT alumni still insist to this day that Steve was still unsure whether he wanted to stay at Apple and that his love was Pixar.

That March, as Apple struggled, Steve's old friend Larry Ellison spotted opportunity: He decided, this time without telling Steve beforehand, to launch a campaign to take over Apple.

"I put Steve in this horrible position," Larry later recalled to *Vanity Fair*. "Steve had a heart attack [when I told him]. We were hiking at Castle Rock Park last weekend. He tried to talk me out of it. He said, 'Is this really what you want to do for the next five years? You could be on a desert island with a girlfriend getting your private life in order! Have kids! Run for governor!' I said, 'Steve, I believe Apple is the only brand in our industry that is cool. I have to do it.'"

The next day, Larry went public with his takeover bid in the *San Jose Mercury News*. He'd gathered investors and was willing to pay more than $1.25 billion for 60 percent of Apple's stock.

"Apple is in desperate need of all-new management and leadership," Larry declared to *The Washington Post*. His first step upon gaining control would be to fire Apple's current management, including Gil.

After the story broke, Larry called Steve to tell him.

"He goes, 'No, you're kidding, you didn't do this,'" Larry said to *Vanity Fair.*

"I said, 'Yeah, I did.'

"'No . . . You didn't mention my name, did you? Tell me you didn't mention my name.'

"'Well, yeah.'

"'Oh, God . . .'"

Steve's name was now publicly linked to a hostile takeover of the company he'd cofounded, the company where he now served as an adviser. Larry pressed him: "Well, Steve, will you [help me]?"

"Yeah," Steve said, sighing. "What are friends for?"

Though Larry claimed Steve agreed to help, Steve told the *San Francisco Chronicle* that he was not involved in the takeover bid and that it was "a soap opera that I frankly don't care about." Steve repeatedly denied wanting to grow his influence at Apple.

Apple's lawyers had a defensive weapon they could activate called a "poison pill," a shareholder rights plan that would flood the market with shares if Larry tried to buy in, making any acquisition exponentially more expensive. Gil saw the timing as predatory. "If you were going to try to take over a company, when would you do it?" he asked reporters. Larry had made the announcement just two weeks before Apple announced another devastating quarterly loss.

If Larry triggered the poison pill plan, Apple's existing shareholders could suddenly buy new stock at a discount from the market price. For Apple supporters, this created an unexpected opportunity. They could potentially profit while defending their beloved company.

But Larry's vision for the company horrified many devoted Apple fans. He planned to pivot the company from consumer-focused computers toward network computers—stripped-down terminals that would replace personal computers and rely on distant servers for their software. They feared Apple's beloved personal computer would morph into an office appliance dependent on Oracle's infrastructure and corporate networks.

Larry's bid split the faithful into warring camps. Within days, a "Save Apple Computer" campaign emerged on a simple website. The group rallied people to stop Larry's bid and "prevent Mr. William Gates III from achieving his dream of total domination."

They urged Apple's sixteen million users to buy stock—even single shares at $25 to $40—to gain democratic control of the company. If half of Apple users bought stock, they calculated, the democratic takeover could control more than management's paltry share of 4.37 percent. They called it a "user buy-in."

The grassroots math was fantasy. Even if eight million users each bought a single share, Larry had more than $1.25 billion ready to deploy—enough to buy 60 percent of the company outright. But corporate takeovers aren't decided by math alone. A hostile bid could trigger a messy public battle between Larry and eight million Apple fans—the optimistic number estimated by the grassroots movement—a public relations nightmare.

"Larry Ellison has the wrong idea of what Macintosh is," wrote one user. "It is a religion. We believe in the icon and the mouse." Another compared Larry's vision to a Procrustean bed, a one-size-fits-all torture device that would "cut off their [victims'] arms, their legs, and pull out their tongues so all will shut up and fit comfortably in the same box."

The other side saw Larry as Apple's only hope. Even if he wasn't perfect, he was a heavyweight with the resources to fight Microsoft. Larry himself began answering this second group's emails, seeking to fire up the troops: "I intend to use the Mac OS to build Mac NCs [network computers] . . . I am a Mac user," he wrote to one person. "Have been since 1984 . . . Big Macs plus little Macs make for good business for Apple. Please spread the word. Larry."

In March, the takeover campaign got more fuel when Saudi Prince al-Waleed bin Talal Al Saud—the forty-one-year-old nephew of Saudi Arabia's King Fahd—quietly acquired 5 percent of Apple for $115 million. "Things could be resurrected [at Apple]," he told Larry at a late-night meeting at his San Francisco apartment, "and we could have the old Apple back."

Michael Milken joined Larry's effort. Even Goldman Sachs and Salomon Brothers advised Gil that Larry had access to "trainloads of money," Gil wrote, and that he had the ability to take over Apple. His threat had teeth.

Gil tried to call Larry but got no response. Instead, Larry waged his war in the press. "Steve's the only one who can save Apple," he told *Fortune*. "We've talked about it seriously many, many times, and I'm ready to help him the minute he says the word. I could raise the money in a week."

"Larry brings this up now and then," Steve told the *San Jose Mercury News*. "I try to explain my role at Apple is to be an adviser." In private, he also told Gil that "I think all this is crazy," but at the same time, he wasn't willing to take a strong stance against the takeover bid in the press, as Gil wanted.

Steve wasn't orchestrating Gil's downfall, but he wasn't rushing to his defense either. Steve's positioning reflected his own ambivalence. Despite the acquisition, NeXT had still been a commercial failure, and after more than a decade away from Apple, he couldn't afford another public misstep.

He was also genuinely torn about whether he wanted the responsibility of rescuing a company that seemed beyond saving.

At Apple's March 25 board meeting, Gil requested an additional $80 million for advertising to boost sales. But the board refused. The rejection knocked the wind out of him, Gil said. He couldn't believe that the board demanded better sales but wouldn't fund the advertising Gil needed to achieve them.

The board sensed that it was the beginning of the end.

Ed Woolard, Apple's chairman, started suggesting other solutions to Gil. Why didn't he hand day-to-day operations off to Fred, the CFO, and focus solely on marketing? Gil responded by trying to explain his philosophy. Running a company was like flying a plane on instruments, he said. It required constant attention to multiple gauges, not fixation on a single metric, like sales or accounting.

Ed had been CEO and then chairman of chemical giant DuPont. An engineer by training with a grandfatherly mien, he had overseen turnarounds at other companies. When a friend suggested he join Apple's board, Ed welcomed the opportunity to help save a company that had been written off.

In Gil's leadership, Ed saw competence but not magic. The man could run a meeting, read a balance sheet, articulate a strategy—but Apple's revenues kept falling and the stock price kept sliding. Every week brought another resignation letter: Of the forty-seven senior executives who'd started with Gil, twenty-nine had fled by March 1997, just thirteen months into his term. Ed had seen enough turnarounds to know that this one wasn't working.

Soon after, Larry's offer to buy Apple fell apart. According to his plan, Apple shareholders would receive only 60 percent of their money in cash, with the remainder paid in equity stakes in Larry's reimagined Apple, journalist Jim Carlton reported. Essentially, Larry was asking investors to bankroll his risky transformation with their own money. Prince al-Waleed's representatives visited Apple headquarters and heard a presentation from Gil, but he never moved forward with the hostile takeover plans, though he kept his Apple stock and remained an influential shareholder.

Then, on April 29, Larry suddenly withdrew his hostile takeover effort altogether. He released the announcement—conveniently enough—while he was traveling abroad and unreachable by the press.

Whether Larry intended it or not, the damage was done. The threat of a takeover had weakened Gil's grip on the company. He could feel the walls closing in.

In June, Apple's board reached all-out crisis mode. Someone had dumped 1.5 million Apple shares at a price of about $14—the lowest tick in company history. And everyone knew that Steve had been granted exactly 1.5 million shares in the NeXT deal, with restrictions lifted at his request.

When Avie asked Steve point-blank if he'd made the sale, Steve wouldn't confirm it but, Avie said, "he led me to believe that it was him." As Avie understood it, this was Steve's "public statement that he was not happy with Gil and the company." It was a vote of no confidence.

Gil suspected the truth, but Steve denied it when he asked. (Steve later told Walter Isaacson that he didn't think Gil needed to know.) During the NeXT negotiations, Gil had explicitly warned Steve that "you have to understand it's very important that you not sell."

"I've got all the money I need," Steve had reassured him. "I'd have no reason for selling."

When the SEC filing came out weeks later, it revealed everything. Steven P. Jobs had, in fact, sold all but one share, keeping it to maintain access to company reports, the same thing he'd done in 1985 to fund NeXT.

Gil confronted Steve with the document, and he came clean. "I was sort of in a fit of depression at the time and I just felt the company was hopeless and so I just did a spontaneous thing and sold my shares," Steve told him.

Steve's stock sale hurt the board's confidence in Gil's leadership even more. Ed declared that Apple was in a "death spiral." He needed to decide once and for all if Gil should go. So he consulted Apple's senior managers, most of whom had already shifted into Steve's camp.

The verdict was unanimous. "We knew [Steve] had the personal credibility with software developers and employees to at least buy us some time," Ed later wrote.

From a family trip to Wimbledon, Ed called Steve—whom he'd

never met in person and had spoken to only once before—to offer him Apple's future as CEO. Steve declined the title but offered to help.

"I can't do that," Steve said. "I'm the CEO of Pixar. It's a publicly traded company. We have all these wonderful employees. We have these shareholders. And I can't go be CEO of another public [company] . . . I can't desert them. So I can't do this. I'll help you any way I can, but I can't."

Though Steve declined, the question gnawed at him. At 8:00 a.m. on a Saturday, Steve called his mentor, Intel cofounder Andy Grove, who was known for his blunt advice. As Steve recounted in a talk at the Stanford Graduate School of Business in 2003:

> And I was thinking about it and called up a friend of mine, a really smart guy, a good friend I'd known for a long time that works at another company in the industry. And I probably woke him up in the morning, about eight o'clock one morning, and I was telling him about my struggles about, should I, could I do this? Should I not? And this and that . . .
>
> And finally, he interrupted me after about four minutes and he said, "Steve, I don't give a shit about Apple. Why are you telling me all this?"
>
> And I said, "Oh, OK. I'm sorry." And I hung up the phone.
>
> And I realized: You know, I do give a shit about Apple.

That's when Steve decided to step into a larger role at Apple. But he put forth precise terms to Ed: He'd remain an adviser only, would not get the CEO title, would not receive a salary, and wouldn't be given any stock compensation. He also reassured his employees at Pixar that he wasn't abandoning them for Apple, that he would remain Pixar CEO. He did agree, however, to join Apple's board.

By July Fourth weekend, the board had made its decision about Gil. But rather than immediately turn to Steve, they installed Fred Anderson as interim CEO and began searching for a permanent replacement. Steve remained an adviser and would help evaluate CEO candidates.

On Sunday morning, Ed called Gil from London: "Gil, the board has been meeting by telephone on and off for the last thirty-six hours. And I'm afraid I don't have a very good message for you. We think you need to step down."

Gil had been promised three years to turn Apple around. He'd gotten five hundred days. "[Steve's] view," Ed explained to Gil, "is that you're a really nice guy, but that you don't really know much about the computer industry."

Gil was perplexed. Steve wasn't even on the board, yet he had somehow been a part of these deliberations while Gil had been pushed to the side. Gil wanted to stay and fight. But he ultimately decided to resign, knowing the battle was over.

Gil recited the arrangement at a press conference: Steve would help search for the new CEO. Fred would handle day-to-day operations. Ed would represent the board for now.

As they had agreed, Steve joined the board—but he didn't respect his fellow directors, and so he made an unusual demand, according to biographer Walter Isaacson. Every member except Ed would have to resign immediately or else he would resign the following Monday. Ed negotiated him down to keeping one other director. The rest agreed to clear out. "It's conceivable Apple could turn around without Steve," Ed told *Time*, "but the probability goes up significantly with Steve."

The ultimatum revealed how seriously Steve took Apple's downfall. According to those who knew him during this period, Steve remained reluctant about deeper involvement with Apple. But when he did engage, he engaged completely. The board purge was about ensuring that if Apple was going to be saved, the people overseeing that effort would be capable of the task.

But Steve still insisted he didn't want to lead Apple over the long term. He was still having a great time running Pixar, and Apple was a mess. Still, Apple employees marveled at how he had consolidated power without appearing to grasp for it. He hadn't needed to convince anyone of anything. His importance to the company spoke for itself.

The timing had been less than ideal, as Steve later acknowledged. In a CBS interview three months later, he explained: "I sold my stock before I got the call from the board that they wanted me to come in and shepherd Apple for this period, and that was unfortunate. I wish the call had come a week earlier, but I wasn't a mind reader, so I didn't know." His June stock sale had come just weeks before Ed's July call asking him to elevate his role. Steve found himself in the contradictory position of being asked to save the company he'd just financially abandoned.

"If [the sale of stock] upsets employees," Steve told *Time*, "I'm perfectly happy to go home to Pixar."

28

COMEBACK KID

Steve's five NeXT cofounders watched him operate from afar. "This was a reverse takeover," Bud Tribble realized from his perch at Sun. "NeXT was actually taking over Apple." His wife, Susan Barnes, who had advised Steve and Larry when they had previously explored a hostile takeover, didn't find Steve's machinations surprising.

For George Crow, former NeXT head of analog hardware engineering and now an engineer at Truevision, which made video editing hardware for PCs, Steve's takeover held the potential to pay off a gamble he'd made four years earlier.

In 1993, Steve had offered to buy back departing employees' NeXT stock at $1 per share—far below its original value. George sold half of his equity but kept the rest. "My attitude was he must know something, or he wouldn't be offering to buy the stock," George reasoned.

Then came the acquisition. George's retained shares converted to cash at Apple's purchase price. "I actually made out really well," George said. Those who had already sold everything back to Steve were out of luck.

Inside Apple, Steve's maneuvering put NeXT refugees in a weird position. Their company had been acquired, but now their former CEO was effectively controlling Apple's direction—purging the board, installing NeXT alumni in key roles, and wielding operational authority that Gil had never possessed. Yet Steve still insisted he was just an adviser helping to find a permanent CEO.

The contradiction was striking. Steve had demanded the power to reshape Apple from top to bottom, but he continued to maintain he didn't want to run the company. For NeXT employees watching this unfold, it raised uncomfortable questions about what they'd gotten themselves into.

Some NeXT alumni saw Steve's growing control as vindication—their leader conquering the company that had exiled them. Others felt betrayed, watching their profitable enterprise software being absorbed into a company that seemed to have lost its way.

The WebObjects team was livid. At NeXT, they had built a profitable enterprise business. Gil had made grand announcements about WebObjects at Macworld, but in the months following the acquisition, those promises seemed to evaporate. Apple's focus was clearly elsewhere.

Nico Popp, one of WebObjects' creators who followed Steve to Apple, quit after six months, convinced that Apple would never embrace WebObjects. "I thought it's not going to lead to anything," he said. He was spectacularly wrong—WebObjects would be later used to help power the iTunes Store—but he wouldn't realize that until it was released five years later.

The remaining team was being absorbed into Apple's chaos—as the company tried to sell everything from confusing computer lines to printers to a digital camera, hemorrhaging cash all the while. Apple had even licensed other companies like Power Computing and Motorola to make "Mac clones"—computers that ran Apple's operating system but weren't made by Apple, letting other companies cannibalize its sales. The company that had once defined simplicity now sold a sprawling mess of products nobody understood.

But the NeXT old-timers, those who'd survived the company's retreat from hardware and still believed in the original vision, saw an opportunity. They hadn't joined NeXT because of a passion for selling enterprise software. They had signed up to reinvent computing. And for all of its problems, Apple was a place where that might finally happen.

Steve had filled out Apple's ranks with ex-NeXTers, as company alumni proudly called themselves. In software, they formed the core of the new operating system team. Bertrand Serlet joined as a VP. Scott Forstall, a young NeXT engineer who had worked on NeXTSTEP's user interface, came aboard to help design Apple's new visual interface—the translucent, colorful digital world that would make computers feel more intuitive and alive.

Mitch Mandich, NeXT's VP of worldwide sales, took over Apple's sales organization to revitalize distribution. Sina Tamaddon, who had run NeXT's professional services and European operations, became Apple's senior VP of worldwide service and support and later led Apple's Applications Division.

Others were less eager to join Apple. Over sushi, Steve had tried to lure Dominique, but he declined. By then Dominique was CEO of Gemplus, a French company that made smart cards, credit card–sized chips that would eventually enable secure digital payments and mobile phone SIM cards. "I don't think I have the Apple DNA in me," he concluded.

NeXT alumni joined Apple bearing the scars of a decade at sea. They had watched their technology dismissed as too expensive and too ambitious. They had endured the humiliation of retreating from hardware, the frustration of seeing inferior products dominate the market, and the exhaustion of constantly justifying the importance of their software.

Now, suddenly, they were in charge of saving Apple, which had fallen to barely 3 percent of the personal computer market share, slipping out of the list of top five global computer manufacturers.

Where their solutions had once been too far ahead of the market, by 1997, the relentless march of technology had caught up. Computer chips had become exponentially faster and cheaper while memory costs plummeted, following the pattern Intel founder Gordon Moore had observed decades earlier: Computing power doubles roughly every two years. As a result, the features that had made NeXTSTEP impossibly expensive in 1988—memory protection, true multitasking, sophisticated graphics—could now run on a regular PC. Features that used to be too much were now just right.

Even though Steve wasn't formally Apple's CEO—he introduced himself at the 1997 Macworld Boston conference as the chairman and CEO of Pixar only—the reverse takeover was nearly complete, and a decade of patient innovation was about to pay off.

Steve spent the summer of 1997 on a listening tour, gathering thoughts from senior managers on what had gone wrong at Apple. All he heard were tales of doom and gloom. He wanted to flip the script to one of optimism. In his presentations, he made it clear Apple had talented people but the wrong strategy. "Somebody taught me a long time ago . . . if you do the right things on the top line, the bottom line will follow," he told CNBC.

In the meantime, Steve pared down Apple's out-of-control product development portfolio. Steve found that about 30 percent of the products were good and held promise. He thought the rest were distractions. So he killed 70 percent of existing product lines, including, eventually, the Newton, and shuttered the entire Advanced Technology Group.

"Apple is executing wonderfully on many of the wrong things," he explained at Macworld that August. But "Apple needs to find where it is still incredibly relevant and focus on those areas."

He identified two areas where Apple still led the industry. First, its neglected brand. Despite its troubles, the Apple logo and name remained as iconic as Coca-Cola, Disney, and Nike. Second, Apple's operating system, which Steve referred to as "still the best thing in the world." He acknowledged the fear that Apple might now abandon Mac OS and then complained that previous leadership had been "walking all over it." But the Mac OS was "one of the core assets of the company" that "has yet to really be fully exploited."

Developers were upset at all of Steve's changes. They had been hard at work creating software for Apple product lines that kept getting changed, upended, and discontinued. At the May 1997 Worldwide Developers Conference, in front of a crowd of hundreds, a developer stood up and said to Steve, "You're a bright and influential man . . . it's sad and clear that on several counts you've discussed, you don't know what you're talking about." Then: "Perhaps you could tell us what you personally have been doing for the last seven years."

The crowd murmured uncomfortably—"the last seven years," was a stinging reference to his failure at NeXT. But Steve didn't blow his cool. Instead, he took a long pause, smiled slightly, and began with an admission. "One of the hardest things when you're trying to effect change is that people like this gentleman are right in some areas," he said.

Then he laid out a principle that would come to define the new Apple. "You've got to start with the customer experience and work backwards to the technology," he said. "You can't start with the technology and try to figure out where you're going to try to sell it."

He continued with humility. "I readily admit there are many things in life that I don't have the faintest idea what I'm talking about. So I apologize for that too."

Apple announced a "dual OS strategy": The company would support two operating systems simultaneously. The existing Mac OS would continue for current users, while a new system called Rhapsody would offer NeXT's advanced capabilities on Apple computers. Rhapsody was essentially NeXTSTEP being ported to run on Apple hardware.

In truth, this "dual OS strategy" was corporate doublespeak designed to soften a harsh reality. Apple wasn't planning to maintain two operating systems indefinitely. Behind the company's reassuring presentations lay the hard truth for developers: The old Mac OS was being phased out, and developers would have to abandon the programming tools they'd spent years mastering to learn NeXT's different approach to building object-oriented software.

Apple tried to make this transition sound gradual and optional. But experienced Mac developers could read between the lines. If they wanted to build anything new and powerful for Apple's future, they'd essentially be starting from scratch with NeXT's development environment. Fortunately, NeXTSTEP's object-oriented programming was designed with an intuitive structure that made it relatively easy to learn.

Avie explained the urgency of this strategy with a *Star Trek*–inspired warning: He cautioned that without the new operating system, Apple would be trapped forever as a niche player. "If we are forced to live within the Windows monopoly, we will all be assimilated," he told the crowd at Apple's 1997 Worldwide Developers Conference. The new operating system was Apple's escape plan.

To turn things around, Steve needed more runway. Apple was on track for a $56 million loss in the third quarter of 1997. Steve later estimated the company was ninety days away from total collapse. He knew just who to turn to—a long-time acquaintance with deep pockets and the potential to offer a newsworthy stamp of approval on Apple's recovery plans. So he made a call that would have been unthinkable to the Steve of 1985, or even 1990.

He dialed Bill Gates to ask for help.

Steve had once positioned himself as the anti-Gates—the humanist challenging the technologist, the artist facing off against the businessman. At NeXT, he'd continued the holy war, even as it became increasingly clear that Microsoft had won. But Steve understood something now that he hadn't twelve years ago: Righteous indignation didn't pay bills.

On the phone, Steve said he wanted to discuss a broad alliance with Microsoft, including a potential Microsoft investment in Apple. Bill dispatched Greg Maffei, Microsoft's CFO, to Cupertino to negotiate. On two successive Sundays, Greg and Steve hammered out a deal.

Steve suggested they work it out over a walk. The Apple adviser grabbed two bottles of mineral water from his refrigerator and headed for the door. "It was an interesting scene," Greg told *Time*. "It was a pretty radical change for relations between the two companies."

Greg strode along in his shoes while Steve padded along barefoot next to him as the terms of a deal began to take shape. During his NeXT years, Steve had worn Armani suits and insisted on Italian marble lobbies. But walking around barefoot was vintage Apple, the same informal approach he'd taken in the 1970s and early 1980s before corporate polish took over. Now, negotiating for his company's survival, he'd reverted to his own skin.

Greg agreed that Microsoft would commit to developing its Office suite for the Mac for five years, matching Windows release schedules.

The two agreed that Internet Explorer would replace Netscape Navigator as the Mac's default web browser.

Greg did express serious concerns about one Steve priority: putting Larry Ellison on Apple's board. Larry was perhaps the fiercest—and certainly the loudest—of Silicon Valley's Microsoft bashers.

Greg pressed Steve directly: What did he think of network computers—the simple, inexpensive devices that Larry championed? "He said he wasn't very optimistic about them," Greg told *The New Yorker.* "He said that making NCs wasn't a very workable business model for Apple."

This assurance mattered enormously. Steve's dismissal of network computers—and the implied distancing from Larry—was crucial to securing Microsoft's investment. It signaled that Apple would remain in the personal computer business rather than joining forces with Oracle to make PCs obsolete. But Steve still planned to put Larry, his best friend, on the board.

By the second Sunday, terms had emerged. "[Steve] was expansive and charming," Greg reflected to *Time*. But more importantly, "he didn't ask for 23,000 terms. He looked at the whole picture, [and] figured out what he needed," Greg said.

Finally, Microsoft would invest $150 million in Apple for nonvoting stock—the public vote of confidence that the company desperately needed. The investment was shrewd self-interest. Microsoft faced mounting antitrust scrutiny from the Department of Justice, which was threatening to break up the company. Keeping Apple alive gave Microsoft a competitor to point to, arguing they were not a monopoly. For $150 million—pocket change for Microsoft—Bill Gates bought himself a defense exhibit.

If Steve was willing to compromise on software, he told Apple executives there was one compromise he would never make again: letting other companies build his hardware. At NeXT, he'd had no choice but to license NeXTSTEP to companies like Sun and HP. But now, back at Apple with real power, he could act on his conviction that great computer companies had to control both hardware and software, end to end.

So he killed Apple's clone program. Every license, every partnership: gone, just like that. The move stunned Silicon Valley analysts. Apple bought out Power Computing's entire Mac operation for $100 million in stock—acquiring all the company's Mac assets and key employees—while ending Apple's relationship with clone makers Motorola and UMAX completely. Steve would control everything that mattered again.

NeXT alumni at Apple knew that the Apple faithful would see his deal with Bill Gates as a betrayal. For twenty years, Apple had defined itself as Microsoft's opposite. Apple users had chosen Macs because they weren't PCs, weren't part of Microsoft's soulless monopoly. Now Steve was about to herald that enemy as Apple's financial savior.

He planned to announce the deal at the Boston Macworld conference in August 1997.

The morning of the conference, Steve paced the convention center stage, finagling final details with Bill over his cell phone, sometimes sitting, sometimes lying on his back staring at the lighting rig above. Before he hung up, he said, "Thank you for your support of this company. I think the world's a better place for it."

That afternoon, standing before thousands of Mac devotees, he prepared for their rage. "I happen to have a special guest with me today via satellite downlink," he told them.

When Bill's face appeared on the giant screen, the crowd erupted. Some booed and jeered, while others laughed and applauded.

Microsoft's chairman was literally looking down on them as Steve announced what they saw as surrender. Some compared it to Apple's famous 1984 Super Bowl commercial, with Big Brother Bill staring down at them, set to control their very thoughts.

"We have to let go of this notion that for Apple to win, Microsoft has to lose," Steve said over the hostile crowd. "I think if we want Microsoft Office on the Mac, we better treat the company that puts it out with a little bit of gratitude."

Then he said, "The era of setting this up as a competition between Apple and Microsoft is over, as far as I'm concerned. This is about getting Apple healthy."

The booing crowd couldn't know how hard-won this pragmatism was. Steve would later admit that idealism was one of his greatest weaknesses. "Sometimes I go for 'best' when I should go for 'better,' and end up going nowhere or backwards," he told an interviewer. He'd learned to question whether he was "blinded by 'what could be' versus 'what is possible,' doing things incrementally versus doing them in one fell swoop."

The Microsoft deal embodied that lesson, choosing better over best and survival over purity. It was the kind of pragmatic decision the younger Steve could never have made.

On August 6, Steve propped his worn sneakers up on Apple's boardroom table.

Empty chairs surrounded him like ghosts. Among those he had purged from the board was Mike Markkula, Apple's third cofounder, who'd written the $250,000 check that had transformed Apple from a garage start-up into a real company. The rupture between Steve and Mike dated back to 1985, when Mike had sided with John Sculley against him.

"I felt betrayed by Mike, but I still had a very warm spot in my heart for him," Steve told *The New York Times* of that episode. Mike, in turn, called Steve's exit "at best ungentlemanly."

The new board consisted of Steve's personally chosen allies: Jerry

York from Chrysler and IBM; Ed Woolard from DuPont; Bill Campbell, his former marketing and sales vice president at Apple in the 1980s; and Larry Ellison. Steve now had a board that stood by his leadership but who had the force of personality to push back against him. According to Ed Catmull, Steve looked for board members who were unafraid to debate and disagree. Still, he knew the board would never sideline him again.

"I wouldn't be honest if some days I didn't question whether I made the right decision in getting involved [in Apple]," Steve admitted to *Time*. "Apple has some tremendous assets, but I believe without some attention, the company could, could, could—I'm searching for the right word—could, could . . . die."

He cared about the company, deeply. And he struggled to find a replacement CEO for Apple. That summer, Apple interviewed Hewlett-Packard executive Antonio M. Perez and Sun president Ed Zander for the job—though as Jon Rubinstein noted, "Steve didn't like any of them."

By mid-August, his software chief Avie, tasked with porting NeXTSTEP to Apple, wrote in an email that he had reached his breaking point. The toxic Apple culture was fighting every attempt at reform. Engineers were threatening to call in sick in protest. Good people were resigning while the worst actors spread poison through the ranks.

On the night of August 14, Avie poured out his frustrations in an email to Steve published in *Make Something Wonderful*. The problems at Apple reminded him of "cancer," he wrote—something they'd put "into remission" months ago that now "came back with a vengeance." Without any emotional tie to Apple, "it gets increasing difficult to come to work each day," he admitted. His conclusion: "It makes me think this company isn't worth saving. At least not for the sake of the employees."

It was a remarkable admission from someone who had survived the tough NeXT years. But Apple was different. At NeXT, everyone understood they were building something new. At Apple, they were fighting to save something that maybe didn't want to be saved.

Steve felt it too. "You know, I have had the same feeling lately," he replied that same August evening. "That Apple employees don't deserve to be saved. They think they work so hard—heck, I don't see it."

But then something shifted in his response. "But, there is something good here worth saving," he wrote. "I don't quite know how to express it, but it has to do with the fact that Apple is the ONLY alternative to Windows and that Apple can inject some new thinking into the equation."

Eleven days later, Avie was still wrestling with his doubts. He was "completely unmotivated," he admitted to Steve—a dangerous state for someone Steve was counting on to rebuild Apple's software foundation. Worse, he confessed, "for the first time in ten years I don't even feel like challenging your ideas when I disagree—which scares me because I believe as a team we work best when we challenge each other and come out all-the-better for it."

"Please continue to challenge me," Steve replied immediately. "It's the way we get to the right decisions, and I enjoy it too." Avie didn't quit. He stayed on, with Steve's support.

But even as he managed the crisis, Steve made it home every night, helping six-year-old Reed pick lemon verbena from their garden for after-dinner tea and tucking his children into bed.

On September 16, 1997, Apple, unsatisfied with its CEO candidates after a three-month search, officially announced Steve as its interim CEO, exactly twelve years to the day after his resignation from Apple.

Why did Steve accept?

"I just thought, 'Well, it will take another ninety days to find somebody.' . . . And I decided right up front that I was just going to act like I was the permanent CEO, because they didn't need a caretaker," Steve recounted at the Stanford Graduate School of Business in 2003. "This thing was in intensive care. It was about ninety days away from bankruptcy. It was in pretty bad shape."

Steve, with his instinct for branding, shortened the new title to iCEO, Apple's first *i* name. "It was kind of like a call option on the job," Avie explained to the Computer History Museum. Steve could test-drive running Apple without staking his reputation on the turnaround. If Apple proved unsalvageable, he could walk away, having only been interim CEO of someone else's disaster.

But Steve didn't walk away.

In twelve years, he'd gone from a boy wonder expelled from his own kingdom to its returning king. But this was not the Steve Jobs of 1985.

That Steve would have probably killed the Microsoft deal over pride. Would have micromanaged Apple's software transformation. Would have built uncompromisingly beautiful products that no one could afford. He would probably have chosen being right over succeeding.

This Steve had learned from his mistakes. Every humiliation, his closest confidants recounted, had taught him something he'd needed to know. The company he'd built after Apple had become the company that saved it—the years he'd spent in exile had taught him how to lead it.

And his new family had shown him what truly mattered.

"I believe life is an intelligent thing," Steve would later tell *Time*, "that things aren't random."

For twelve years, he had wandered. He had been cast out of the company he built, mocked for chasing impossible dreams, humbled by failure, and remade by loss. Now, on September 16, 1997, he returned as a man forged in the fires of exile. His wilderness years had done their work. He had been broken and remade. He was prepared to lead a company strong enough to last.

Apple was his again. And this time, he was ready.

Epilogue

THE LONG ROAD HOME

Fourteen years after leaving NeXT, Paul Vais started a wine business in the Sonoma Valley. He maintained ties to fellow NeXT alumni—including Steve—through their children's school. One day in September 2011, he caught up with Laurene at a back-to-school event.

She invited him over to the Jobs family home. Paul accepted, planning to bring his company's wine over.

On October 5, 2011, Paul loaded wine bottles into his car and hit the road for Steve and Laurene's. As he was driving, Laurene called him.

Steve had just died, she said. At around 3:00 p.m. that day, he had succumbed to pancreatic cancer, a condition he had initially left untreated.

The news spread fast across the NeXT community, first through text messages and phone calls, and then on the alumni mailing list. Many felt a complicated grief. They had worked for a genius who'd treated them as expendable, who'd humiliated them in meetings, who'd made the best and brightest feel small. Many of them carried those wounds for decades, unable to forgive him for what he'd done.

His passing began to change that.

Former NeXT sales manager Mark Hayes couldn't remember where he was when he heard the news, but he remembered exactly what happened inside him. "I was able to release a lot of anger that I had bottled up inside me," he recounted. Twenty years of resentment suddenly had nowhere to go. "I started to look more favorably at all of his gifts, and the things he did accomplish."

When former NeXT marketing director Ron Weissman heard that Steve had died, he left a client meeting and sat paralyzed in his car for forty minutes. "I couldn't imagine a world without Steve," he said.

At Steve's private commemoration service on October 16, Mike Slade felt both grief and anger. "It was very, very moving and very hard," he recalled of the intimate gathering at Stanford Memorial Church. Mike sat with Bill Gates among a few hundred mourners.

Steve had hidden his illness from almost everyone, even his closest friends and colleagues, including Mike. He had maintained a reality distortion field until the very end. The deception left many feeling betrayed alongside their sorrow.

Mike thought back to thirteen years before, in 1998, when Steve had called him up to propose a reunion at Apple. "I'll take as much of your brain as I can get," Steve told him.

Mike, now based in Seattle and working for Disney, had left NeXT following the collapse of the hardware division. Microsoft cofounder Paul Allen had then hired him to run a web company called Starwave, which was sold to Disney for slightly more than $1 billion. It was one of the successes of the dot-com boom.

Steve pitched Mike on a special assistant role, advising him on Apple product strategy and branding. Mike, burned out from corporate politics at Disney, saw Steve as a safe harbor. He loved working with him—"We had a crush on each other," Mike said.

But Mike had young kids and couldn't uproot his family from Seattle. So Steve accommodated him, offering a part-time job. Mike accepted, calling it "the most relaxing, fun thing I'd done in my whole career."

For the next six years, Mike flew down from Seattle every Monday morning and returned Wednesdays. He shadowed Steve through meetings to help design the new Mac OS X—built with NeXTSTEP technology—and craft the apps that would define Apple's renaissance.

Because of his web experience, Mike brought a unique perspective to the company. "At first, nobody at Apple knew anything about the internet except me," Mike said. While everyone else was still figuring out the web, Mike helped Steve plan for an online future that would transform everything from music distribution to software updates.

Despite this, most Apple executives had no idea who Mike was or why he was in their meetings. He'd sit quietly as senior staff argued for hours, then Steve would suddenly turn to him: "What do you think, Mike?"

Cue confused looks from around the table.

Mike also took a front-row seat to Steve's transformation. He saw the ways in which this Steve was not the same man who had nearly driven NeXT into the ground.

He watched as some of his most challenging traits receded. The "you're fired" tantrums ebbed. Steve remained a tough boss, always demanding perfection. But he no longer humiliated people in the process. He also shelved the public salary policy from NeXT that had ended up spawning resentment and petty politics.

He learned to let go, placing his faith in lieutenants like Avie, Jon, Mike, and Bud (who returned to Apple in 2002 as VP of software technology, reporting to Avie, his former protégé). During Monday morning staff meetings, Steve listened to them and implemented their advice. He learned to delegate and focus on what he loved.

As the environment improved, he managed to shut down Apple's revolving door of executives. He marshaled in eight years of executive team stability at Apple. "Unbelievable," Mike called it.

"He had made a lot of mistakes [at NeXT]," Mike observed, "and he decided not to make any of them again."

NeXT LESSON ONE: Don't Repeat Your Failures

For weeks, the executive team debated over whether Apple needed to develop an entry-level, easy-to-use product, rather than the upmarket computers it had been pushing. Steve was entertaining the creation of diskless network computers—the terminals that his friend Larry Ellison proposed for Apple that would pull everything from the internet.

Jon disagreed. Because they would lack disks, it reminded him of the NeXT Cube optical-drive debacle. "The NeXT machine with no hard drive didn't work out well," Jon argued. "This isn't going to work well."

The tension finally exploded in what Jon called a "knock-down, drag-out" fight. Then a breakthrough compromise emerged. What if they kept the network computer's motherboard but grew their planned translucent case just enough to contain a hard drive?

Most audaciously, Jon promised to build it in under fourteen months instead of Apple's usual three years. The engineers stared at him in disbelief.

"Everyone goes, 'That's impossible,'" Jon recounted. Thus, the legendary iMac was born.

NeXT LESSON TWO: Sometimes You Have to Bend Your Vision

As Avie worked to make NeXTSTEP run on Apple's computers through the Rhapsody project, he had to come up with a creative solution to keep Mac developers like Adobe and Microsoft happy. They would balk at the idea of rewriting everything from scratch for the new operating system.

So his team built what they called the "Blue Box," essentially the old Mac operating system running inside the new one, letting ancient software breathe while the new world booted up around it.

This same pragmatic approach would define how Apple handled NeXT's development tools. Over the next decade, Apple refined NeXT's software-building frameworks into two tool kits—Cocoa for Mac computers and the touch-optimized Cocoa Touch for iPhones.

The NeXT revolution that Steve hoped would happen in 1988 came to fruition with the introduction of the first iPhone nineteen years later.

Allowing a workaround like the Blue Box was uncharacteristic for Steve. At NeXT, he had demanded developers build software exclusively for his platform, and his purist approach had starved the system of applications. Now at Apple, he embraced pragmatism. More software meant more users, which attracted more developers, and created the virtuous cycle that had eluded NeXT.

NeXT LESSON THREE: Listen to Your People

After NeXT, Steve came to fully understand that being right isn't enough. You could build the most beautiful computer ever conceived and watch it gather dust because you failed to take customers into account.

Jon and Steve applied this learning to Apple's sprawling product mess. Out went the underperforming models and legacy cruft bleeding Apple dry. In their place, Apple focused all its resources on building the iMac, the translucent, Bondi-blue homage to NeXT's simplicity.

While other computers in the early 1990s displayed text with jagged edges and crude pixels, NeXT screens showed fonts so crisp they looked like they'd been typeset for a magazine. Steve had licensed the same PostScript technology that professional printing presses used for Apple's desktop computers. The result was gorgeous but expensive fonts on the screen, requiring chips that cost more than most people's entire computers.

By the time the iMac was launched in 1998, computer chips had become dramatically faster and cheaper; what once required expensive custom hardware could now run on standard processors. The technology that made NeXT machines prohibitively expensive had become affordable enough for consumer products.

Three decades later, when you pinch to zoom on your iPhone and watch text stay razor-sharp at any size, you're seeing Display PostScript's great-grandchildren—Quartz and Core Graphics—freed from their luxury price tag.

The iMac included no floppy drive (heresy!) and only USB ports. It was purpose-built for getting regular people online effortlessly. And at $1,299, the computer's price undercut its competitors. Steve had finally learned how to market hardware for regular people.

Released in August 1998, the iMac sold 800,000 units in its first five months and brought Apple back to profitability for the first time since the NeXT acquisition.

At the same time, NeXT's expensive technologies found new life in Apple's product portfolio. WebObjects, the enterprise framework that had cost more than $50,000 per license at NeXT, now powered Apple's online store invisibly. By 1999, Apple sold the same WebObjects software for just $699 and eventually gave it away for free. It became the invisible nervous system connecting iTunes purchases to the iPod.

With the release of Mac OS X Server in March 1999—two years before the release of Mac OS X itself—Apple brought NeXT's software foundation to a broader audience. Dozens of Apple and former NeXT engineers recounted that Mac OS X Server was essentially NeXTSTEP with a familiar Mac interface layered on top.

The ghost of the NeXT Cube itself reemerged in 2000, when Steve launched the Power Mac G4 Cube, a powerful, translucent crystal computer. "Yeah, we did one before," he told *Newsweek*. "Cubes are very efficient spaces."

At $1,799 without a monitor, it flopped just like its predecessor at NeXT. Some habits die harder than others.

NeXT LESSON FOUR: Total Control Requires Total Capability

In the 1990s, using a personal computer was like driving a car that might randomly stall in traffic. The old Mac OS crashed so routinely that people saved their work every few minutes out of paranoia. NeXT machines, built on the same Unix bedrock that ran Wall Street's trading systems, didn't break as easily.

The catch was that Unix spoke only to computer scientists who understood cryptic commands. Apple's masterstroke was putting a friendly face on this bulletproof foundation. It's the same magic that would later make smartphones feel simple despite their breathtaking complexity.

In March 2001, Apple released Mac OS X—essentially NeXTSTEP with a Mac makeover. This was exactly what Apple had bought NeXT for, a modern foundation to replace its aging operating system. Steve marketed it as "the world's most advanced operating system." It was stable, powerful, beautiful.

It also laid the groundwork for a breakthrough that would complete Apple's reversal of fortune. When Jon went on a routine business trip to Japan, Toshiba executives showed him a tiny hard drive that didn't have enough capacity for PCs. A light bulb went off in Jon's head. "This is how to make an iPod," he said.

Steve happened to be in Japan too, so Jon called him right away. "Steve, I need a $10 million check to go do development on this," he said. Steve didn't hesitate: "No problem."

The iPod demonstrated NeXT's philosophy of hardware, software, and services working as a seamless whole. Its software drew from OS X, with an interface intuitive enough for a child to use, and it connected to iTunes easily. For the first time, you could carry a thousand songs in your pocket and never worry about file formats or compatibility. Technology became so good it had become practically invisible—exactly what Steve had dreamed of.

In April 2003, Apple launched the iTunes Music Store. Steve had managed to convince paranoid record labels to sell songs online for ninety-nine cents each, but the real triumph was on the store's backend. The store ran on WebObjects, scaled up to handle a massive number of transactions. After selling more than a million songs in its first week, it proved that NeXT's enterprise-grade tools could be adapted for regular consumers at scale.

For NeXT veterans watching from the sidelines, the vindication tasted delicious. Their "failed" company's framework had become the invisible engine driving Apple's revolution. The strategy of hardware and software integration that had nearly killed NeXT finally found its moment.

Steve reflected on what he learned from NeXT at his graduation speech at Stanford University in 2005:

> I didn't see it then, but it turned out that getting fired from Apple was the best thing that could have ever happened to me. The heaviness of being successful was replaced by the lightness of being a beginner again, less sure about everything. It freed me to enter one of the most creative periods of my life.
>
> During the next five years, I started a company named NeXT, another company named Pixar, and fell in love with an amazing woman who would become my wife. Pixar went on to create the world's first computer-animated feature film, *Toy Story*, and is now the most successful animation studio in the world.
>
> In a remarkable turn of events, Apple bought NeXT, and I returned to Apple. And the technology we developed at NeXT is at the heart of Apple's current renaissance. And Laurene and I have a wonderful family together.
>
> I'm pretty sure none of this would have happened if I hadn't been fired from Apple. It was awful-tasting medicine, but I guess the patient needed it.

Sometimes life's gonna hit you in the head with a brick. Don't lose faith.

At Macworld on January 9, 2007, Steve took the stage again. "Today, we're introducing three revolutionary products," he began. "The first one is a widescreen iPod with touch controls. The second is a revolutionary mobile phone. And the third is a breakthrough internet communications device."

He paused. "Are you getting it?" he asked. "These are not three separate devices. This is one device. And we are calling it iPhone."

Behind the scenes, the day before this launch, Steve had shown the iPhone to AT&T's board of directors. According to Bud, who helped develop it, "their jaws hit the floor."

The iPhone story was one of patience. At NeXT, Steve had been forced to compromise to stay alive, building software for Intel chips and beige-box PC manufacturers whose designs he abhorred. According to NeXT alumni and Apple executives, when he returned to Apple in 1997, he made tactical retreats from that vision—keeping Intel processors, maintaining carrier relationships, working within existing supply chains. But each compromise bought Steve the time and resources to build something larger.

By 2007, a decade of patient institution building paid off. With the iPhone, Steve finally could control everything that mattered. Apple would eventually design the chip architecture. Apple controlled the manufacturing through carefully managed partners. Apple dictated terms to cellular carriers—forcing AT&T to accept the phone before it even saw it. The software, the hardware, the services, even the retail stores answered to Apple headquarters in Cupertino.

At NeXT, Steve had tried to control everything from day one with insufficient resources. At Apple, he built the resources first then seized control. The iPhone proved that the whole stack strategy could work so long as you had the power to enforce it.

When the iPhone launched in 2007, NeXT alumni swapped emails on a mailing list called "ex-NeXTers," trading sarcastic humor whenever Apple unveiled some "revolutionary" feature they had built at NeXT in 1994.

The iPhone's operating system, its development tools, and much of its underlying architecture traced back to code and apps they had written a decade earlier. In fact, buried in some of Apple's code were the initials "NS," a marker that stood for "NeXTSTEP." NeXT had become what Steve once predicted his life's work would amount to: a sediment layer in computing history.

By then, company alumni had scattered across Silicon Valley like seeds, their NeXT pedigree opening doors everywhere. Dan'l had been hired as a corporate vice president by Microsoft CEO Steve Ballmer. Susan became CFO of Intuitive Surgical, a surgical robotics company. Rich chaired Chowbotics, maker of "Sally the salad-making robot," a vending machine that could assemble salads with a thousand combinations, which DoorDash acquired in 2021. Having NeXT on your resume became Silicon Valley shorthand: You were a survivor of Steve's gauntlet.

A few weeks after Steve's death, almost two hundred ex-NeXTers gathered at the Sofitel San Francisco Bay hotel in Redwood City, the location of the original NeXT headquarters, to commemorate their departed chairman. The room held a complicated energy—grief mixed with old grievances, love tangled with unresolved anger. These were the survivors of Steve's cruelest years.

Former sales vice president Todd Rulon-Miller took the podium. He looked out at faces he'd known for decades.

"I haven't found my way through this one yet," he began. "I'm still working on it."

Todd recounted the IBM meeting where Steve tossed aside a 125-page contract while IBM executives watched in horror. Chuckles spread across the room. He replayed the endless arguments over which color the Cube would take and recalled Ross Perot screaming at Todd about NeXT's inability to sell computers. Todd did a brief impression of Ross's Texas drawl that drew laughs.

"[Steve] demanded an opinion, a point of view—declare, decide, do," Todd said. "They were all active verbs under Steve."

The audience knew this Steve well, the demanding perfectionist. But then Todd's voice softened.

"He had a big heart," he said, then a long pause. "Carefully hidden."

Somewhere, they knew about this Steve too.

Todd reminded the crowd of a business dinner twenty-one years ago, where NeXT university customers waited and Steve never showed. He had chosen to blow it off to have dinner with a graduate student named Laurene Powell.

Some cynics, Todd said, had called Steve's transformation staged. But the people at NeXT had watched him for two decades afterward. They knew it was real. As the father of three children, he became a man who remembered birthdays and coached soccer games.

"Something I would have never forecast in Steve Jobs," Todd admitted.

Todd paused.

"He created my future for me. So I summarize: bold and determined, creative and artistic, tough as nails and caring. Yes, he was my friend, and I miss him terribly."

AFTERWORD

At NeXT and Pixar, the period from 1985 to 1997 was our crucible. Three key events transformed our companies and, by extension, the computer and entertainment industries at large. First, Pixar cultivated a bonded team that changed animation forever. Second, NeXT developed an operating system—NeXTSTEP—that led to its acquisition by Apple. And most importantly, Steve himself changed, returning to Apple equipped with the skills he needed to lead a revolution.

This is the version of Steve that has been memorialized in countless books, articles, films, and podcasts. As his legend has grown, I've noticed competing narratives emerge. Some cast him as superhuman, airbrushing his shortcomings. Others focus on those shortcomings to the exclusion of everything else, overlooking Steve's generosity and deep loyalty. Both versions deprive Steve of his humanity. Worse, they neglect the improbable story of his evolution. For those looking to glean insights from Steve's life, I believe this story contains his greatest lesson: the importance—and the discipline—of embracing personal transformation.

During these years, I watched Steve travel the Hero's Journey. He was cast out of his own kingdom, condemned to struggle in the wilderness, but he was forged by that struggle and emerged as a once-in-a-generation leader. While the process of transformation is fascinating in its own right, it raises a more profound question: What characteristics lead someone to pursue personal transformation while working to create something of lasting value?

Foremost for Steve, I believe, was his relentless commitment to truth-seeking. During his decade-long tenure as CEO of Pixar as a public company, our board meetings were a testament to that, featuring extraordinarily intense and lively debate. When Steve decided to fire two members of the board, his reasoning surprised me: They never disagreed with him. If they never disagreed, he asked, then what value did they bring to the company? Steve always sought difficult feedback and responded accordingly.

In parallel to his professional transformation, Steve's family life blossomed in 1991. That's the year he married Laurene Powell and welcomed his wonderful son, Reed, into the world. As a new husband and father, Steve cultivated a trait that I initially doubted he could learn: genuine empathy. I was very wrong about that. When employees faced serious health challenges, Steve went out of his way to give them access to the best medical care in the world. When he saw people smoking outside Pixar's headquarters, Steve would warn them about the risk of lung cancer, which had taken the life of his beloved mother, Clara. He began to stop and chat with assistants.

In work meetings, his infamously hard edges softened. While he never shied away from difficult conversations, he learned to take care with how he delivered feedback, recognizing the impact on the person receiving it. When film directors felt hurt by what he had said, Steve would walk with them around the campus to hear them out and offer reassurance.

Steve also developed a newfound sense of humor. For his keynote at

Macworld 1999, he invited the actor Noah Wyle, who had just played Steve in an unflattering TV movie called *Pirates of Silicon Valley*, to open with a Steve impersonation. It was so convincing that many people in the room believed Noah was, in fact, Steve. As their laughter and applause swelled, the real Steve suddenly whirled onto the stage, feigning displeasure. "That's not me at all!" he said to Noah, eyes twinkling. "You're blowing it!"

Over the course of several years, Steve had developed a shrewder business mind and, at a personal level, had become a better boss. Gone was the mercurial CEO who NeXT's cofounders had fallen out with one by one. In his place was someone more fun, more empathetic, and less bruising to work for. As time went on, he began to shed his reputation for high turnover. By the late nineties, most of his top executives would be the people who would work with him for the rest of his life.

I'm proud to count myself among that cohort, though our professional relationship began earlier. It started in 1986 when Steve purchased the computer division of Lucasfilm, which would become Pixar. He was the rare technology leader who could see, early on, just how important computer graphics were going to become. His intelligence outpaced his interpersonal skills when I first knew him, but unlike many other brilliant people, he applied his formidable intelligence to change the way he worked.

After signing the papers to acquire Pixar, Steve put his arms around me and my colleague Alvy Ray Smith. Eager to avoid a repeat of his ouster at Apple, he said to us, "As we're going through this, there's one thing I ask. And that is that we be loyal to each other."

Steve lived up to his end of the pact and then some. Over the nine years leading up to Pixar's 1995 IPO, he personally funded our work to the tune of $54 million. I primarily remember NeXT's offices as the destination of my monthly pilgrimage to update him and, with difficulty, to get him to issue yet another check to fund our operations. I later discovered that Steve's investment in Pixar represented around half of his net worth at the time, which was even more extraordinary considering that he was bankrolling not one but two failing companies. Two giant bets, each demanding his attention, each holding gems that would transform industries.

Steve's role at Pixar was distinct from that of a computer company CEO. For the most part, Steve stayed away from our creative process. I even asked him never to come to our brain trust meetings—a gathering of senior executives that solved difficult creative problems. He agreed. When Steve did provide feedback on in-progress films at board meetings, he prefaced it by telling the directors that he wasn't a filmmaker and that they could ignore everything he said. They knew he meant it.

Steve's distance from Pixar's day-to-day work allowed him to bring fresh eyes to the process. It was remarkable to me how well he understood the mechanics of narrative storytelling despite not being a filmmaker. And, as the fastest thinker in any room, he delivered his thoughts with a confidence that cut through the noise. In truth, there were often elements of Pixar films that Steve didn't like, but he never assumed that his judgment was better. He welcomed opposing ideas. Our team understood that disagreements were never personal—if you could convince Steve that your idea was stronger, he would turn on a dime and give it his full-throated support.

Our arrangement with Steve was ideal: He believed in our work, funded it generously, and left us to do it largely uninterrupted. Meanwhile, his periodic feedback became an essential part of our development process.

I am deeply grateful for Steve's unwavering support of Pixar. And I thoroughly admired his no-ego attitude, his genuine curiosity, and his willingness to learn from failure. It was these tools that allowed him to make the personal transformation chronicled in this book. And I believe it is these qualities that most distinguished Steve's leadership.

The lesson for the rest of us is clear: Don't attempt to emulate Steve's final form. Instead, embrace the work of personal transformation. Develop the intense curiosity to learn from mistakes and adjust course accordingly. Test your ideas against those of others. Be open to being proved wrong. Above all, when you fail, always be willing to begin again.

Ed Catmull

cofounder of pixar

ACKNOWLEDGMENTS

The friends, guides, and collaborators behind this story

This book exists because the passionate and exceptionally talented people who built NeXT—engineers, designers, marketers, and visionaries who gathered in that creative crucible—opened their memories to me. NeXT attracted some of the most gifted and determined people in Silicon Valley, and I was honored to be given the privilege to document their stories of ambition, innovation, and the turbulent years that ultimately reshaped Apple. Their insights—some technical, some deeply personal—became the foundation for the stories that followed.

I'm deeply grateful to the 111 individuals who gave their time for interviews, with special thanks to Dan'l Lewin (who generously opened his private archives to me and introduced me to key people), Bud Tribble, Susan Barnes, Rich Page, George Crow, Ed Catmull, Jon Rubinstein, Mike Slade, Paul Vais, Dominique Trempont, Todd Rulon-Miller, Bertrand Serlet, William Parkhurst, Warren "Bunny" Weiss, Deac Manross (who shared hours of rare video from NeXT's internal meetings), Kevin Compton, Doug Menuez, Leo Hourvitz, Gary Moore, Jean-Louis Gassée, and so many others. Their candor and insight became the backbone of this narrative.

Some people in this story—including Steve Jobs himself—passed away before this project began or while it unfolded. Pat Crecine, Ross Perot, Morton Meyerson, Andy Grove, Paul Strassman, Herb Philpott, Paul Rand, Richard Crandall, Keith Ohlfs, Brent Schlender, Jean-Marie Hullot, and Paul Berg are among those whose legacy lives on through the memories of friends and colleagues.

In February 2023, as I was preparing to reach out to Paul Berg, the Nobel Prize–winning biochemist who met with Steve Jobs in 1985 as Jobs was first imagining NeXT, I learned he had died only three weeks earlier. That loss crystallized the urgency of capturing this story while the people who lived it are still with us.

I'm also grateful to my friend and business partner Benjamin F. Carlson and our team at Alembic Partners, our executive branding firm, whose editorial wisdom guided me like no other adviser, always honest about what worked and what fell flat.

This book builds on the foundation laid by earlier biographers and journalists: Walter Isaacson, Brent Schlender, Rick Tetzeli, Michael Moritz, Jim Carlton, Michael S. Malone, Frank Rose, and others who chronicled different chapters of Steve's story.

My agent, David Halpern, has championed my work and—through the tough stretches of being a writer—spent years helping me develop ideas toward this book. I'm equally grateful to my team at Portfolio: Noah Schwartzberg, executive editor; Niki Papadopoulos, VP and editor in chief, who immediately saw the insight and value in this project; and Brian Borchard, editorial assistant. Your rigor and patience shaped this book at every turn.

Ben Kalin, my fact-checker, brought his sharp eye to every statement, every number, every quote, rigorously challenging me to substantiate what I put in print. I also want to thank my friend Jimmy Soni, tech historian and author of *The Founders* and *A Mind at Play*, whose research with me informed this book's arc and argument. And thanks to Laura Yorke for kind support along the way.

My deepest thanks to the archivists who safeguarded the record: Emily Davis at Carnegie Mellon's Hunt Library; Leif Anderson and

Tim Noakes at Stanford's Special Collections; Penny Ahlstrand at the Computer History Museum; and Rachel Mihalko, project archivist for the Paul Rand papers at Yale University's Arts Library Special Collections.

I'm also grateful to court archivists and clerks Kenyon Kubo, Allan B. Goodrich Jr., Mark Romyn, Tammy Duvall, and Robt. Stephens, who helped me locate the few surviving records of NeXT's legal battles after many federal court files had already been destroyed in 2011. Their persistence in pulling what remained underscored how fragile the historical record can be, and why documenting it matters.

I am also grateful to the Steve Jobs Archive, launched by Laurene Powell Jobs in 2022 and led by historian Leslie Berlin, for its thoughtful curation and publication of Steve's emails, speeches, and reflections. Their exhibits and ebook *Make Something Wonderful* preserved Steve's own words and provided essential context for this book.

Preserving history, of course, requires people willing to fight for it. A special note to the Stanford team who rescued what we now call the Apple Archive.

In 1997, amid Apple's sweeping layoffs and restructuring, company librarians received a sudden order to vacate the off-site warehouse holding Apple's informal "museum collection"—hundreds of boxes of historic documents, prototypes, and rare hardware—within twenty-four hours or see them destroyed. Apple's librarians raced to the warehouse, salvaged every box they could, and stashed them in a back room at the Apple headquarters.

Days later, as the library itself was closed as part of those broader layoffs, they phoned the curator of technology history at Stanford University Libraries, who arrived with moving boxes. On Halloween, their final day, the librarians marked the moment with tongue-in-cheek pink-slip costumes: They dyed slips of fabric bright pink and wore them as a nod to their layoff notices while they finished packing the collection for Stanford. The Apple Archive remains there today because of them.

I'm also grateful to the Wine School of Philadelphia, where I trained as a sommelier. Alana Zerbe, a careful reader and lover of a good story, and Keith Wallace, a former journalist and kindred spirit, both read portions of this manuscript and offered detailed feedback. Keith taught me the ways of wine while swapping vivid tales of reporting on drug epidemics and dodging gang warfare—stories as unforgettable as any grand cru.

Much of this book was written at my family's cabin on the shores of Lake Vermilion in northern Minnesota, built by my grandparents Don and Shirlee Hamlin. The lake was once described by the Ojibwa with a phrase meaning "Where sunset painted the water red." Many evenings I worked at a desk looking through birch trees as the water turned red at dusk, proud to write in a place that carries my family's history.

Other chapters took shape on Anna Maria Island, Florida, where I wrote overlooking a canal while an egret, nicknamed "Sticks" by my family, showed up each morning, gently asking for a snack. These settings, each with its own quiet rhythm, gave me the stillness to sift through hundreds of thousands of pages of interview transcripts, archival documents and videos, product launches, unbroadcast recordings of Steve and his colleagues, historical news reports, and technical documentation on NeXT hardware and software—and to hold fast to the stories that might otherwise slip away.

For detailed endnotes, a list of interviews, and the bibliography, visit stevejobs.tech.

IMAGE CREDITS

p. xiii: **Steve Jobs Returning from a Visit to the New Factory. Fremont, California, 1987**

Crammed into a rented school bus with his NeXT team, Steve erupts in laughter on the ride back from the factory site. (PHOTO © DOUG MENUEZ)

p. 3: **Apple Computer Rolls Out the Macintosh**

Cupertino, CA, January 24: Steve Jobs, left, and John Sculley host the annual Apple Computer show at the Flint Center at De Anza College. Sculley is leaning on the Apple Lisa personal computer, which succeeded the original Macintosh, on which Jobs is leaning. The 1984 annual meeting was the predecessor of what would become the Macworld show the next year.

(PHOTO BY CAP CARPENTER/MEDIANEWS GROUP/THE MERCURY NEWS VIA GETTY IMAGES)

p. 15: **Jean-Louis Gassée**

President of the products division of Apple Computer Inc. Jean-Louis Gassée sits on his car January 27, 1986, in California. Gassée started the French subsidiary of Apple, which has become the largest business unit outside of the US for Apple.

(PHOTO BY ED KASHI/LIAISON/HULTON ARCHIVE VIA GETTY IMAGES)

p. 27: **Steve Jobs**

Apple cofounder Steve Jobs poses for a portrait on September 21, 1985.

(PHOTO BY STEVE RINGMAN/SAN FRANCISCO CHRONICLE/ HEARST NEWSPAPERS VIA GETTY IMAGES)

p. 35: **Steve Jobs Introduces NeXT Computer**

The NeXT senior staff poses for a photograph on October 12, 1988, in San Francisco. Jobs, cofounder of Apple Computer, left the company after a power struggle with John Sculley to create NeXT.

Back row (left to right): Larry Sonsini, Rich Page, Steve Jobs, George Crow, Gary Moore, and Bud Tribble

Front row (left to right): Dan'l Lewin, Susan Barnes

(GETTY IMAGES/STRINGER/HULTON ARCHIVE)

p. 49: **Steve Jobs Views the NeXT Computer Case Prototype. Santa Cruz, California, 1987**

Steve runs his fingers across the magnesium cube, dissecting every millimeter of its anodized surface with Ken Haven, NeXT's director of mechanical engineering.

(PHOTO © DOUG MENUEZ)

p. 63: **The End of the Beginning. Washington, DC, 1988**

Three days after the glittering San Francisco launch, Steve walks with Ross Perot and NeXT marketing executive Kathy Kilcoyne at the EDUCOM conference in 1988.

(PHOTO © DOUG MENUEZ)

p. 77: **Steve Jobs Outlining the Digital Revolution. Sonoma, California, 1986.**

At a company retreat in Sonoma, Steve maps out what's left to conquer. He's cataloging everything still trapped in the analog world—music, video, publishing, design—and showing his team where the work remains. (PHOTO © DOUG MENUEZ)

p. 97: **Silicon Beach. Palo Alto, California, 1987**

The engineers claimed the top-floor office as their own, naming it Silicon Beach and working there whenever the Palo Alto sun broke through. Here, Trey Matteson rests on the floor while Chris Franklin codes standing up. (PHOTO © DOUG MENUEZ)

p. 109: **Steve Jobs, Cofounder of Apple Computer, Announcing the NeXT Computer in San Francisco, California, 1988**

Steve Jobs stands behind his NeXT computer during the NeXT launch event at Davies Symphony Hall, San Francisco, 1988. Behind Jobs are NeXT employees and at the far right Ross Perot, who had invested $20 million in NeXT Inc.

Left to right: Bud Tribble, board member Pat Crecine, board member Ross Perot.

Front: Steve Jobs (CHUCK NACKE/ALAMY)

p. 119: **Ninety Hours a Week to Change the World. Palo Alto, California, 1986**

Steve stops mid-presentation with an idea: Why don't they all work nights and weekends until Christmas, then take a week off? A tired voice from the back: "We're already doing that, Steve." Laughter ripples through the room. (PHOTO © DOUG MENUEZ)

p. 137: **Steve Jobs Pretending to Be Human. Menlo Park, California, 1987**

Steve kicks a beach ball at the company picnic, smiling for the camera. It looks like fun, but something's off. He's performing relaxation rather than experiencing it. The man who operated at maximum intensity constantly understood, at least intellectually, that his team needed downtime to survive the marathon ahead. So here he is, playing the role of casual boss at a company outing. (PHOTO © DOUG MENUEZ)

p. 147: **Steve Jobs Is Thinking. Santa Cruz, California, 1987**

Steve leans back, eyes distant, working through a problem only he can see.
(PHOTO © DOUG MENUEZ)

p. 161: **At the 1990 PC Forum**

Vittorio Cassoni, from Olivetti & Co., speaks with Steve Jobs, from Apple Computer, at the annual PC Forum, Tucson, AZ, 1990.
(PHOTO BY ANN E. YOW-DYSON/ARCHIVE PHOTOS/GETTY IMAGES)

p. 169: **British Physicist-Turned-Programmer Tim Berners-Lee Devised Much**

British physicist-turned-programmer Tim Berners-Lee devised much of the programming language that made the internet accessible to the broad public.
(PHOTO BY CATRINA GENOVESE/HULTON ARCHIVE/GETTY IMAGES)

p. 177: **Becoming Steve Jobs**

Steve and Bill pose together at Steve's Palo Alto home for a *Fortune* cover shoot in 1991. The frenemies traded barbs between shots for George Lange's camera. But the tension breaks occasionally. Here, something actually strikes them both as funny.
(PHOTO © GEORGE LANGE)

p. 185: **Steve Jobs, NeXT Computer**

Personal computer pioneer Steve Jobs, of NeXT Computer Inc., delivers his keynote address during the Unix expo at the Javits Convention Center in New York City on October 30, 1991. (AP PHOTO/RICHARD DREW. © 1991 AP. ALL RIGHTS RESERVED.)

p. 193: **At the 1991 PC Forum**

Dan'l Lewin (left), from GO Corporation/Microsoft, and John Perry Barlow (center), from Electronic Frontier Foundation/Berkman Center for Internet & Society, listen to Mitch Kapor, from Electronic Frontier Foundation/Kapor Enterprises, at the annual PC Forum, Tucson, AZ, March 10–13, 1991.
(PHOTO BY ANN E. YOW-DYSON/ARCHIVE PHOTOS/GETTY IMAGES)

p. 207: **Steve Jobs Introduces NeXT**

Steve Jobs at the NeXTWORLD Expo in San Francisco, January 22, 1992. NeXT, Inc. was an American computer and software company founded in 1985 by Apple Computer cofounder Steve Jobs. (AP PHOTO/NEWSBASE © NEWSBASE 2020.)

p. 223: **The Burning Cube**

By 1993, the NeXT Cube had become a symbol of beautiful failure, a machine too expensive, too late, and too uncompromising for the market it was meant to serve. Simson Garfinkel, writing for *NeXTWORLD* magazine, decided to give it a Viking funeral. He hauled a Cube chassis to Lawrence Livermore National Laboratory and had scientists incinerate it. It took multiple tries, since Steve had chosen an exotic magnesium alloy that didn't easily catch fire in everyday settings. Steve had shuttered the hardware division a few weeks earlier. (PHOTO © SIMSON L. GARFINKEL)

p. 235: **Former NeXT Software Head Bud Tribble Joins Sun, 1993**

Bud Tribble led software development at NeXT, overseeing the creation of object-oriented programming tools that were years ahead of the competition. But brilliant code doesn't pay the bills when nobody's buying the hardware. Bud jumped to Sun Microsystems, one of NeXT's fiercest rivals, in 1993. From inside Sun, Bud helped broker licensing deals that funneled desperately needed cash back to Steve's struggling company. (PHOTO © DOUG MENUEZ)

p. 243: **Steve Jobs and Laurene Powell Jobs**

Apple Computer head Steve Jobs and wife Laurene Powell relax in their garden in Palo Alto, CA on August 4, 1997. (PHOTO BY DIANA WALKER/SJ/CONTOUR BY GETTY IMAGES)

p. 251: **Apple and Ellison**

Larry Ellison, chief executive of the computer software company Oracle Corp., gestures during a news conference on May 20, 1997, in Redwood City, CA. According to a financial newspaper report on Friday, August 1, 1997, Ellison says he will join the board of Apple Computer Inc.

(AP PHOTO/PAUL SAKUMA. © 1997 AP. ALL RIGHTS RESERVED.)

p. 261: **Steve Jobs at Pixar**

Steve Jobs, founder of Apple, bought animation company Pixar off George Lucas in 1986 and turned it into a Academy-Award-winning studio. (© LOUIE PSIHOYOS)

p. 271: **Steve Jobs**

Personal computer pioneer Steve Jobs is shown in this 1993 photo.

(AP PHOTO/KRISTY MACDONALD. © 1993 AP. ALL RIGHTS RESERVED.)

p. 279: **Gil Amelio**

Gil Amelio, chief executive officer of Apple Computer, sits where many Apple decisions are hashed out—the company's boardroom in Cupertino.

(PHOTO BY ANNA MARIE REMEDIOS/MEDIANEWS GROUP/
THE MERCURY NEWS VIA GETTY IMAGES)

p. 293: **USA Apple Arbeitsplaetze**

Apple Chairman Gil Amelio, right, shows Apple cofounder Steve Jobs, center left, into Apple headquarters in Cupertino, CA, Friday evening, December 20, 1996, as they arrive for a news conference. Apple and NeXT Software Inc., the company Jobs cofounded, have reached an agreement to help on Apple's operating system.

(AP PHOTO/PAUL SAKUMA. © 1996 AP. ALL RIGHTS RESERVED.)

p. 303: **Apple Macworld**

Steve Jobs, right, the former cofounder and chairman of Apple, talks about his plans for Apple's new system software as Apple Inc.'s Chairman Gil Amelio, left, looks on at the Macworld trade show in San Francisco, January 7, 1997. Apple recently acquired NeXT Software Inc., which was run by Jobs.

(AP PHOTO/ERIC RISBERG. © 1997 AP. ALL RIGHTS RESERVED.)

p. 319: **Steve Jobs, *Time*, September 18, 1997**

Apple CEO Steve Jobs onstage at Macworld Expo in Boston on August 8, 1997.

(PHOTO BY DIANA WALKER/SJ/CONTOUR BY GETTY IMAGES)

p. 333: **Apple Computer, *Fortune*, 2002**

Steve Jobs with key members of his brain trust (from left): Design Chief Jonathan Ive, Software Guru Avie Tevanian, Hardware Chief Jon Rubinstein, and Applications Czar Sina Tamaddon are photographed for *Fortune* magazine on December 19, 2001.

(PHOTO BY MICHAEL O'NEILL/CONTOUR RA BY GETTY IMAGES)

p. 345: **The 77th Annual Academy Awards—Executive Arrivals**

Steve Jobs of Pixar and wife Laurene, Ed Catmull of Pixar and daughter Jeannie, Rob Cook of Pixar, Sarah McArthur, and Lois Scali during the 77th Annual Academy Awards at the Kodak Theatre in Hollywood, CA.

(PHOTO BY JEFF VESPA/WIREIMAGE VIA GETTY IMAGES)

INDEX